Seventh International Conference on Dependency Linguistics (Depling 2023)

Washington, DC, USA
9-12 March 2023

ISBN: 978-1-7138-9034-8

Printed from e-media with permission by:

Curran Associates, Inc.
57 Morehouse Lane
Red Hook, NY 12571

CURRAN ASSOCIATES INC. proceedings .com

Some format issues inherent in the e-media version may also appear in this print version.

Printed with permission by Curran Associates, Inc. (2024)

Association for Computational Linguistics
209 N. Eighth Street
Stroudsburg, Pennsylvania 18360

Phone: 1-570-476-8006
Fax: 1-570-476-0860

acl@aclweb.org

Additional copies of this publication are available from:

Curran Associates, Inc.
57 Morehouse Lane
Red Hook, NY 12571 USA
Phone: 845-758-0400
Fax: 845-758-2633
Email: curran@proceedings.com
Web: www.proceedings.com

Depling 2023

The Seventh International Conference on Dependency Linguistics (Depling, GURT/SyntaxFest 2023)

Proceedings of the Conference

March 9-12, 2023

The Depling organizers gratefully acknowledge the support from the following sponsors.

The Georgetown College of Arts & Sciences, the Georgetown Faculty of Languages and Linguistics, and the Georgetown Department of Linguistics

GURT 2023
SYNTAXFEST
Washington, D.C.

1789
GEORGETOWN UNIVERSITY

Introduction

The Seventh edition of the International Conference on Dependency Linguistics (Depling 2023) follows a biannual series that started in 2011, in Barcelona, and continued in Prague (2013), Uppsala (2015), Pisa (2017), Paris (2019) and Sofia (2021/22). The series responds to the growing need for linguistic meetings dedicated to approaches in syntax, semantics, and the lexicon that are centered around dependency structures as a central linguistic notion. For the first time, Depling is part of GURT2023, an annual linguistics conference held at Georgetown University, which this year co-locates four related but independent events:

- The Seventh International Conference on Dependency Linguistics (Depling 2023)
- The 21st International Workshop on Treebanks and Linguistic Theories (TLT 2023)
- The Sixth Workshop on Universal Dependencies (UDW 2023)
- The First International Workshop on Construction Grammars and NLP (CxGs+NLP 2023)

The Georgetown University Round Table on Linguistics (GURT) is a peer-reviewed annual linguistics conference held continuously since 1949 at Georgetown University in Washington DC, with topics and co-located events varying from year to year.

In 2023, under an overarching theme of 'Computational and Corpus Linguistics', GURT/SyntaxFest continues the tradition of SyntaxFest 2019 and SyntaxFest 2021/22 in bringing together multiple events that share a common interest in using corpora and treebanks for empirically validating syntactic theories, studying syntax from quantitative and theoretical points of view, and for training machine learning models for natural language processing. Much of this research is increasingly multilingual and cross-lingual and requires continued systematic analysis from various theoretical, applied, and practical perspectives. New this year, the CxGs+NLP workshop brings a usage-based perspective on how form and meaning interact in language.

For these reasons and encouraged by the success of the previous editions of SyntaxFest, we —the chairs of the four events— decided to facilitate another co-located event at GURT 2023 in Washington DC.

As in past co-located events involving several of the workshops, we organized a single reviewing process, with identical paper formats for all four events. Authors could indicate (multiple) venue preferences, but the ultimate assignment of papers to events for accepted papers was made by the program chairs.

33 long papers were submitted, 11 to Depling, 16 to TLT, 10 to UDW and 10 to CxGs+NLP. The program chairs accepted 27 (82%) and assigned 7 to Depling, 6 to TLT, 5 to UDW and 9 to CxGs+NLP.

16 short papers were submitted, 6 of which to Depling, 6 to TLT, 10 to UDW and 2 to CxGs+NLP. The program chairs accepted 9 (56%) and assigned 2 to Depling, 2 to TLT, 3 to UDW, and 2 to CxGs+NLP.

Our sincere thanks go to everyone who is making this event possible: everybody who submitted their papers; Georgetown University Linguistics Department students and staff—including Lauren Levine, Jessica Lin, Ke Lin, Mei-Ling Klein, and Conor Sinclair—for their organizational assistance; and of course, the reviewers for their time and their valuable comments and suggestions. Special thanks are due to Georgetown University, and specifically to the Georgetown College of Arts & Sciences and the Faculty of Languages and Linguistics for supporting the conference with generous funding. Finally, we would also like to thank ACL SIGPARSE for its endorsement and the ACL Anthology for publishing the proceedings.

Owen Rambow, François Lareau (Depling2023 Chairs)
Daniel Dakota, Kilian Evang, Sandra Kübler, Lori Levin (TLT2023 Chairs)
Loïc Grobol, Francis Tyers (UDW2023 chairs)
Claire Bonial Harish Tayyar Madabushi (CxG+NLP2023 Chairs)
Nathan Schneider, Amir Zeldes (GURT2023 Organizers)
March 2023

Organizing Committee

Depling2023 Chairs

Owen Rambow, Stony Brook University
François Lareau, Université de Montréal

TLT2023 Chairs

Daniel Dakota, Indiana University
Kilian Evang, Heinrich Heine University Düsseldorf
Sandra Kübler, Indiana University
Lori Levin, Carnegie Mellon University

UDW2023 Chairs

Loïc Grobol, Université Paris Nanterre
Francis Tyers, Indiana University

CxGs+NLP2023 Chairs

Claire Bonial, U.S. Army Research Lab
Harish Tayyar Madabushi, The University of Bath

GURT2023 Organizers

Amir Zeldes, Georgetown University
Nathan Schneider, Georgetown University

GURT2023 Student Assistants

Lauren Levine, Georgetown University
Ke Lin, Georgetown University
Jessica Lin, Georgetown University

Program Committee

Program Committee for the Whole of GURT2023

Lasha Abzianidze, Utrecht University
Patricia Amaral, Indiana University
Valerio Basile, University of Turin
Emily Bender, University of Washington
Bernd Bohnet, Google
Claire Bonial, Army Research Lab
Gosse Bouma, University of Groningen
Miriam Butt, Universität Konstanz
Marie Candito, Université de Paris
Giuseppe G. A. Celano, Universität Leipzig
Xinying Chen, Xi'an Jiaotong University
Silvie Cinkova, Charles University Prague
Cagri Coltekin, Universität Tübingen
Stefania Degaetano-Ortlieb, Universität des Saarlandes
Éric Villemonte de la Clergerie, INRIA
Miryam de Lhoneux, KU Leuven
Valeria de Paiva, Topos Institute
Lucia Donatelli, Saarland University
Timothy Dozat, Google
Kim Gerdes, Université Paris-Saclay
Koldo Gojenola, University of the Basque Country
Loïc Grobol, Université Paris Nanterre
Bruno Guillaume, INRIA
Dag Trygve Truslew Haug, University of Oslo
Jena Hwang, Allen Institute for Artificial Intelligence
András Imrényi, Eötvös Lorand University
Alessandro Lenci, University of Pisa
Lori Levin, Carnegie Mellon University
Markéta Lopatková, Charles University Prague
Sylvain Kahane, Université Paris Nanterre
Jordan Kodner, State University of New York, Stony Brook
Sandra Kübler, Indiana University
Jan Macutek, Mathematical Institute, Slovak Academy of Sciences
Harish Tayyar Madabushi, University of Sheffield
Nicolas Mazziotta, Université de Liège
Alexander Mehler, Johann Wolfgang Goethe Universität Frankfurt am Main
Simon Mille, Dublin City University
Pierre André Ménard, Computer research institute of Montréal
Yusuke Miyao, The University of Tokyo
Simonetta Montemagni, ILC-CNR
Alexis Nasr, Aix Marseille Univ
Joakim Nivre, Uppsala University
Pierre Nugues, Lund University
Timothy John Osborne, Zhejiang University
Petya Osenova, Bulgarian Academy of Sciences
Robert Östling, Stockholm University

Simon Petitjean, Heinrich-Heine Universität Düsseldorf
Dirk Pijpops, Université de Liège
Michael Regan, University of Colorado, Boulder
Mathilde Regnault, Universität Stuttgart
Laurence Romain, University of Birmingham
Rudolf Rosa, Charles University Prague
Haruko Sanada, Rissho University
Beatrice Santorini, University of Pennsylvania
Giorgio Satta, Università degli studi di Padova
Sebastian Schuster, Universität des Saarlandes
Olga Scrivner, Rose-Hulman Institute of Technology
Ashwini Vaidya, Indian Institute of Technology, Delhi
Remi van Trijp, Sony Computer Sciences Laboratories Paris
Giulia Venturi, Institute for Computational Linguistics "A. Zampolli" (ILC-CNR)
Nianwen Xue, Brandeis University
Eva Zehentner, University of Zurich
Amir Zeldes, Georgetown University
Daniel Zeman, Charles University Prague
Heike Zinsmeister, Universität Hamburg
Hongxin Zhang, Zhejiang University

Table of Contents

The development of dependency length minimization in early child language: A case study of the dative alternation

Zoey Liu
Department of Linguistics
University of Florida
liu.ying@ufl.edu

Stefanie Wulff
Department of Linguistics
University of Florida
UiT The Arctic University of Norway
swulff@ufl.edu

Abstract

How does the preference for dependency length minimization (DLM) develop in early child language? This study takes up this question with the dative alternation in English as the test case. We built a large-scale dataset of dative constructions using transcripts of naturalistic child-parent interactions. Across different developmental stages of children, there appears to be a strong tendency for DLM. The tendency emerges between the age range of 12-18 months, slightly decreases until 30-36 months, then becomes more pronounced afterwards and approaches parents' production preferences after 48 months. We further show the extent of DLM depends on how a given dative construction is realized: the tendency for shorter dependencies is much more pronounced in double object structures, whereas the prepositional object structures are associated with longer dependencies.

1 Introduction

The principle of Dependency Length Minimization (DLM) (Ferrer-i Cancho, 2004), originally developed based on the framework of Dependency Grammar (Tesnière, 1959), predicts that words or phrases that are syntactically dependent on each other prefer to appear closer in order to minimize the overall dependency distance, thereby reducing its structural complexity.

While research on DLM thus far has been fruitful (Hawkins, 1990; Gildea and Temperley, 2010; Gulordava and Merlo, 2015; Liu, 2020, 2022), one crucial question remains: how does the preference for shorter dependencies develop in early child language? Given that the preference for DLM has been well-documented in the literature, we would expect to see similar preferences in child production as well. That said, it is unclear (1) at what developmental stage the preference for DLM emerges; (2) whether and how the extent of DLM varies along the developmental trajectory; (3) when children's production of DLM reaches a comparable level to that in parent/adult production.

This study addresses the aforementioned questions using the dative construction in English as the test case. Here (1a) and (1b) are different syntactic variants of the same dative construction: (1a) is a double object construction, (1b) is a prepositional object construction. Within the verb phrase (VP) of (1a), the head verb has two noun phrase (NP) dependents, one as the direct object (*the toy*) and one as the indirect object (*me*); the semantic roles for the two are theme and recipient, respectively. By comparison, in (1b), the direct object dependent of the head verb, *the toy*, is the same as that in (1a), whereas the recipient is realized as a prepositional phrase (PP) dependent instead.

(1) a. **give** [$_{NP}$ the girl] [$_{NP}$ the lunch box]
b. **give** [$_{NP}$ the lunch box] [$_{PP}$ to the girl]

Leveraging transcripts of naturalistic child-parent interactions and computational techniques, we analyze the developmental patterns of DLM in child production of the dative alternation. We foresee two possible directions regarding the extent of DLM across children's developmental stages. On one hand, at earlier stages, utterances produced by children are comparatively shorter (Brown, 1973); based on evidence from written data that there is a positive correlation between overall dependency length and sentence length (Ferrer-i Cancho et al., 2020; Futrell et al., 2020), this means that during these stages the preference for DLM is potentially weaker, and would gradually increase as utterance lengths increase when children reach later developmental stages. On the other hand, if the primary motivation for DLM is to lessen cognitive load (Gibson et al., 2019; Hawkins, 2007, 2015), then at earlier developmental stages, when children have shorter working memory (Hudson Kam, 2019; Austin et al., 2022), they may have a stronger preference for shorter dependencies than they do in later stages of development.

Proceedings of the Seventh International Conference on Dependency Linguistics (Depling, GURT/SyntaxFest 2023), pages 1 - 8
March 9-12, 2023

2 Related work

The dative alternation in English (Levin, 1993), has been studied extensively, specially in first language adult production (Bresnan et al., 2007; Bresnan, 2007; Szmrecsanyi et al., 2017; Engel et al., 2022). In addition, a number of studies have looked into the production patterns of the dative constructions in child (and child-directed) spoken language in English, though from different angles. One line of work probes the generalization (Goldberg et al., 2005; Conwell and Demuth, 2007; Shimpi et al., 2007) and learnability (Gropen et al., 1989; Yang and Montrul, 2017) of the dative structures in children's production. Others attended to the developmental order of the different variants of the dative construction (Campbell and Tomasello, 2001; Snyder and Stromswold, 1997). With syntactic orders in particular, De Marneffe et al. (2012) investigated what structural constraints, such as animacy and pronominality, affect children's syntactic choices.

3 Experiments

3.1 Data and preprocessing

Although prior work has studied the dative alternation in child production, their constructed datasets are not publicly available. In addition, they tended to focus on narrower age ranges of only a handful of children. Therefore we turned to building a dataset of our own. For child (and parent) production data, we resorted to the CHILDES database (MacWhinney, 2000), which contains transcripts of naturalistic child-parent conversational speech. We focused on (monolingual) children with typical development. Child and parent utterances were first taken from the English-NA and the English-UK sections of CHILDES via the `childes-db` interface (Sanchez et al., 2019). We then automatically assigned part-of-speech (POS) tags as well as syntactic dependencies to each utterance in order to derive morphosyntactic information; the former was performed using Stanza (Qi et al., 2020), a publicly open library for natural language processing; and the latter was achieved using DiaParser (Attardi et al., 2021), which has recently been shown to yield good dependency parsing performance for child spoken language in English (Liu and Prud'hommeaux, 2022).

We relied on the classes of dative ($N = 336$) and benefactive ($N = 177$) verbs from Levin (1993) as references when extracting utterances that potentially contain a dative structure from the parsed data described above. We searched for VPs where the head verb occurs in either the double object structure (V-NP-NP) or the prepositional object structure (V-NP-PP). (See Appendix A for details on our data extraction process).

Here we used children's age as an index of their developmental stage; therefore we removed utterances where the age information of the corresponding child is not provided. This resulted in an initial dataset of 43,156 utterances. In what follows, we describe our annotation procedures for deciding whether an utterance contains a dative construction. Given the size of the dataset, manually annotating each instance is plausible yet not practical. To remedy that, we also illustrate a simple automatic approach for the identification of dative structures.

3.2 Annotation criteria and process

We determined whether an utterance includes a dative structure or not based on the following two criteria: (1) the verb takes a direct object which is the theme, as well as an indirect object or a prepositional object that serves as either the recipient or the beneficiary; (2) the verb can be understood as expressing some action of transfer from the subject/agent of the sentence to the recipient/beneficiary, even if the action is metaphorical (e.g., (2b)). These restrictions naturally ruled out cases where the head verb takes a verbal complement (which was erroneously parsed as the object by the dependency parser; e.g., 2c); they also excluded cases where the head verb has a PP dependent occurring after the theme, but the semantic role of the PP is purpose (e.g., (2d)) or goal/direction (e.g., (2e)). That said, the annotation criteria were to some extent relaxed for utterances produced by children. For example, while the recipient of the verb is preferred to be animate (Bresnan et al., 2007), if based on preceding context of the utterance, the recipient could be interpreted as being personified (e.g., 2f), we deemed those cases as appropriate dative constructions as well.

(2) a. she **brings** lots of lego to me. [1]
b. **carry** your dream for you.
c. *say thank you to your friend
d. *I **took** him for a walk.
e. *Daddy **sent** me to school.
f. I **made** some lunch for my teddy.

[1]Examples provided here are adapted from utterances initially extracted from CHILDES; * marks the types of instances that we did not consider in this study.

Our annotation process for identifying the dative constructions is as follows. From the initial dataset derived from Section 3.1, we constructed three small practice sets for annotators to familiarize themselves with the annotation criteria described above; each practice set contained 50 utterances. Two annotators with advanced training in linguistics independently annotated one practice set first. They were instructed to annotate an instance as *yes*, if they considered the instance as having a dative structure, *no* if they considered the opposite, and *unsure* if they were uncertain about what decision to make. They then cross-checked their own annotations with each other and settled on the unsure cases along with other questions encountered during the annotation process. The annotation procedures for the other two practice sets were the same. Afterwards, the two annotators along with the senior author of this paper each annotated a subset (of different sizes) of the initial dataset, using the same three annotation labels. We ensured that there was overlap between each of these subsets such that a total of 1,000 utterances were independently annotated by two annotators (regardless of which two). Agreement score for these 1,000 utterances, which was measured as the percentage of times when the two annotators agree, was 95.20%. Discrepancies in annotations, including the unsure cases, were eventually resolved through discussions. Given the high agreement score, each annotator continued to independently examine more instances.

In total, we annotated 10,709 utterances taken from the initial dataset (Section 3.1), which we refer to hereafter as the gold-standard. Among these cases, 8,718 have an annotation label of *yes* whereas the remainder have the label *no*.

3.3 Automatic identification of the dative constructions

Using the gold-standard utterances, we explored automatic approaches in order to identify which of the remaining utterances in the initial dataset contain dative structures. Specifically, we treated this task as a binary classification task. We randomly split all the gold-standard data into training/test sets at a 4:1 ratio, 3 times. Our classifier was trained with BERT (Devlin et al., 2019) using the default parameters from MaChamp v0.3beta (van der Goot et al., 2021), an open-access multi-task learning toolkit. The input to the classifier was the utterance concatenated with the speaker of the utterance (child or parent) and the head verb. The performance of the classifier was measured as its prediction accuracy averaged across the three test sets.

Label	Accuracy (%)
yes	98.43
no	84.05

Table 1: Classification accuracy for each label for the gold-standard dative utterances.

Role	Structure	N
Child	double object	5,645
	prepositional object	2,401
Parent	double object	21,865
	prepositional object	8,793

Table 2: Descriptive statistics for the dative constructions in child and parent production.

The classifier was able to perform reasonably well (average accuracy = 94.36%; see also Table 1). Hence we trained the same classifier using all the gold-standard data, then applied it to the remaining instances in the initial dataset. We excluded cases in the original dataset with an annotation label of *no*, whether manually or automatically identified, eventually yielding a dataset of 38,704 utterances (Table 2; see also Figure 3 in Appendix C). Compared to previous work on constituent orderings of the dative alternation in child language development (De Marneffe et al., 2012), our dataset is of much larger scale (including utterances produced by over 900 children from 54 corpora).

3.4 Measures for DLM

Since we used children's age as a proxy of developmental stage, to avoid data sparsity, we set every 6 months as one age bin, then separated all the dative constructions produced by children (and by parents accordingly) into their corresponding age bins. As illustration of our computations for the extent of DLM, consider the examples below. Say the original utterance appears in the double object structure (e.g., (3a)). To check whether DLM is observable in the utterance, we first measured its overall dependency length ($DL\_observed$). Then we automatically constructed the syntactic alternative of the utterance (e.g., (3b)). [2] and measured its overall dependency length as well ($DL\_alternative$); if the value of $DL\_observed$ is smaller than that of

[2]See Appendix B for discussion about using sentences with the heavy NP shift (Wasow, 1997) as syntactic alternatives for the prepositional object structure.

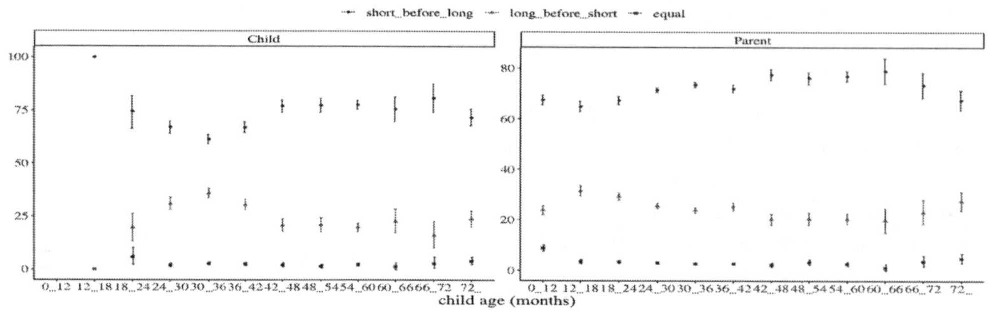

Figure 1: DLM in the dative constructions in child and parent production.

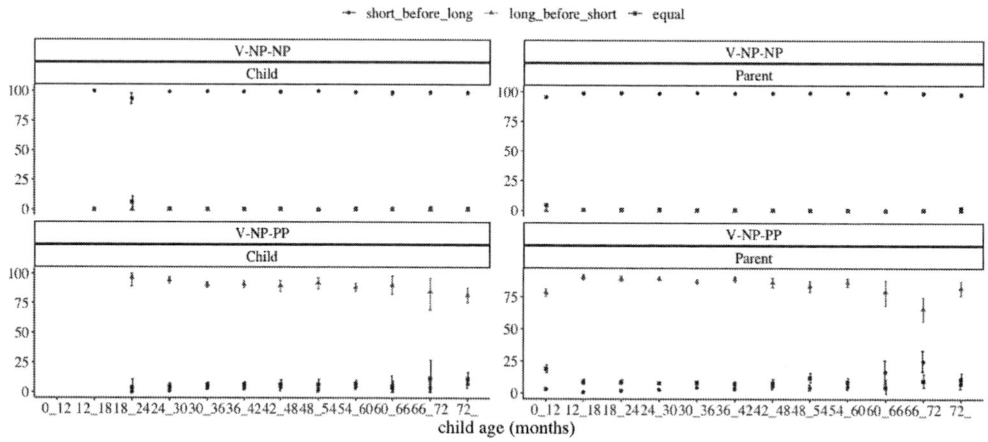

Figure 2: DLM in the double object structure (V-NP-NP) and the prepositional object structure (V-NP-PP) in child and parent production.

$DL\_alternative$, we consider the original utterance to show DLM. For all the utterances produced by children within a certain age bin, we measured the proportion of instances where a preference for shorter dependencies exists, the proportion of cases where the opposite pattern holds, and the proportion of sentences where the overall dependency lengths of the syntacic alternatives are the same. Significance testing was conducted using bootstrapping (Efron and Tibshirani, 1994).

(3)

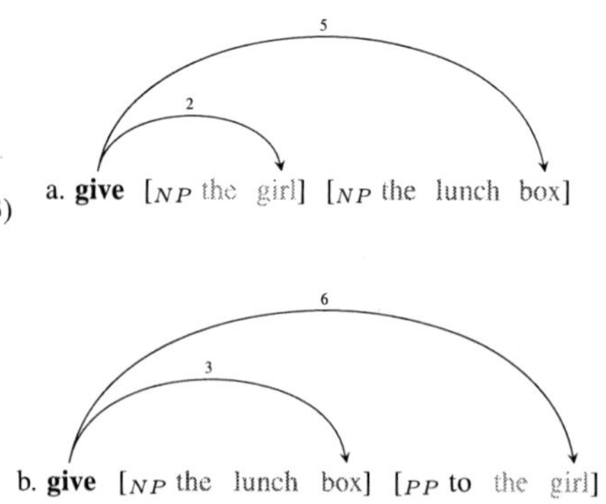

4 Results

Here we used the production patterns in parent data as benchmarks for analysis of the developmental trajectory of DLM in child data; thus the subplots in each figure often contrast child production patterns with those of parent production. As illustrated in Figure 1, there is consistently a pronounced preference for shorter dependencies across different stages of children's developmental trajectory. This preference seems to emerge in child production between the age range of 12 to 18 months; during this range the proportion of utterances that demonstrate a tendency for DLM is 100%, where all the utterances (N=14) have the double object structures (Figure 3). The overall tendency for DLM is also observable when looking at a few of the most frequent head verbs in the dative dataset, such as *give* and *get* (see Appendix D).

When comparing the extent of DLM in child production across different age ranges, it appears that the preference for shorter dependencies gradually gets weaker from 12 to 36 months, then grows noticeably stronger afterwards. In fact, the preference for DLM is the weakest when children are between 30-36 months old; that said, during that age range, the proportion of cases that demonstrate DLM is still 3.09 times that of the utterances that show the opposite observations. When children reach 42-48 months old, their production of DLM becomes more stable and is approaching the production levels in parent data.

When taking a closer look at DLM in the two structural alternatives of the dative constructions, respectively, we see different patterns (Figure 2). In the double object structures, again, there appears to be a strong tendency for shorter dependencies across the developmental trajectory of children. The preference for DLM in child production approximates that in parent production around the age range of 24-30 months.

By contrast, we observe the opposite tendency for the prepositional object structure, that is, across children's age ranges, there seems to be a significant preference *against* DLM instead. In other words, the observed V-NP-PP utterances produced by children actually have longer dependency length compared to their syntactic alternatives. We conjectured several explanations for this discrepancy and verified them with our data. First, the difference in the overall dependency length between the V-NP-PP instances and their double object alternatives is mostly small. Indeed, in about 63.10% of the prepositional object structures in child production (N=2,401), the overall dependency length difference between them and their structural alternations is equal to one. Second, the direct object/theme of the V-NP-PP utterances is relatively short (De Marneffe et al., 2012); in approximately 67.43% of all these instances, the theme consists of just one word. Third, in 77.14% of cases where the theme is composed of one word, the word is usually pronominal (Bresnan et al., 2007).

The patterns based on the prepositional object structures in turn shed light on the overall developmental trajectory of the preference for DLM in Figure 1: between the age range of 12 to 36 months, the proportion of the V-NP-PP structures in children's production gradually increases (from 20.44% to 39.61%), leading to overall weaker extents of shorter dependencies during this age range; the proportion of the V-NP-PP instances then gradually decreases after 36 months, thereby making the age range of 30-36 months a "turning point" in the development of DLM in child production.

5 Discussion

This study analyzed the developmental trajectory of the preference for DLM in child production using the dative alternation in English as the test case. Our findings illustrated that the tendency for shorter dependencies emerges in child production during the age range of 12-18 months. The extent of the tendency decreases until 30-36 months, then gradually increases and approximates the production level in parent data around 42-48 months.

In this work, we used age as the index of children's developmental stages. For future experiments, we plan to investigate how other alternatives, such as the mean length of utterance, affect observations of children's developmental trajectories of DLM. We would also like to analyze the development of children's syntactic choices via enriching the dataset with annotations for other constraints such as verb semantics. These factors could potentially provide additional explanations for the varying extents of DLM in children's early development. Lastly, given that our dative dataset is much larger than prior ones, we hope that it will be useful to research topics related to acquisition of syntactic alternations more broadly.

References

Jennifer E. Arnold, Anthony Losongco, Thomas Wasow, and Ryan Ginstrom. 2000. Heaviness vs. newness: The effects of structural complexity and discourse status on constituent ordering. *Language*, 76(1):28–55.

Giuseppe Attardi, Daniele Sartiano, and Zhang Yu. 2021. Diaparser attentive dependency parser.

Alice Austin, Kathryn D. Schuler, S Furlong, and Elissa L. Newport. 2022. Learning a language from inconsistent input: Regularization in child and adult learners. *Language Learning and Development*, 18:249 – 277.

Joan Bresnan. 2007. Is syntactic knowledge probabilistic? Experiments with the English dative alternation. *Roots: Linguistics in Search of its Evidential Base*, 96:77–96.

Joan Bresnan, Anna Cueni, Tatiana Nikitina, and R Harald Baayen. 2007. Predicting the dative alternation. In *Cognitive foundations of interpretation*, pages 69–94. KNAW.

Roger Brown. 1973. *A first language: The early stages.* Harvard University Press.

Aimee L Campbell and Michael Tomasello. 2001. The acquisition of English dative constructions. *Applied psycholinguistics*, 22(2):253–267.

Erin Conwell and Katherine Demuth. 2007. Early syntactic productivity: Evidence from dative shift. *Cognition*, 103(2):163–179.

Marie-Catherine De Marneffe, Scott Grimm, Inbal Arnon, Susannah Kirby, and Joan Bresnan. 2012. A statistical model of the grammatical choices in child production of dative sentences. *Language and Cognitive Processes*, 27(1):25–61.

Jacob Devlin, Ming-Wei Chang, Kenton Lee, and Kristina Toutanova. 2019. BERT: Pre-training of deep bidirectional transformers for language understanding. In *Proceedings of the 2019 Conference of the North American Chapter of the Association for Computational Linguistics: Human Language Technologies, Volume 1 (Long and Short Papers)*, pages 4171–4186, Minneapolis, Minnesota. Association for Computational Linguistics.

Bradley Efron and Robert J Tibshirani. 1994. *An introduction to the bootstrap*. CRC press.

Alexandra Engel, Jason Grafmiller, Laura Rosseel, and Benedikt Szmrecsanyi. 2022. Assessing the complexity of lectal competence: the register-specificity of the dative alternation after give. *Cognitive Linguistics*.

Ramon Ferrer-i Cancho. 2004. Euclidean distance between syntactically linked words. *Physical Review E*, 70(5):056135.

Ramon Ferrer-i Cancho, Carlos Gómez-Rodríguez, Juan Luis Esteban, and Lluís Alemany-Puig. 2020. The optimality of syntactic dependency distances. *arXiv preprint arXiv:2007.15342*.

Richard Futrell, Roger P Levy, and Edward Gibson. 2020. Dependency locality as an explanatory principle for word order. *Language*, 96(2):371–412.

Edward Gibson, Richard Futrell, Steven Piantadosi, Isabelle Dautriche, Kyle Mahowald, Leon Bergen, and Roger Levy. 2019. How efficiency shapes human language. *Trends in Cognitive Sciences*, 23(5):389–407.

Daniel Gildea and David Temperley. 2010. Do Grammars Minimize Dependency Length? *Cognitive Science*, 34(2):286–310.

Adele E Goldberg, Devin M Casenhiser, and Nitya Sethuraman. 2005. The role of prediction in construction-learning. *Journal of Child Language*, 32(2):407–426.

Jess Gropen, Steven Pinker, Michelle Hollander, Richard Goldberg, and Ronald Wilson. 1989. The learnability and acquisition of the dative alternation in English. *Language*, pages 203–257.

Kristina Gulordava and Paola Merlo. 2015. Structural and lexical factors in adjective placement in complex noun phrases across Romance languages. In *Proceedings of the Nineteenth Conference on Computational Natural Language Learning*, pages 247–257.

John A Hawkins. 1990. A Parsing Theory of Word Order Universals. *Linguistic Inquiry*, 21(2):223–261.

John A. Hawkins. 2007. Processing typology and why psychologists need to know about it. *New Ideas in Psychology*, 25(2):87–107.

John A. Hawkins. 2015. Typological Variation and Efficient Processing. In *The Handbook of Language Emergence*, chapter 10, pages 215–236. John Wiley Sons, Ltd.

Carla L. Hudson Kam. 2019. Reconsidering retrieval effects on adult regularization of inconsistent variation in language. *Language Learning and Development*, 15(4):317–337.

Beth Levin. 1993. *English verb classes and alternations: A preliminary investigation*. University of Chicago press.

Zoey Liu. 2020. Mixed evidence for crosslinguistic dependency length minimization. *STUF - Language Typology and Universals*, 73(4):605 – 633.

Zoey Liu. 2022. A multifactorial approach to crosslinguistic constituent orderings. *Linguistics Vanguard*.

Zoey Liu and Emily Prud'hommeaux. 2022. Data-driven parsing evaluation for child-parent interactions. *arXiv preprint arXiv:2209.13778*.

Brian MacWhinney. 2000. *The CHILDES Project: Tools for analyzing talk. transcription format and programs*, volume 1. Psychology Press.

Peng Qi, Yuhao Zhang, Yuhui Zhang, Jason Bolton, and Christopher D. Manning. 2020. Stanza: A Python Natural Language Processing Toolkit for Many Human Languages. In *Proceedings of the 58th Annual Meeting of the Association for Computational Linguistics: System Demonstrations*, pages 101–108, Online. Association for Computational Linguistics.

Alessandro Sanchez, Stephan C Meylan, Mika Braginsky, Kyle E MacDonald, Daniel Yurovsky, and Michael C Frank. 2019. childes-db: A flexible and reproducible interface to the child language data exchange system. *Behavior research methods*, 51(4):1928–1941.

Priya M Shimpi, Perla B Gámez, Janellen Huttenlocher, and Marina Vasilyeva. 2007. Syntactic priming in 3-and 4-year-old children: evidence for abstract representations of transitive and dative forms. *Developmental psychology*, 43(6):1334.

William Snyder and Karin Stromswold. 1997. The structure and acquisition of English dative constructions. *Linguistic inquiry*, pages 281–317.

Lynne M Stallings, Maryellen C MacDonald, and Padraig G O'Seaghdha. 1998. Phrasal ordering constraints in sentence production: Phrase length and verb disposition in heavy-NP shift. *Journal of Memory and Language*, 39(3):392–417.

Benedikt Szmrecsanyi, Jason Grafmiller, Joan Bresnan, Anette Rosenbach, Sali Tagliamonte, and Simon Todd. 2017. Spoken syntax in a comparative perspective: The dative and genitive alternation in varieties of English. *Glossa: a journal of general linguistics*, 2(1):1–27.

Lucien Tesnière. 1959. *Eléments de Syntaxe Structurale*. Paris: Klincksieck.

Rob van der Goot, Ahmet Üstün, Alan Ramponi, Ibrahim Sharaf, and Barbara Plank. 2021. Massive choice, ample tasks (MaChAmp): A toolkit for multi-task learning in NLP. In *Proceedings of the 16th Conference of the European Chapter of the Association for Computational Linguistics: System Demonstrations*, pages 176–197, Online. Association for Computational Linguistics.

Thomas Wasow. 1997. End-Weight from the Speaker's Perspective. *Journal of Psycholinguistic Research*, (3):347–361.

Charles Yang and Silvina Montrul. 2017. Learning datives: The tolerance principle in monolingual and bilingual acquisition. *Second Language Research*, 33(1):119–144.

A Notes on data preprocessing

After parsing data from the English sections of the CHILDES database (Section 3.1), we searched for VPs where the head verb takes either a double object structure (V-NP-NP) or a prepositional object structure (V-NP-PP). The part-of-speech (POS) tag of the head verb was VERB, which only includes lexical verbs (as opposed to auxiliaries). For double object structures, we selected VP instances in which the head verb has one direct object and one indirect object, which were identified based on their dependency relations with the head verb (*obj* and *iobj*, respectively). For the prepositional object structure, we selected VP instances where the head verb takes one direct object as well as one PP oblique immediately following the direct object; the dependency relation between the PP and the head verb was *oblique*, and the nominal head of the PP had one of four POS tags: NOUN (lexical noun), NUM (numeral), PRON (pronoun), and PROPN (proper noun). For verbs that only belong to the dative class, the adposition, or the function head of the PP was restricted to *to*, and for the benefactive verbs, the adposition was *for*; for verbs that are included in both classes, the adposition was either *to* or *for*.

Levin class verbs were taken from `http://www-personal.umich.edu/~jlawler/levin.verbs`; there are 23 verbs overlapped in both classes. Note that in the final dative dataset (Section 3.3), there were 67 dative verbs, 52 benefactive verbs, and 15 verbs that belong to both classes.

B Notes on syntactic alternatives for the prepositional object structure

Based on literature related to the heavy NP shift in English (Stallings et al., 1998; Arnold et al., 2000), one might posit that the alternative of an observed prepositional object structure can be constructed another way. For example, if the original sentence is ***give*** *[$_{NP}$ the bread that she bought at the store yesterday] [$_{PP}$ to her]*, one grammatical alternative, besides the direct object structure, can also be ***give*** *[$_{PP}$ to her] [$_{NP}$ the bread that she bought at the store yesterday]*. Nevertheless, structures with (heavy) NP shift as such are rare in child production. We searched for VP instances where the head verb takes one direct object and one prepositional oblique phrase dependent (PP); in addition, the PP has to precede the direct object. This only yielded 128 utterances produced by 56 children. Therefore we left these cases out from our analysis.

C Descriptive statistics for our dative dataset

Visualizations of the frequency distribution of the double object structure and the prepositional object structure in child and parent speech are presented in Figure 3.

D DLM for specific head verbs

We present the preferences for DLM in the dative constructions headed by *give* (Figure 4) and *get* (Figure 5) in child and parent production. Of all the head verbs for the dative alternation in our dataset, these two verbs are attested most frequently.

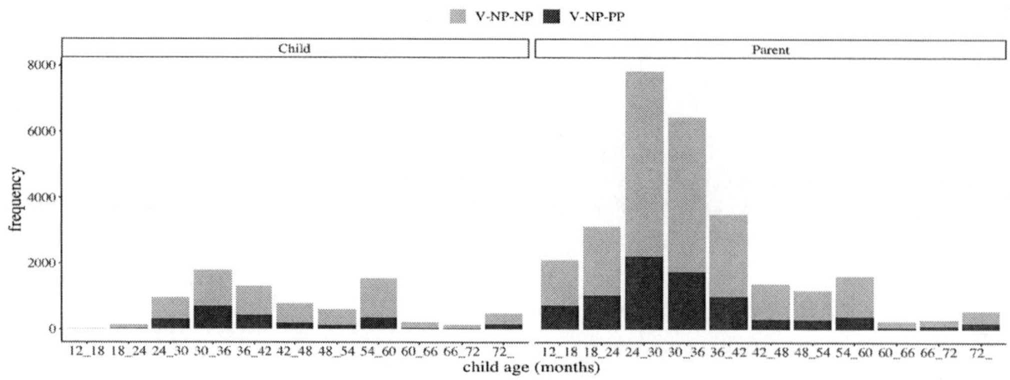

Figure 3: Frequency distribution of the double object structure (V-NP-NP) and the prepositional object structure (V-NP-PP) in child and parent production.

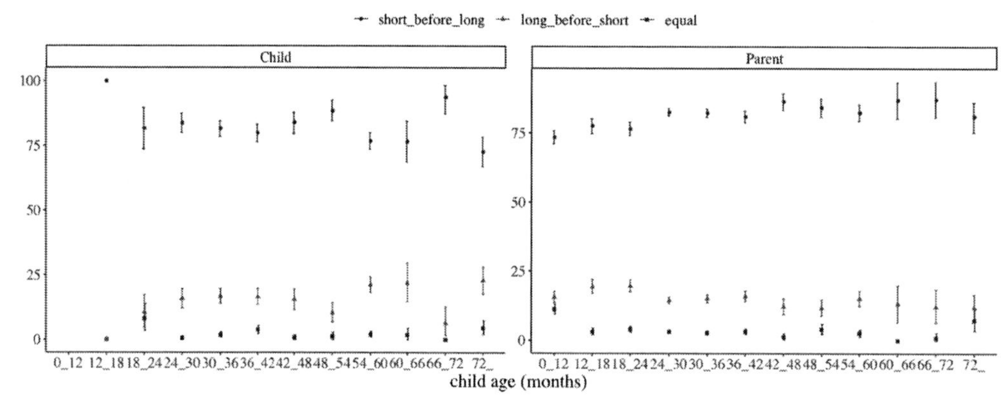

Figure 4: DLM in the dative constructions headed by *give* in child and parent production (Child: N=3,338; Parent: N=12,246).

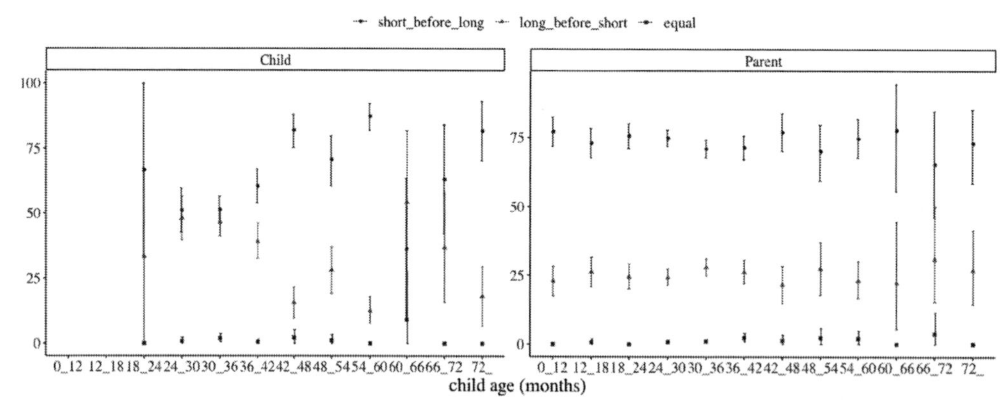

Figure 5: DLM in the dative constructions headed by *get* in child and parent production (Child: N=1,158; Parent: N=3,414).

Which Sentence Representation is More Informative: An Analysis on Text Classification

Necva Bölücü
Computer Engineering
Adana Alparslan Turkes
Science and Technology University
Adana, Turkey
nbolucu@atu.edu.tr

Burcu Can
Department of Computing Science and Mathematics
University of Stirling
Stirling, UK
burcu.can@stir.ac.uk

Abstract

Text classification is a popular and well-studied problem in Natural Language Processing. Most previous work on text classification has focused on deep neural networks such as LSTMs and CNNs. However, text classification studies using syntactic and semantic information are very limited in the literature. In this study, we propose a model using Graph Attention Network (GAT) that incorporates semantic and syntactic information as input for the text classification task. The semantic representations of UCCA and AMR are used as semantic information and the dependency tree is used as syntactic information. Extensive experimental results and in-depth analysis show that UCCA-GAT model, which is a semantic-aware model outperforms the AMR-GAT and DEP-GAT, which are semantic and syntax-aware models respectively. We also provide a comprehensive analysis of the proposed model to understand the limitations of the representations for the problem.

1 Introduction

The text classification problem has been widely studied in the literature (Yao et al., 2019; Malekzadeh et al., 2021) in the field of Natural Language Processing (NLP).

The text classification problem has been recently used as a downstream task in SentEval (Conneau and Kiela, 2018), a toolkit for evaluating sentence representations. In the literature, studies on Semantic Textual Similarity (STS) (Reimers et al., 2019; Gao et al., 2021) have used the text classification to evaluate the sentence embeddings learned by their proposed models using the datasets provided by the SentEval toolkit (Conneau and Kiela, 2018).

For text classification, traditional deep learning models such as Long Short-Term Memory (LSTM) Networks (Hochreiter and Schmidhuber, 1997) and Convolutional Neural Networks (CNN) (Kim, 2014) have been adopted. These deep learning models capture the local semantic and syntactic information by using the input as a sequence of words but they ignore the semantic and syntactic information of the input (Peng et al., 2018). Recently, Graph Neural Networks (GNNs) (Battaglia et al., 2018; Cai et al., 2018) have been used for text classification (Yao et al., 2019; Malekzadeh et al., 2021), sequence labeling (Marcheggiani and Titov, 2017; Zhang et al., 2018a), and question answering (Song et al., 2018; De Cao et al., 2019).

In dependency parsing the aim is to find a tree that represents dependencies between words in a sentence. On the contrary, semantic parsing maps a text to its formal representation that provides an abstraction of its meaning. There has been a recent increase in the studies that propose various neural network architectures such as tree-LSTM (Takase et al., 2016), Heterogeneous Graph Transformer (Li et al., 2020), and Transformer (Xie et al., 2021) that integrate semantic and syntactic information. GNN models that integrate external representations into deep learning models referred to as semantic and syntax-aware models, are the well-studied models in the literature for various NLP problems such as Neural Machine Translation (NMT) (Bastings et al., 2017) and text classification (Elbasani and Kim, 2022). These models have gained attention because they are capable of capturing information over long distances, especially between discontinuous constituents (Wang and Li, 2022).

In this study, we analyzed the impact of semantic and syntactic representations within Graph Attention Networks (GAT), particularly for the text classification problem. We used the dataset provided by SentEval toolkit (Conneau and Kiela, 2018). We constructed the GAT model by integrating Abstract Meaning Representation (AMR) (Banarescu et al., 2013) and the Universal Conceptual Cognitive Annotation (UCCA) (Abend and Rappoport, 2013) as graph-based semantic representations and the dependency tree as syntactic representation. Since the size of the datasets in SentEval toolkit (Con-

Proceedings of the Seventh International Conference on Dependency Linguistics (Depling, GURT/SyntaxFest 2023), pages 9 - 21
March 9-12, 2023

neau and Kiela, 2018) is different, we evaluated the results of our proposed model with the studies that use the SentEval toolkit (Conneau and Kiela, 2018). [1]

The rest of the paper is organized as follows. Section 2 reviews similar semantic and syntax-aware models. Section 3 describes our methodology for addressing the text classification problem using semantic and syntactic parser models. Section 4 presents our experimental results along with a detailed analysis of the proposed models. Finally, Section 5 concludes the paper with insights on the impact of the semantic and syntactic information on the classification problem.

2 Related Work

In addition to the traditional neural networks that simply rely on neural language models, semantic and syntax-aware models have been recently used effectively in NLP problems such as text classification (Ahmed et al., 2018; Huang et al., 2020; Liang et al., 2022; Elbasani and Kim, 2022), natural language generation (Guo et al., 2021), question answering (Schlichtkrull et al., 2020), semantic role labeling (SRL) (Schlichtkrull et al., 2020; Mohammadshahi and Henderson, 2021), reading comprehension (Sachan and Xing, 2016; Galitsky, 2020), text summarization (Takase et al., 2016; Dohare and Karnick, 2017), language modelling (Zhang et al., 2020), and machine translation (Qin and Liang, 2020; Slobodkin et al., 2021; Nguyen et al., 2021; Li and Flanigan, 2022).

Dependency trees usually provide sufficient syntactic information in various NLP tasks (Huang et al., 2020; Liang et al., 2022; Guo et al., 2021) and improve the performance of the models considerably. As for the external resource of semantic information, the most popular semantic representation is the AMR (Hardy and Vlachos, 2018; Elbasani and Kim, 2022; Kouris et al., 2022).

In particular, GNNs (Bastings et al., 2017; Marcheggiani and Titov, 2019; Schlichtkrull et al., 2020; Guo et al., 2021; Elbasani and Kim, 2022) have been used as models into which syntactic and semantic information are easily integrated. In addition to GNNs, Transformers have also been used to integrate such external resources such as syntax-aware word representation (SAWR) (Xie et al., 2021), syntax-aware local attention (SLA) (Li et al., 2020), syntax-graph guided self-attention (SGSA) (Gong et al., 2022), Scene-Aware Self-Attention (SASA), and Scene-Aware Cross-Attention (SACrA) head (Slobodkin et al., 2021). Last but not least, the Heterogeneous Graph Transformer (Hu et al., 2020), a customized version of the Transformer (Vaswani et al., 2017), has been recently introduced as a model with semantic AMR information (Yao et al., 2020).

3 Methodology

In this section, we describe the proposed semantic- and syntax-aware GAT models that integrate semantic and syntactic information as external resources into the model. First, we explain the preprocessing step that is performed to convert the text into the required form to be processed by the GAT model.

3.1 Preprocessing

GAT models use adjacency and feature matrices that are extracted from graphs as input. There are several approaches to transform a text into a graph, such as digitizing text (Hamid et al., 2020), statistical methods (PMI, TF-IDF) (Yao et al., 2019), dependency trees (Zhang et al., 2018b) or semantic graphs (AMR) (Elbasani and Kim, 2022).

In this study, we use dependency trees and semantic graphs. Here we explain the preprocessing step along with the parser model that is used to convert datasets into dependency trees and semantic graphs, as well as the details of extracting adjacency and feature matrices from graphs and trees.

Converting datasets into graphs/trees The parser models that are employed to extract the graphs and trees from the datasets are described below:

- **UCCA Semantic Parser** We use the self-attentive semantic parser model by Bölücü and Can (2021) to extract the UCCA-based semantic representations. The model is based on a graph-based approach with an encoder-decoder architecture, where the encoder is a Transformer (Vaswani et al., 2017) with 2 MLP classifiers and the decoder corresponds to the CYK algorithm (Chappelier and Rajman, 1998) that generates a constituency tree with the maximum score using the per-span scores obtained from the transformer encoder.

[1]The code is publicly available at https://github.com/adalin16/depling-GAT

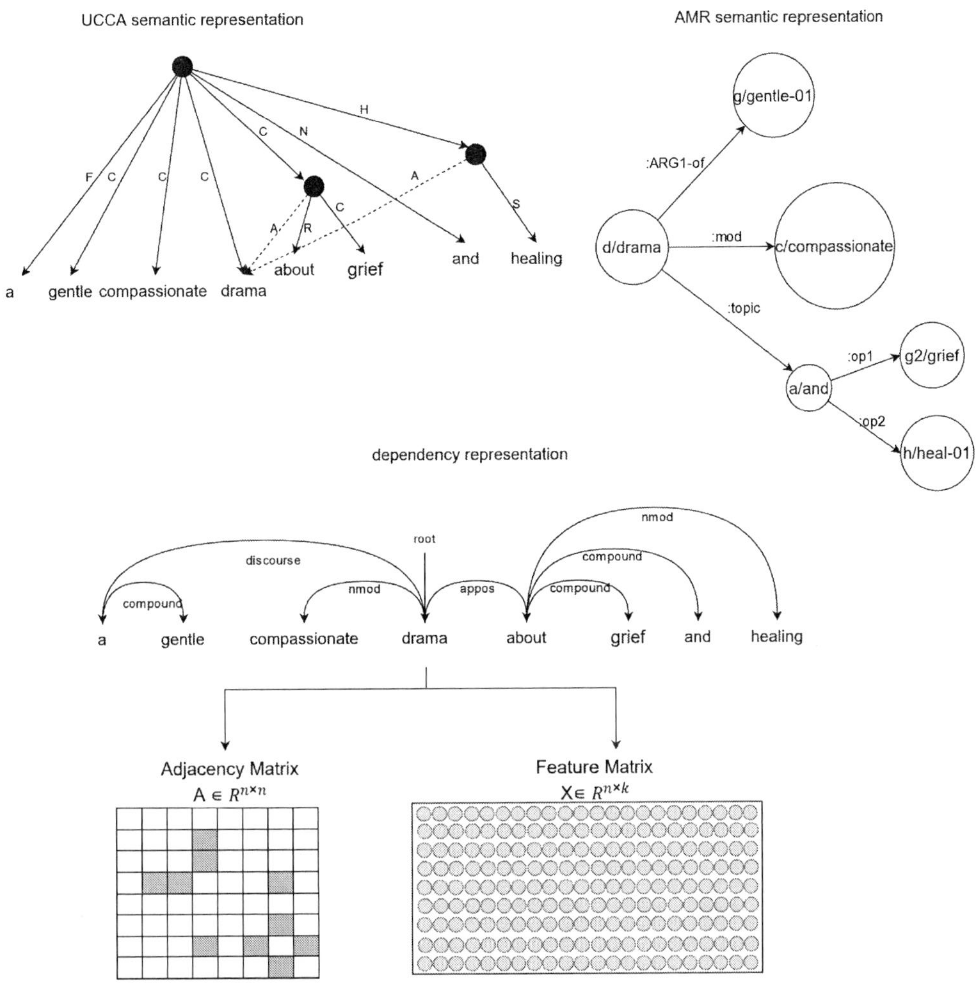

Figure 1: UCCA, AMR semantic graphs, and the dependency trees along with the feature and adjacency matrices that are used as input to the GAT model are illustrated for the example phrase *"a gentle compassionate drama about grief and healing"* from the MR dataset (Pang and Lee, 2005). The gray color in the matrix represents the value of 1 and the white color represents the value of 0. Each row in the feature matrix corresponds to the pre-trained word embedding of a node in the graph/tree.

- **AMR Semantic Parser** As an AMR semantic parser, we use the T5 parser (Roberts et al., 2020). The model is based on a language model that is fine-tuned on English. The model is integrated into the spaCy library (Honnibal and Montani, 2017) and is called AMRLib[2].

- **Dependency Parser** We use the Deep Biaffine dependency parser model Dozat and Manning (2016) to extract the dependency trees. The model is based on a graph-based approach where BiLSTM with biaffine classifiers is used as an encoder and MST is used as a decoder that generates dependency trees from predicted arcs and labels in the encoder. We use the model[3] integrated within the Stanza library (Qi et al., 2020).

Extracting adjacency and feature matrices from graphs/trees Since the inputs of the proposed model are adjacency and feature matrices, we extracted the matrices from graphs and trees. The semantic representations of UCCA and AMR are based on DAG, and the dependency trees are represented by trees. We followed the same proce-

[2] https://spacy.io/universe/project/amrlib

[3] https://stanfordnlp.github.io/stanza/depparse.html

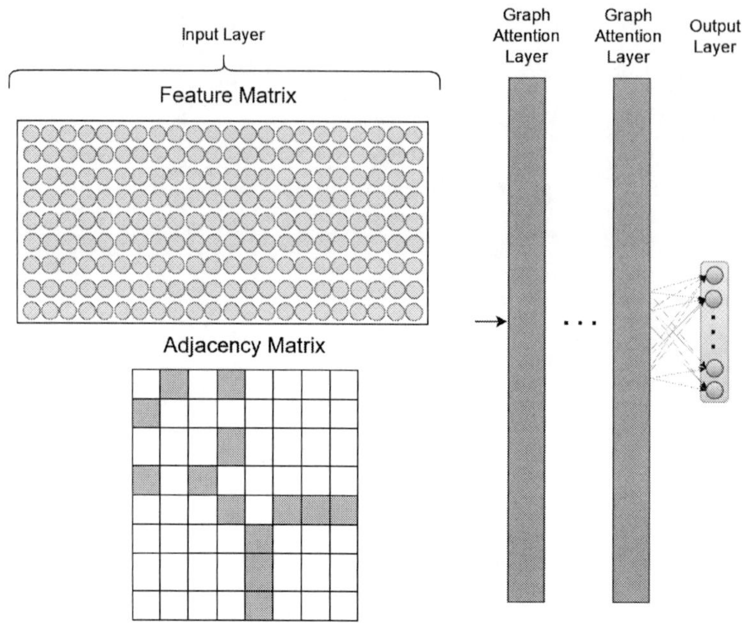

Figure 2: Overview of the GAT model along with its input in the form of a feature and adjacency matrix. The matrices correspond to semantic and syntactic information in the form of a UCCA or an AMR graph, or a dependency tree.

Dataset	Train	Dev	Test
Movie Review (MR) (Pang and Lee, 2005)	10,662	train in k-fold	test in k-fold
Customer Review (CR) (Hu and Liu, 2004)	3,770	train in k-fold	test in k-fold
Subjectivity / Objectivity (SUBJ) (Pang and Lee, 2004)	10,000	train in k-fold	test in k-fold
Multi-Perspective Question and Answering (MPQA) (Wiebe et al., 2005)	10,606	train in k-fold	test in k-fold
Stanford Sentiment Analysis 2 (SST-2) (Socher et al., 2013)	67,349	872	1,821
Text Retrieval Conference (TREC) (Voorhees and Tice, 2000)	5,452	train in k-fold	500
The Microsoft Research Paraphrase Corpus (MRPC) (Dolan et al., 2004)	4,726	train in k-fold	1,725

Table 1: The details of the datasets given in the downstream tasks in SentEval toolkit.

dure for all of the representations considering all as graphs.

For a given graph $G = (V, E)$, V is the set of nodes and E is the set of labeled edges (UCCA - edges, AMR - relations between nodes, dependency tree - dependency relations). We extracted:

- the feature matrix X ($n \times k$, where n is the number of nodes (UCCA - terminal and non-terminal nodes, AMR - words, dependency tree - words except the `ROOT` node) in the graph and k is the embedding dimension),
- the adjacency matrix A ($n \times n$, where n is the number of nodes in the graph), which is not trainable.

For the feature matrix, we used pre-trained word embeddings (BERT (Devlin et al., 2019), RoBERTa (Liu et al., 2019), and XLNet (Yang et al., 2019)) for nodes (UCCA - terminal nodes, AMR - words, dependency tree - words) and a randomly generated embedding with the same embedding dimension of the pre-trained word embeddings for non-terminal nodes in UCCA.

UCCA, AMR, and dependency tree representations of the phrase *"a gentle compassionate drama about grief and healing"* from the Movie Review (MR) dataset (Pang and Lee, 2005) with extracted adjacency and feature matrices are given in Figure 1.

3.2 Graph Attention Network

In order to incorporate external semantic information, we adopted Graph Attention Networks (GAT) (Veličković et al., 2017) that are based on self-attention layers. We used GATs for the text classification problem since they provide a straightforward method to utilise semantic information in the form of a semantic graph (UCCA/AMR) or a dependency tree. The overview of the model is given in Figure 2.

GNN models have different types of updating mechanisms for nodes. The basic version of updating, as applied in this study, updates each node i in the l-th layer, H^{l+1} as follows:

$$H^{l+1} = \sigma(AH^{l}W^{l}) \quad (1)$$

where $\sigma(\cdot)$ refers to ReLU non-linear activation function, A is the adjacency matrix, W^l is the attention weights in the l-th layer. H^l is the feature matrix of the l-th layer ($H^0 = X$, where X is the feature matrix extracted from a semantic graph or a dependency tree) where l is a hyperparameter that needs to be finetuned for the graph.

We fed the output of the node in the final layer into the output layer that applies the softmax function to generate the output class of a given text either as a binary or a multi-class classification:

$$Z = softmax(H^{o}) \quad (2)$$

where H^o is the feature matrix of the final GAT layer.

4 Experiments and Results

4.1 Datasets

We evaluated the model on 7 downstream tasks given in the SentEval toolkit (Conneau and Kiela, 2018). The details of the datasets are given in Table 1.

4.2 Experimental Setting

We used PyTorch 3.7 to implement the model. We used cross-entropy loss for both binary and multi-class classification. The Adam (Kingma and Ba, 2014) was used as the optimizer in all models with $\epsilon = 1e - 8$, and the default max grad norm for gradient clipping.

We used the monolingual (BERT (Devlin et al., 2019), RoBERTa (Liu et al., 2019), XLNet (Yang et al., 2019)) and multilingual pre-trained language models (M-BERT (Devlin et al., 2019), XLM-R (Conneau and Lample, 2019), XLM-R-large (Conneau et al., 2020)) in order to build the feature matrices as described in Section 3.1. All hyperparameters along with their values are given in Appendix A.

We evaluated the models applied to binary and multi-class classification problems using the SentEval toolkit (Conneau and Kiela, 2018). We used accuracy metric in all downstream tasks and reported Precision, Recall, and F1 for a detailed analysis of the class-wise results for TREC.

4.3 Results

The results obtained from the semantic and syntax-aware GAT models (UCCA-GAT, AMR-GAT, and Dep-GAT) on 7 datasets in SentEval toolkit (Conneau and Kiela, 2018) along with the state-of-the-art results are given in Table 2. The results show that the performance of the GAT models is slightly behind the state-of-the-art results (Cer et al., 2018; Gao et al., 2021; Reimers et al., 2019). The main reason is that these models learn sentence embeddings and then apply the learned sentence embeddings to the downstream tasks (Reimers et al., 2019; Gao et al., 2021). Here, the main aim is to investigate the external usage of semantic and syntactic information without performing separate learning for sentence embeddings but solely relying on the existing semantic and syntactic information. Therefore, we only compare the performance of the semantic- and syntax-aware GAT models with each other for 7 downstream tasks. The results show that the UCCA-GAT model performs better than the AMR-GAT and the Dep-GAT models. The analysis of the adjacency matrices extracted from the AMR semantic parser and the UCCA semantic parser shows that the relations such as "about", "like", "of", etc. are defined as concepts and used as edge labels instead of nodes in the AMR representation. Since our models use the nodes without edge labels, the model misses the concepts that might give a clue about the target class. This also leads to sparse adjacency matrices for AMR graphs compared to other adjacency matrices extracted from UCCA graphs and dependency trees.

We analyse the class-wise results obtained from the three models using the TREC dataset (Voorhees and Tice, 2000) (multi-class classification problem). The results are given in Table 3. It can be clearly seen that UCCA-GAT is particularly good at predicting the classes "num" and "loc", since the number of relations in the UCCA graphs is higher in these classes than in other classes. The performance of AMR-GAT is worse than the other models (UCCA-GAT, Dep-GAT) because we lose the relations represented as labels in the AMR semantic representation and we used only the nodes in the semantic and syntactic representations in the preprocessing step during the extraction of the adjacency matrices for the AMR-GAT model. The Dep-

	Our proposed models							
	MR	CR	SUBJ	MPQA	SST-2	TREC	MRPC	Avg.
UCCA-GAT	82.04	83.37	90.38	87.29	89.35	81.92	73.50	83.98
AMR-GAT	81.55	81.11	88.98	83.94	85.83	79.65	72.87	83.42
Dep-GAT	80.66	81.62	89.10	85.76	88.03	81.06	75.25	83.07
	State-of-the-art							
BERT-CLS embedding ♡	78.68	84.85	94.21	88.23	84.13	**91.40**	71.13	84.66
BiLSTM ♢	81.1	86.3	92.4	90.2	-	-	-	-
Universal Sentence Encoder ♣	80.09	85.19	93.98	86.70	86.38	93.2	70.14	85.10
SimCSE-BERT$_{base}$ ♠	83.64	89.43	94.39	89.86	88.96	89.60	**76.00**	87.41
SBERT-NLI-large ♡	**84.88**	**90.07**	**94.52**	**90.33**	**90.66**	87.4	75.94	**87.69**

Table 2: Accuracy results of the downstream tasks using the proposed models and the other state-of-the-art models. The highest scores are given in bold. (♣ results from (Cer et al., 2018); ♠ results from (Gao et al., 2021); ♡ results from (Reimers et al., 2019); ♢ results from (Conneau et al., 2017))

	UCCA-GAT			AMR-GAT			Dep-GAT		
Class	Precision	Recall	F1	Precision	Recall	F1	Precision	Recall	F1
num	0.97	0.89	**0.93**	0.90	0.84	0.87	0.91	0.82	0.87
loc	0.86	0.79	**0.83**	0.86	0.78	0.82	0.82	0.80	0.81
hum	0.80	0.80	0.80	0.74	0.80	0.77	0.77	0.85	**0.81**
desc	0.85	0.83	0.84	0.82	0.83	0.82	0.87	0.87	**0.87**
enty	0.70	0.85	0.77	0.77	0.83	0.80	0.81	0.87	**0.84**
abbr	0.86	0.67	**0.75**	0.64	0.78	0.70	0.67	0.67	0.67
avg.	0.84	0.81	0.82	0.79	0.81	0.80	0.81	0.81	0.81

Table 3: Class-wise results on the TREC dataset (Voorhees and Tice, 2000)

PLM	MR	CR	SUBJ	MPQA	SST-2	TREC	MRPC
	Monolingual Embeddings						
BERT	78.33	79.15	87.80	82.78	85.01	80.40	69.68
RoBERTa	80.16	79.89	89.11	**87.29**	**89.35**	79.11	72.52
XLNet	74.62	75.99	83.15	77.46	80.56	76.82	67.71
	Multilingual Embeddings						
M-BERT	79.27	81.94	88.15	83.11	83.14	81.00	72.35
XLM-R	**82.04**	82.23	89.48	84.76	85.01	**81.92**	72.93
XLM-R-large	78.78	**83.37**	**90.38**	85.82	87.59	81.42	**73.50**

Table 4: Accuracy results obtained with monolingual and multilingual embeddings in UCCA-GAT model. The best values are in bold.

GAT model achieves better overall results since the dependency trees can capture long-distance information. The only class that Dep-GAT cannot capture is "abbr", compared to the success achieved with other classes in the TREC dataset (Voorhees and Tice, 2000).

Figure 3 illustrates the confusion matrices of the semantic and syntax-aware GAT models for the TREC dataset. The results show that the UCCA-GAT model predicts the class "num" better than other models. In addition, the Dep-GAT model is better at predicting the class "desc". For all models, there is a general confusion between the classes "desc" and "ent".

We also analyse the models deeply in terms of the impact of the layers and embeddings.

- **Embeddings** We present an analysis of the pre-trained language models used in the extraction of feature matrix X from UCCA, AMR, and dependency

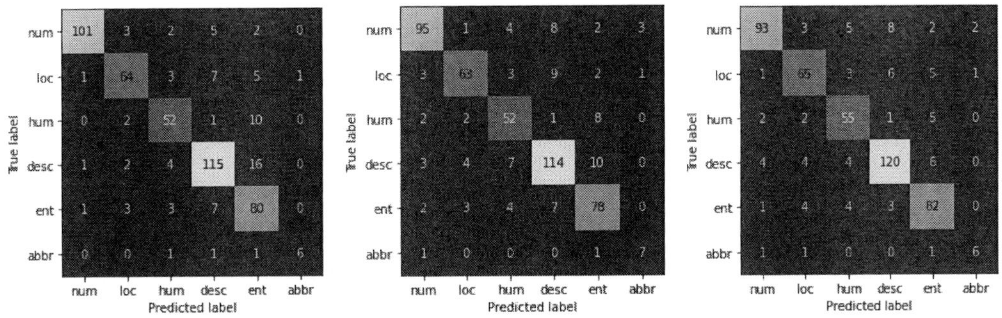

(a) UCCA-GAT (b) AMR-GAT (c) Dep-GAT

Figure 3: Confusion matrices of the semantic and syntax-aware GAT models on TREC dataset (Voorhees and Tice, 2000)

PLM	MR	CR	SUBJ	MPQA	SST-2	TREC	MRPC
			Monolingual Embeddings				
BERT	77.68	**81.11**	83.98	83.11	82.48	75.61	70.43
RoBERTa	**81.55**	79.44	85.44	83.44	**85.83**	**79.65**	70.78
XLNet	72.64	72.12	82.56	78.15	79.68	71.95	68.87
			Multilingual Embeddings				
M-BERT	78.77	79.71	87.45	82.17	83.91	76.42	71.19
XLM-R	79.49	79.28	**88.98**	83.56	84.46	78.20	**72.87**
XLM-R-large	80.10	80.08	87.95	**83.94**	85.01	78.62	72.35

Table 5: Accuracy results obtained with monolingual and multilingual embeddings in AMR-GAT model. The best values are in bold.

PLM	MR	CR	SUBJ	MPQA	SST-2	TREC	MRPC
			Monolingual Embeddings				
BERT	77.30	79.50	86.43	82.99	83.64	78.80	70.78
RoBERTa	78.95	**80.11**	89.10	83.14	**88.03**	79.62	71.59
XLNet	72.45	74.40	82.47	78.04	81.38	75.27	69.51
			Multilingual Embeddings				
M-BERT	79.39	79.55	84.69	82.64	84.51	79.89	73.51
XLM-R	80.19	81.62	87.59	83.84	85.78	**81.06**	74.09
XLM-R-large	**80.66**	81.14	**88.11**	**85.76**	86.49	79.49	**75.25**

Table 6: Accuracy results obtained with monolingual and multilingual embeddings in Dep-GAT model. The best values are in bold.

tree. We used BERT (Devlin et al., 2019) (`bert-base-cased`), RoBERTa (Liu et al., 2019) (`roberta-base`), and XLNet (Yang et al., 2019) (`xlnet-base-cased`) monolingual embeddings with base variants consisting of 768 hidden dimensions, whereas we used multilingual version of BERT (M-BERT) (Devlin et al., 2019), and RoBERTa (XLM-R) (Conneau and Lample, 2019) and its large version (XLM-R-large) (Conneau and Lample, 2019).

The results obtained using monolingual and multilingual pre-trained embeddings are given in Table 4, 5 and 6 for UCCA-GAT, AMR-GAT, and Dep-GAT respectively. The re-

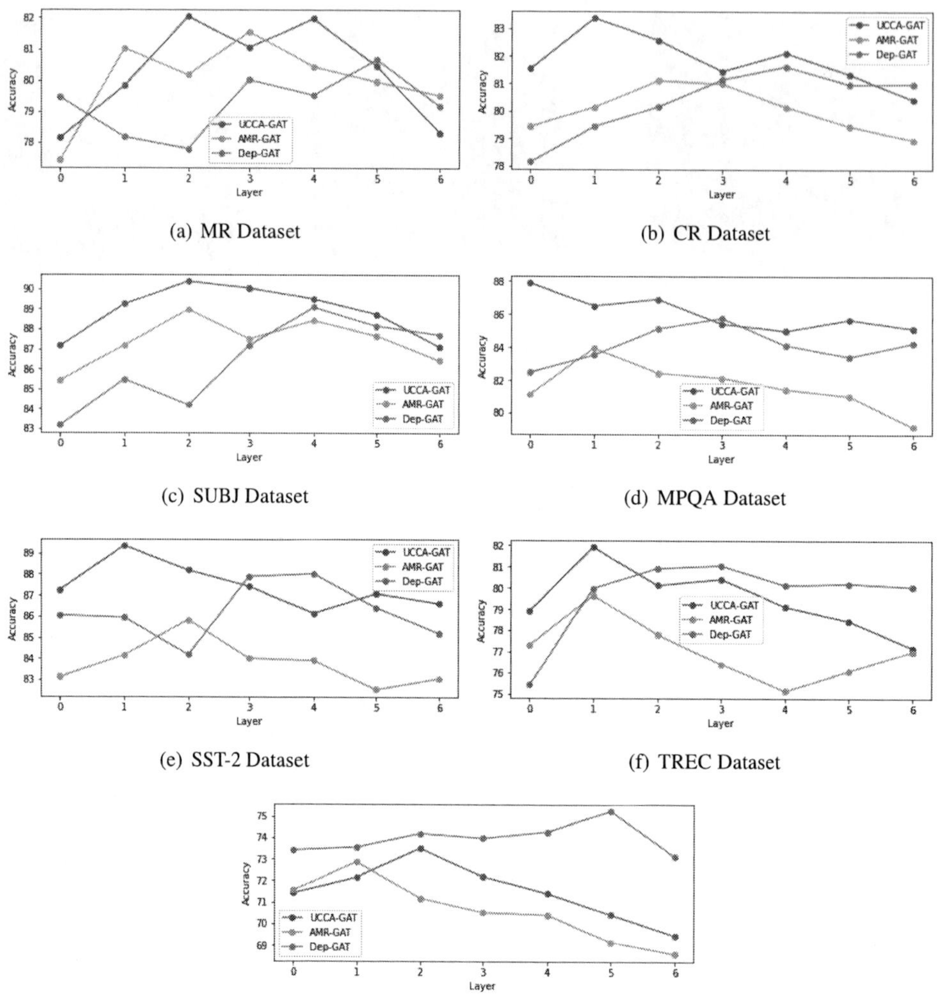

(a) MR Dataset

(b) CR Dataset

(c) SUBJ Dataset

(d) MPQA Dataset

(e) SST-2 Dataset

(f) TREC Dataset

(g) MRPC Dataset

Figure 4: Accuracy scores based on the number of layers in the proposed models.

sults show that multilingual embeddings are more effective for both proposed semantic and syntax-aware models. In monolingual embeddings, the results obtained from the models RoBERTa pre-trained word embeddings are higher than that of the others (BERT, XLNet).

- **Impact of the layers** We also analyse the impact of the number of layers in the proposed models (UCCA-GAT, AMR-GAT, Dep-GAT) on the performance of the models. We perform the experiments with embeddings with which we obtained the best results. We vary the number of the layers from 1 to 7 and report the results in Figure 4 for all datasets with UCCA-GAT, AMR-GAT, and Dep-GAT models. The results show that the syntax-aware model (Dep-GAT) learns in deeper layers, and semantic-aware models (UCCA-GAT and AMR-GAT) tend to learn in shallow layers or in the middle layers. The previous studies already show that syntactic features are encoded in the shallow layers and semantic features are encoded in the deeper layers of the pre-trained language models (Conneau et al., 2018; Jawahar et al., 2019), and here we also obtained better results with deeper layers in the syntax-aware model and with shallow layers in the semantic-aware models (UCCA-GAT and AMR-GAT).

5 Conclusion

Semantic and syntax-aware models have recently been proposed for various NLP problems, that especially require long-distance information, especially between discontinuous constituents, in addition to the local information captured by sequential models. In this paper, we propose a graph neural network model that incorporates semantic and syntactic information for the text classification task. To the best of our knowledge, this is the first study that compares semantic and syntactic information used in a graph neural network, specifically for the task of text classification. We present a detailed analysis of the results, showing that the UCCA semantic information improves the performance of the classification model compared to syntactic information (i.e. dependency tree). However, we were not able to obtain similar results with the model using the AMR semantic representation. This shows that the preprocessing step to convert the graph into adjacency and feature matrices is a very important step in GNN models.

As future work, we plan to improve the preprocessing step to obtain more informative adjacency and feature matrices.

References

Omri Abend and Ari Rappoport. 2013. UCCA: A Semantics-based Grammatical Annotation Scheme. In *Proceedings of the 10th International Conference on Computational Semantics (IWCS 2013)–Long Papers*, pages 1–12.

Usman Ahmed, Lubna Zafar, Faiza Qayyum, and Muhammad Arshad Islam. 2018. Irony Detector at SemEval-2018 Task 3: Irony Detection in English Tweets using Word Graph. In *Proceedings of the 12th international workshop on semantic evaluation*, pages 581–586.

Laura Banarescu, Claire Bonial, Shu Cai, Madalina Georgescu, Kira Griffitt, Ulf Hermjakob, Kevin Knight, Philipp Koehn, Martha Palmer, and Nathan Schneider. 2013. Abstract meaning representation for sembanking. In *Proceedings of the 7th linguistic annotation workshop and interoperability with discourse*, pages 178–186.

Jasmijn Bastings, Ivan Titov, Wilker Aziz, Diego Marcheggiani, and Khalil Sima'an. 2017. Graph Convolutional Encoders for Syntax-aware Neural Machine Translation. *CoRR*, abs/1704.04675.

Peter W. Battaglia, Jessica B. Hamrick, Victor Bapst, Alvaro Sanchez-Gonzalez, Vinícius Flores Zambaldi, Mateusz Malinowski, Andrea Tacchetti, David Raposo, Adam Santoro, Ryan Faulkner, Çaglar Gülçehre, H. Francis Song, Andrew J. Ballard, Justin Gilmer, George E. Dahl, Ashish Vaswani, Kelsey R. Allen, Charles Nash, Victoria Langston, Chris Dyer, Nicolas Heess, Daan Wierstra, Pushmeet Kohli, Matthew M. Botvinick, Oriol Vinyals, Yujia Li, and Razvan Pascanu. 2018. Relational inductive biases, deep learning, and graph networks. *CoRR*, abs/1806.01261.

Necva Bölücü and Burcu Can. 2021. Self-Attentive Constituency Parsing for UCCA-based Semantic Parsing.

Hongyun Cai, Vincent W Zheng, and Kevin Chen-Chuan Chang. 2018. A comprehensive survey of graph embedding: Problems, techniques, and applications. *IEEE Transactions on Knowledge and Data Engineering*, 30(9):1616–1637.

Daniel Cer, Yinfei Yang, Sheng-yi Kong, Nan Hua, Nicole Limtiaco, Rhomni St. John, Noah Constant, Mario Guajardo-Cespedes, Steve Yuan, Chris Tar, Yun-Hsuan Sung, Brian Strope, and Ray Kurzweil. 2018. Universal Sentence Encoder. *CoRR*, abs/1803.11175.

J-C Chappelier and Martin Rajman. 1998. A generalized CYK algorithm for parsing stochastic CFG. In *Proc. of 1st Workshop on Tabulation in Parsing and Deduction (TAPD'98)*, CONF, pages 133–137.

Alexis Conneau, Kartikay Khandelwal, Naman Goyal, Vishrav Chaudhary, Guillaume Wenzek, Francisco Guzmán, Edouard Grave, Myle Ott, Luke Zettlemoyer, and Veselin Stoyanov. 2020. Unsupervised Cross-lingual Representation Learning at Scale. In *Proceedings of the 58th Annual Meeting of the Association for Computational Linguistics*, pages 8440–8451, Online.

Alexis Conneau and Douwe Kiela. 2018. SentEval: An Evaluation Toolkit for Universal Sentence Representations. In *Proceedings of the Eleventh International Conference on Language Resources and Evaluation (LREC 2018)*.

Alexis Conneau, Douwe Kiela, Holger Schwenk, Loïc Barrault, and Antoine Bordes. 2017. Supervised Learning of Universal Sentence Representations from Natural Language Inference Data. In *Proceedings of the 2017 Conference on Empirical Methods in Natural Language Processing*, pages 670–680.

Alexis Conneau, Germán Kruszewski, Guillaume Lample, Loïc Barrault, and Marco Baroni. 2018. What you can cram into a single $ &!#* vector: Probing sentence embeddings for linguistic properties. In *Proceedings of the 56th Annual Meeting of the Association for Computational Linguistics (Volume 1: Long Papers)*, pages 2126–2136.

Alexis Conneau and Guillaume Lample. 2019. Cross-lingual Language Model Pretraining. *Advances in neural information processing systems*, 32.

Nicola De Cao, Wilker Aziz, and Ivan Titov. 2019. Question Answering by Reasoning Across Documents with Graph Convolutional Networks. In *Proceedings of NAACL-HLT*, pages 2306–2317.

Jacob Devlin, Ming-Wei Chang, Kenton Lee, and Kristina Toutanova. 2019. BERT: Pre-training of Deep Bidirectional Transformers for Language Understanding. In *Proceedings of the 2019 Conference of the North American Chapter of the Association for Computational Linguistics: Human Language Technologies, Volume 1 (Long and Short Papers)*, pages 4171–4186.

Shibhansh Dohare and Harish Karnick. 2017. Text Summarization using Abstract Meaning Representation. *CoRR*, abs/1706.01678.

William B Dolan, Chris Quirk, and Chris Brockett. 2004. Unsupervised Construction of Large Paraphrase Corpora: Exploiting Massively Parallel News Sources. In *COLING 2004: Proceedings of the 20th International Conference on Computational Linguistics*, pages 350–356.

Timothy Dozat and Christopher D Manning. 2016. Deep biaffine attention for neural dependency parsing. *arXiv preprint arXiv:1611.01734*.

Ermal Elbasani and Jeong-Dong Kim. 2022. AMR-CNN: Abstract Meaning Representation with Convolution Neural Network for Toxic Content Detection. *Journal of Web Engineering*, pages 677–692.

Boris Galitsky. 2020. Employing Abstract Meaning Representation to Lay the Last-Mile Toward Reading Comprehension. In *Artificial Intelligence for Customer Relationship Management*, pages 57–86. Springer.

Tianyu Gao, Xingcheng Yao, and Danqi Chen. 2021. SimCSE: Simple Contrastive Learning of Sentence Embeddings. *CoRR*, abs/2104.08821.

Longchao Gong, Yan Li, Junjun Guo, Zhengtao Yu, and Shengxiang Gao. 2022. Enhancing low-resource neural machine translation with syntax-graph guided self-attention. *Knowledge-Based Systems*, 246:108615.

Qipeng Guo, Xipeng Qiu, Xiangyang Xue, and Zheng Zhang. 2021. Syntax-guided text generation via graph neural network. *Science China Information Sciences*, 64(5):1–10.

Abdullah Hamid, Nasrullah Sheikh, Naina Said, Kashif Ahmad, Asma Gul, Laiq Hassan, and Ala I. Al-Fuqaha. 2020. Fake News Detection in Social Media using Graph Neural Networks and NLP techniques: A COVID-19 use-case. *CoRR*, abs/2012.07517.

Hardy and Andreas Vlachos. 2018. Guided Neural Language Generation for Abstractive Summarization using Abstract Meaning Representation. *CoRR*, abs/1808.09160.

Sepp Hochreiter and Jürgen Schmidhuber. 1997. Long short-term memory. *Neural computation*, 9(8):1735–1780.

Matthew Honnibal and Ines Montani. 2017. spaCy 2: Natural language understanding with Bloom embeddings, convolutional neural networks and incremental parsing. *To appear*, 7(1):411–420.

Minqing Hu and Bing Liu. 2004. Mining and summarizing customer reviews. In *Proceedings of the tenth ACM SIGKDD international conference on Knowledge discovery and data mining*, pages 168–177.

Ziniu Hu, Yuxiao Dong, Kuansan Wang, and Yizhou Sun. 2020. Heterogeneous graph transformer. In *Proceedings of The Web Conference 2020*, pages 2704–2710.

Lianzhe Huang, Xin Sun, Sujian Li, Linhao Zhang, and Houfeng Wang. 2020. Syntax-aware graph attention network for aspect-level sentiment classification. In *Proceedings of the 28th international conference on computational linguistics*, pages 799–810.

Ganesh Jawahar, Benoît Sagot, and Djamé Seddah. 2019. What does BERT learn about the structure of language? In *ACL 2019-57th Annual Meeting of the Association for Computational Linguistics*.

Yoon Kim. 2014. Convolutional Neural Networks for Sentence Classification.

Diederik P. Kingma and Jimmy Ba. 2014. Adam: A Method for Stochastic Optimization.

Panagiotis Kouris, Georgios Alexandridis, and Andreas Stafylopatis. 2022. Text summarization based on semantic graphs: An abstract meaning representation graph-to-text deep learning approach.

Changmao Li and Jeffrey Flanigan. 2022. Improving Neural Machine Translation with the Abstract Meaning Representation by Combining Graph and Sequence Transformers. In *Proceedings of the 2nd Workshop on Deep Learning on Graphs for Natural Language Processing (DLG4NLP 2022)*, pages 12–21.

Zhongli Li, Qingyu Zhou, Chao Li, Ke Xu, and Yunbo Cao. 2020. Improving BERT with Syntax-aware Local Attention. *CoRR*, abs/2012.15150.

Shuo Liang, Wei Wei, Xian-Ling Mao, Fei Wang, and Zhiyong He. 2022. BiSyn-GAT: Bi-Syntax Aware Graph Attention Network for Aspect-based Sentiment Analysis. In *Findings of the Association for Computational Linguistics: ACL 2022*. Association for Computational Linguistics.

Yinhan Liu, Myle Ott, Naman Goyal, Jingfei Du, Mandar Joshi, Danqi Chen, Omer Levy, Mike Lewis, Luke Zettlemoyer, and Veselin Stoyanov. 2019. RoBERTa: A Robustly Optimized BERT Pretraining Approach. *CoRR*, abs/1907.11692.

Masoud Malekzadeh, Parisa Hajibabaee, Maryam Heidari, Samira Zad, Ozlem Uzuner, and James H Jones. 2021. Review of graph neural network in text classification. In *2021 IEEE 12th Annual Ubiquitous Computing, Electronics & Mobile Communication Conference (UEMCON)*, pages 0084–0091. IEEE.

Diego Marcheggiani and Ivan Titov. 2017. Encoding Sentences with Graph Convolutional Networks for Semantic Role Labeling. In *Proceedings of the 2017 Conference on Empirical Methods in Natural Language Processing*, pages 1506–1515.

Diego Marcheggiani and Ivan Titov. 2019. Graph Convolutions over Constituent Trees for Syntax-Aware Semantic Role Labeling. *CoRR*, abs/1909.09814.

Alireza Mohammadshahi and James Henderson. 2021. Syntax-Aware Graph-to-Graph Transformer for Semantic Role Labelling. *CoRR*, abs/2104.07704.

Long HB Nguyen, Viet H Pham, and Dien Dinh. 2021. Improving neural machine translation with AMR semantic graphs. *Mathematical Problems in Engineering*, 2021.

Bo Pang and Lillian Lee. 2004. A Sentimental Education: Sentiment Analysis Using Subjectivity Summarization Based on Minimum Cuts. In *Proceedings of the 42nd Annual Meeting of the Association for Computational Linguistics (ACL-04)*, pages 271–278.

Bo Pang and Lillian Lee. 2005. Seeing Stars: Exploiting Class Relationships for Sentiment Categorization with Respect to Rating Scales. In *Proceedings of the 43rd Annual Meeting of the Association for Computational Linguistics (ACL'05)*, pages 115–124.

Hao Peng, Jianxin Li, Yu He, Yaopeng Liu, Mengjiao Bao, Lihong Wang, Yangqiu Song, and Qiang Yang. 2018. Large-scale hierarchical text classification with recursively regularized deep graph-cnn. In *Proceedings of the 2018 world wide web conference*, pages 1063–1072.

Peng Qi, Yuhao Zhang, Yuhui Zhang, Jason Bolton, and Christopher D. Manning. 2020. Stanza: A Python Natural Language Processing Toolkit for Many Human Languages. *CoRR*, abs/2003.07082.

Ying Qin and Ye Liang. 2020. Semantic Analysis and Evaluation of Translation Based on Abstract Meaning Representation. In *International Conference on Web Information Systems and Applications*, pages 268–275. Springer.

Nils Reimers, Iryna Gurevych, Nils Reimers, Iryna Gurevych, Nandan Thakur, Nils Reimers, Johannes Daxenberger, and Iryna Gurevych. 2019. Sentence-BERT: Sentence Embeddings using Siamese BERT-Networks. In *Proceedings of the 2019 Conference on Empirical Methods in Natural Language Processing*. Association for Computational Linguistics.

Adam Roberts, Colin Raffel, and Noam Shazeer. 2020. How Much Knowledge Can You Pack Into the Parameters of a Language Model? *CoRR*, abs/2002.08910.

Mrinmaya Sachan and Eric Xing. 2016. Machine comprehension using rich semantic representations. In *Proceedings of the 54th Annual Meeting of the Association for Computational Linguistics (Volume 2: Short Papers)*, pages 486–492.

Michael Sejr Schlichtkrull, Nicola De Cao, and Ivan Titov. 2020. Interpreting Graph Neural Networks for NLP With Differentiable Edge Masking. *CoRR*, abs/2010.00577.

Aviv Slobodkin, Leshem Choshen, and Omri Abend. 2021. Semantics-aware Attention Improves Neural Machine Translation. *CoRR*, abs/2110.06920.

Richard Socher, Alex Perelygin, Jean Wu, Jason Chuang, Christopher D Manning, Andrew Y Ng, and Christopher Potts. 2013. Recursive deep models for semantic compositionality over a sentiment treebank. In *Proceedings of the 2013 conference on empirical methods in natural language processing*, pages 1631–1642.

Linfeng Song, Zhiguo Wang, Mo Yu, Yue Zhang, Radu Florian, and Daniel Gildea. 2018. Exploring Graph-structured Passage Representation for Multi-hop Reading Comprehension with Graph Neural Networks. *CoRR*, abs/1809.02040.

Sho Takase, Jun Suzuki, Naoaki Okazaki, Tsutomu Hirao, and Masaaki Nagata. 2016. Neural headline generation on abstract meaning representation. In *Proceedings of the 2016 conference on empirical methods in natural language processing*, pages 1054–1059.

Ashish Vaswani, Noam Shazeer, Niki Parmar, Jakob Uszkoreit, Llion Jones, Aidan N Gomez, Łukasz Kaiser, and Illia Polosukhin. 2017. Attention is all you need. In *Advances in Neural Information Processing Systems*, pages 5998–6008.

Petar Veličković, Guillem Cucurull, Arantxa Casanova, Adriana Romero, Pietro Liò, and Yoshua Bengio. 2017. Graph Attention Networks.

Ellen M Voorhees and Dawn M Tice. 2000. Building a question answering test collection. In *Proceedings of the 23rd annual international ACM SIGIR conference on Research and development in information retrieval*, pages 200–207.

Haitao Wang and Fangbing Li. 2022. A text classification method based on LSTM and graph attention network. *Connection Science*, 34(1):2466–2480.

Janyce Wiebe, Theresa Wilson, and Claire Cardie. 2005. Annotating expressions of opinions and emotions in language. *Language resources and evaluation*, 39(2):165–210.

Defeng Xie, Jianmin Ji, Jiafei Xu, and Ran Ji. 2021. Combining Improvements for Exploiting Dependency Trees in Neural Semantic Parsing. In *Pacific Rim International Conference on Artificial Intelligence*, pages 58–72. Springer.

Zhilin Yang, Zihang Dai, Yiming Yang, Jaime Carbonell, Russ R Salakhutdinov, and Quoc V Le. 2019. XLNet: Generalized Autoregressive Pretraining for Language Understanding. *Advances in neural information processing systems*, 32.

Liang Yao, Chengsheng Mao, and Yuan Luo. 2019. Graph convolutional networks for text classification. In *Proceedings of the AAAI conference on artificial intelligence*, volume 33, pages 7370–7377.

Shaowei Yao, Tianming Wang, and Xiaojun Wan. 2020. Heterogeneous graph transformer for graph-to-sequence learning. In *Proceedings of the 58th Annual Meeting of the Association for Computational Linguistics*, pages 7145–7154.

Yue Zhang, Qi Liu, and Linfeng Song. 2018a. Sentence-state LSTM for text representation. *CoRR*, abs/1805.02474.

Yuhao Zhang, Peng Qi, and Christopher D. Manning. 2018b. Graph Convolution over Pruned Dependency Trees Improves Relation Extraction. *CoRR*, abs/1809.10185.

Zhuosheng Zhang, Yuwei Wu, Hai Zhao, Zuchao Li, Shuailiang Zhang, Xi Zhou, and Xiang Zhou. 2020. Semantics-aware BERT for language understanding. In *Proceedings of the AAAI Conference on Artificial Intelligence*, volume 34, pages 9628–9635.

A Hyperparameter Values

Table 7, 8, and 9 list the hyperparameter values used in the UCCA-GAT, AMR-GAT and Dep-GAT models, respectively, for downstream tasks.

Parameters	MR	CR	SUBJ	MPQA	SST-2	TREC	MRPC
weight decay	0.2	0.1	0.2	0.2	0.2	0.1	0.1
batch size	1	1	1	1	1	1	1
learning rate	1e-4	1e-4	1e-4	1e-4	1e-4	1e-4	1e-4
dropout rate	0.1	0.1	0.1	0.2	0.1	0.1	0.1
number of hidden	800	800	800	800	400	800	800
number of head	2	1	2	2	4	1	1

Table 7: Hyperparameters used for the UCCA-GAT for downstream tasks in experiments

Parameters	MR	CR	SUBJ	MPQA	SST-2	TREC	MRPC
weight decay	0.1	0.1	0.2	0.1	0.2	0.1	0.1
batch size	1	1	1	1	1	1	1
learning rate	1e-4	1e-4	1e-4	1e-4	1e-4	1e-4	1e-4
dropout rate	0.2	0.1	0.2	0.1	0.2	0.1	0.1
number of hidden	800	400	800	800	800	400	800
number of head	2	1	2	2	4	1	1

Table 8: Hyperparameters used for the AMR-GAT for downstream tasks in experiments

Parameters	MR	CR	SUBJ	MPQA	SST-2	TREC	MRPC
weight decay	0.1	0.1	0.2	0.1	0.2	0.1	0.1
batch size	1	1	1	1	1	1	1
learning rate	2e-5	2e-5	2e-5	2e-5	2e-5	2e-5	2e-5
dropout rate	0.1	0.1	0.2	0.1	0.2	0.1	0.1
number of hidden	800	400	800	800	800	400	800
number of head	2	1	2	2	4	1	1

Table 9: Hyperparameters used for the Dep-GAT for downstream tasks in experiments

Formal Semantics for Dependency Grammar

Dag T. T. Haug and Jamie Y. Findlay
Department of Linguistics and Nordic Studies
University of Oslo

Abstract

In this paper, we provide an explicit interface to formal semantics for Dependency Grammar, based on Glue Semantics. Glue Semantics has mostly been developed in the context of Lexical Functional Grammar, which shares two crucial assumptions with Dependency Grammar: lexical integrity and allowance of non-binary-branching syntactic structure. We show how Glue can be adapted to the Dependency Grammar setting and provide sample semantic analyses of quantifier scope, control infinitives and relative clauses.

1 Introduction

Although the name *Dependency Grammar* suggests a theory covering everything that could reasonably be understood as *grammar* (often, these days, phonology, morphology, syntax and semantics), it is fair to say that the focus has to a large extent been on *syntax*. Nevertheless, there have been some attempts to extend the idea to phonology (e.g. Dresher and van der Hulst 1998) and semantics (e.g. the tectogrammatical layer of Functional Generative Description: Sgall et al. 1986). In Section 2, we argue that such frameworks lack some important desiderata of semantic theories and suggest that it is reasonable for Dependency Grammar to remain agnostic about semantics and instead attempt to build an interface between dependency syntax and established semantic theories. The main contribution of the paper is to provide such an interface to one influential semantic theory, compositional (also known as formal or logical) semantics in the tradition going back to Frege. We take inspiration from the implementation described in Gotham and Haug (2018), but the focus here is on how Glue Semantics can provide a general interface to semantics for Dependency Grammar, irrespective of this concrete implementation that is tied to a particular meaning language (partial CDRT, Haug 2014) and a particular version of Dependency Grammar (Universal Dependencies, de Marneffe et al. 2021), which deviates from most theoretical versions of Dependency Grammar in various respects.

In Section 3 we briefly introduce compositional semantics and the constraints it puts on the interface to syntax. Then we introduce Glue Semantics as a way of satisfying those constraints in Section 4. Finally, in Section 5 we show how Glue Semantics can be applied to dependency syntax. Section 6 concludes.

2 Previous work

The fundamental concept of Dependency Grammar is of course *dependencies*. But these are in themselves nothing but asymmetric, binary relations as we find them in many domains. For example, a phrase structure tree can be defined in terms of two such relations, dominance and precedence. The characteristic feature of dependency syntax is therefore not just that it is based on dependencies, but that those dependencies are taken to hold between *words*.[1] This can be seen as a strong version of the Lexical Integrity Hypothesis (Bresnan and Mchombo, 1995): not only are words atomic with respect to syntax, but they are the only atoms of syntax.

One intuitive way to extend dependency syntax to semantics, therefore, is to find an analogue to words on which to build semantic graphs. Indeed, Koller et al. (2019) provide a useful classification of graph-based semantic representations by the degree to which the nodes of the graph are anchored in the words of the sentence: some representations, such as CCG word-word dependencies (Hockenmaier and Steedman, 2007), just use the words as nodes; others, such as Prague Tectogrammatical Graphs (Zeman and Hajic, 2020) allow for a looser correspondence where nodes can also rep-

[1] Obviously we can also define notions derived from word-word dependencies, such as the transitive closure of the dominance relation, yielding something similar to constituents.

Proceedings of the Seventh International Conference on Dependency Linguistics (Depling, GURT/SyntaxFest 2023), pages 22 - 31
March 9-12, 2023

resent elided material (e.g. pro-drop, ellipsis), or copied material (e.g. words that are interpreted twice in a coordination structure); and yet others, most prominently Abstract Meaning Representations (Banarescu et al., 2013) are fully unanchored: there is no explicit correspondence between words and nodes.

While such frameworks have shown themselves useful for various computational tasks, including natural language inference, we argue that they currently lack two features that a semantic theory should have: compositionality and an explicit proof theory.

By compositionality we mean that, given a representation of the syntax (in our case, a dependency graph) and of the lexical items in the sentence, it should be possible to enumerate the possible semantic representations of the sentence. This is a weak notion of compositionality: we do not require that there are interpretations of parts of the dependency graph, nor that syntax and lexicon determine a unique meaning, only that there is some form of systematicity in the mapping between complete syntactic and semantic representations. Notice that this is a theoretical desideratum rather than a practical one: given a large dataset of hand-annotated semantic representations, it might make more sense to train a semantic parser directly rather than going via syntax, and this is in fact a common approach in natural language inference these days. Nevertheless it is clear that if we want to construct a semantic *theory* for Dependency Grammar, the semantic representations must be constrained by the syntactic representations we assume if the theory is to have any empirical bite. And yet not all graph-based semantic theories have this: Abstract Meaning Representation, for example, is hand-annotated without regard to any particular syntactic representation. While this does not make it less useful, it does make it hard to use as a semantic theory for Dependency Grammar. The Prague tectogrammatical layer, on the other hand, is a graph-based semantic representation that is explicitly linked to a surface dependency syntax representation, the analytical layer. Similarly, Meaning-Text Theory develops an interface between syntax and a graph-based semantic representation (see Kahane 2003 for an introduction).

By explicit proof theory, we mean that the semantic representations must be able to answer questions like "if a set of sentences P is true, does it follow that sentence h is true?". We take the ability to answer such questions to be a core property of human reasoning. Again, this is a theoretical desideratum: in natural language inference tasks, we are typically only given a few explicit sentences p_1, p_2 from P, whereas an inference to h relies on implicit propositions $p_3, \ldots, p_n$, which could be either just world knowledge or somehow be made salient/likely by the explicit premises p_1, p_2. In this situation, rather than trying to enumerate the possible background knowledge on which an inference may draw, it may easier to predict directly whether p_1 and p_2 make h likely. But this cannot be the basis for a semantic theory.

We are not aware of any graph-based semantic frameworks that provide a sound and complete inference system for computing entailments, though some come close. Graphical Knowledge Representation (Kalouli and Crouch, 2018; Crouch and Kalouli, 2018) explicitly views "graphs as first-class semantic objects that should be directly manipulated in reasoning and other forms of semantic processing". The semantic graphs of Meaning-Text theory are more directed towards tasks like paraphrasing rather than logical deduction, but Kahane (2005) explores the connection to logic.

Indeed, basing semantic representations on logic is one straightforward way to provide a proof theory. This is a long tradition reflected in many theories such as Montague's intensional logic (Montague, 1973), Discourse Representation Theory (Kamp and Reyle, 1993) and Minimal Recursion Semantics (Copestake et al., 2005). Linking dependency syntax to this line of work therefore provides the advantage of being able to connect to a large body of semantic work. But to do this, we must solve the compositionality problem: how do we systematically build formulae in some logic-based formalism from a dependency graph? To our knowledge, Dependency Tree Semantics (Robaldo, 2006) was the first attempt to provide such an interface between dependency syntax and formal semantics. However, Robaldo only deals with quantifiers and quantifier scope ambiguity, and it is not obvious how to generalize his work to other phenomena. The aim of this paper, then, is to provide a general solution to the compositionality problem which would allow dependency syntacticians to connect their syntactic analyses to existing work in formal semantics, or indeed to develop their own semantic analyses in parallel with syntax.

3 Formal semantics and the syntax-semantics interface

As we pointed out above, basing semantic theory on logic provides an immediate proof theory. Indeed, the very development of formal logic from Aristotle onwards can be seen as a way to provide a proof theory for natural language. The real problem, then, is compositionality: how do we systematically constrain the logical formulae that are licit translations of a given natural language sentence? One influential way to achieve this is to provide meanings for lexical items and let the syntactic structure of the sentence guide how we assemble them into a meaning for the whole. This is known as Frege's principle of compositionality (although it is not clear that Frege endorsed it in this form): the meaning of a (syntactically complex) whole is a function only of the meanings of its (syntactic) parts together with the manner in which these parts were combined. This is a much stronger notion of compositionality than what we saw in Section 2, but it has guided much previous work in formal semantics.

One immediate problem is that it is not always clear what the meanings of the parts should be. For example, it seems intuitive that the meaning of *Every man loves Chris* is something like $\forall x.man(x) \rightarrow love(x, c)$. Here it seems obvious that the verb *loves* contributes the predicate *love*, the word *man* contributes the predicate man, and the name *Chris* provides the constant c; but that then leaves the determiner *every* to contribute the rest of the meaning, i.e. the quantifier $\forall x$ and the ocurrences of x that it binds, as well as the implication $\rightarrow$, although these parts are scattered around in the sentence in a way which makes it unclear how we can provide a systematic procedure for combining the meanings.

Yet Montague's (1973) insight was that the lambda calculus *can* provide such a systematic procedure. Intuitively, the scattered meaning of *every* can be represented as $\forall x.? \rightarrow ?$, where the two question marks represent predicates containing x. In the lambda calculus we can represent this as $\lambda P.\lambda Q.\forall x.P(x) \rightarrow Q(x)$. This means that *every* is a function that takes two predicates and says that for any x, if the first predicate (the noun P that *every* combines with) applies, then the second predicate (the verb that *every P* is an argument of) also applies.

Montague's system based on the lambda calculus achieves compositionality, but it imposes strong constraints on the syntax-semantics interface that are problematic from the point of view of Dependency Grammar.

First, the *homomorphism problem*: compositionality in the strict sense requires that syntax and lexicon jointly *determine* meaning: meaning differences between two sentences must be attributed either to the parts of the sentences (i.e. the lexicon), or the manner in which they are combined (i.e., the syntax). Therefore, if a sentence with no ambiguous words is semantically ambiguous, that difference must necessarily be reflected in the syntax. This is the case, for example, with different quantifier scopings. More generally, homomorphism requires that the syntactic tree is strictly binary branching, which is typically not the case in dependency structures. For example, the lambda calculus requires that a verb combine with its subject and object in a particular order (it must combine with one before the other), whereas Dependency Grammars typically assume no hierarchical difference between subject and object, with both being sister nodes under the verb.

One way to go would be to use the *syntactic function* to distinguish the two, for example by replicating the view of most phrase structure grammars that the object bears a closer relation to the verb than the subject. This is the approach taken in UDepLambda (Reddy et al., 2017), where a syntactic function hierarchy is used to binarize the dependency tree before it is fed to the composition process. But given that many languages exhibit subject-object scope ambiguities, it makes more sense to interpret the flat dependency tree as an underspecified representation, which entails giving up on the view that syntax and lexicon determine meaning.

Second, *lexical integrity* is another problem. It is often natural that single lexical items provide two or more different meanings that do not directly combine with each other, but interact with other elements of the sentence in complex ways. For example, the verb introduces the basic predicate-argument structure, but in many languages also temporal and modal meanings, and we cannot necessarily just combine these first: modal meanings, for example, may need to take scope over the arguments of the verb. If these composition patterns are to be directly determined by the syntax, we need to assume abstract syntactic heads for modality, tense etc. This is indeed often done in Chomskyan approaches, but is alien to dependency syntax, which normally assumes lexical integrity, i.e. that words are the atoms of the syntactic structure.

In sum, "standard" formal semantics in the tradition after Montague relies on strictly binary syntax and syntactic decomposition of lexical items. This makes it hard to adapt to Dependency Grammar. But fortunately these problems have been tackled within the tradition of another lexicalist theory of syntax that also does not enforce binary syntax, namely Lexical Functional Grammar (Kaplan and Bresnan, 1982; Dalrymple et al., 2019), via the theory of the syntax-semantics interface called Glue Semantics (Glue: Dalrymple et al., 1993; Asudeh, 2022).

4 Basic Glue Semantics

The semantic building blocks in Glue are called meaning constructors; these are expressions consisting of two parts: a meaning, given in the lambda calculus over some formal language; and a formula of another logic, so-called linear logic (Girard, 1987), which constrains but does not necessarily uniquely determine the valid patterns of combination between meaning constructors. Semantic composition is logical deduction, driven by the linear logic parts of meaning constructors.

Before we get into the technical details of how this works, let us consider how it helps with the problems just described. Treating semantic composition as logical deduction helps to loosen the conection between meaning composition and syntax: provided the logic we use has the property of commutativity, then the order in which we combine meanings is driven wholly by the types of the meanings themselves, and not by the order the words they correspond to happen to occur in the string. Since we therefore no longer require the syntax itself to impose a strict order of combination, it also frees us from the obligation to limit our syntactic trees to binary branching ones. Finally, it means that semantic ambiguities, such as scope ambiguities, need not correspond to syntactic ambiguities: since the order of combination in syntax and semantics can vary independently, there can be semantic ambiguities which have no syntactic correlate. We will present an explicit example of how this works shortly.

Linear logic is chosen as the logic of semantic combination because it has the property of resource sensitivity: premises cannot be reused or discarded in linear logic, unlike in classical logic. This is because linear logic lacks the structural rules of Weakening and Contraction (Restall, 2000). If a logic contains the rule of Weakening, then premises can be freely added; this is shown schematically below, where A and B represent individual premises, and Γ represents a set of premises:

$$\frac{\Gamma \vdash B}{\Gamma, A \vdash B}$$

That is, if we can prove B from the set of premises in Γ, we can also prove it from Γ and some other premise A. If a logic contains the rule of Contraction, extra occurences of a premise can be freely discarded:

$$\frac{\Gamma, A, A \vdash B}{\Gamma, A \vdash B}$$

That is, if we can prove B from Γ and two instances of A, we can also prove it from Γ and just one instance of A.

By removing these rules, a logic becomes resource sensitive in the sense that premises are resources that must be kept track of and accounted for: they can be "used up" in a way that is not the case in classical logic. This is evident in the behaviour of implication, for example. If we apply the rule of *modus ponens* in classical logic, we can prove not only the consequent of the conditional, but also retain both of the premises in the conclusion if we so wish:

$$\begin{array}{rcl} A, A \to B & \vdash & B \\ & \vdash & A \wedge (A \to B) \wedge B \end{array}$$

By contrast, in linear logic, *modus ponens* uses up both premises in proving the consequent, so that the consequent alone is left over ($\multimap$ is linear implication, and $\otimes$ is multiplicative conjunction, which for present purposes can be thought of as the linear logic equivalent of $\wedge$):

$$\begin{array}{rcl} A, A \multimap B & \vdash & B \\ & \nvdash & A \otimes (A \multimap B) \otimes B \end{array}$$

All of this means that, as Dalrymple et al. (1999, 15) put it, premises in linear logic "are not context-independent assertions that may be used or not", as in classical logic, but rather "*occurrences* of information which are generated and used exactly once" (emphasis in original). This seems to be a good

Application : implication elimination

$$\frac{f : A \multimap B \qquad a : A}{f(a) : B} \multimap_{\mathcal{E}}$$

Abstraction : implication introduction

$$\frac{\begin{array}{c}[\mathbf{x_1} : A]^1 \\ \vdots \\ f : B\end{array}}{\lambda x.f : A \multimap B} \multimap_{\mathcal{I},1}$$

Figure 1: Correspondences between operations in the lambda calculus and proof rules in linear logic

fit with how linguistic meaning contributions behave, since they too are resource sensitive (Asudeh, 2012, ch. 5). For example, the sentence *Naomi loves James* cannot have the meaning $love(n, n)$ (i.e. 'Naomi loves herself'), where we ignore the meaning of *James* and use the meaning of *Naomi* twice.

Returning to Glue Semantics, the linear logic formulae of the meaning constructors contributed by the words of a sentence (and sometimes also by structural properties of the sentence) are premises which must all be used up in constructing a proof of the linear logic formula corresponding to the sentence as a whole. Thanks to the correspondence between rules of logical deduction and operations in the lambda calculus known as the Curry-Howard isomorphism (Curry and Feys, 1958; Howard, 1980), each step in this proof also provides instructions for what to do with the meaning expression that forms the other part of a meaning constructor, thus providing us with the compositional semantics we are looking for.

The two most important rules of linear logic which we make use of are those of implication elimination (i.e. *modus ponens*) and implication introduction (i.e. hypothetical reasoning). In the lambda calculus, these correspond to the operations of function application and lambda abstraction, respectively, as shown in Figure 1. In these proofs, meaning constructors are written with a colon separating the meaning expression on the left-hand side and the linear logic formula on the right-hand side. As mentioned above, the symbol $\multimap$ represents linear implication. Figure 2 gives a more linguistic example, combining a transitive verb with its two arguments. We use the following conventions when writing proofs: unannotated

$$\frac{\dfrac{\lambda x.\lambda y.love(x, y) : A \multimap B \multimap C \qquad n : A}{\lambda y.love(n, y) : B \multimap C} \qquad j : B}{love(n, j) : C}$$

Figure 2: Glue proof for *Naomi loves James*

proof steps correspond to implication elimination, and β-reduction is performed silently. For now, we continue to use arbitrary labels for the atoms in the linear logic formulae; in Section 5 we will see how these can be connected (or 'glued') to the syntax.

As mentioned, one of the strengths of the logical deduction approach to semantic composition is that scope ambiguities need not correspond to syntactic ambiguities. Instead, they emerge from the fact that distinct proofs can (sometimes) be obtained from the same set of premises. Figure 3 shows an example of this phenomenon for the scopally ambiguous sentence *Someone loves everyone*. From the same three lexical premises (shown in labelled boxes), we can obtain two distinct proofs, via hypothetical reasoning, where the quantifiers scope in different orders: on top, we see the proof of the surface scope reading ('there is a person who loves everyone'), where *everyone* is applied before *someone*, so that the latter scopes over the former; below, we see the inverse scope reading ('everyone is loved by someone'), where the quantifiers are applied in the opposite order. Both possibilities are afforded by the linear logic, without requiring different premises to begin with, which means that the same syntactic analysis can serve for both readings.

5 Application to Dependency Grammar

The next question that arises is: how do we connect the linear logic formulae in meaning constructors to such a syntactic analysis, specifically in a Dependency Grammar setting? In the previous section, we simply used atomic formulae like A and B, but we cannot assume that the lexical entries of e.g. a verb and its subject know each other's types absolutely. Instead, the formulae must be made relative, and based on the syntactic structure.

There are several ways this can be done: here we adopt so-called "first-order Glue" (Kokkonidis, 2007). As the name says, this is a first-order logic, where the predicates are type-constructors and the terms are nodes of the syntactic trees. By convention, we use type constructors that are mnemonic for the corresponding Montagovian type on the lambda calculus side, so that e.g. E takes a tree

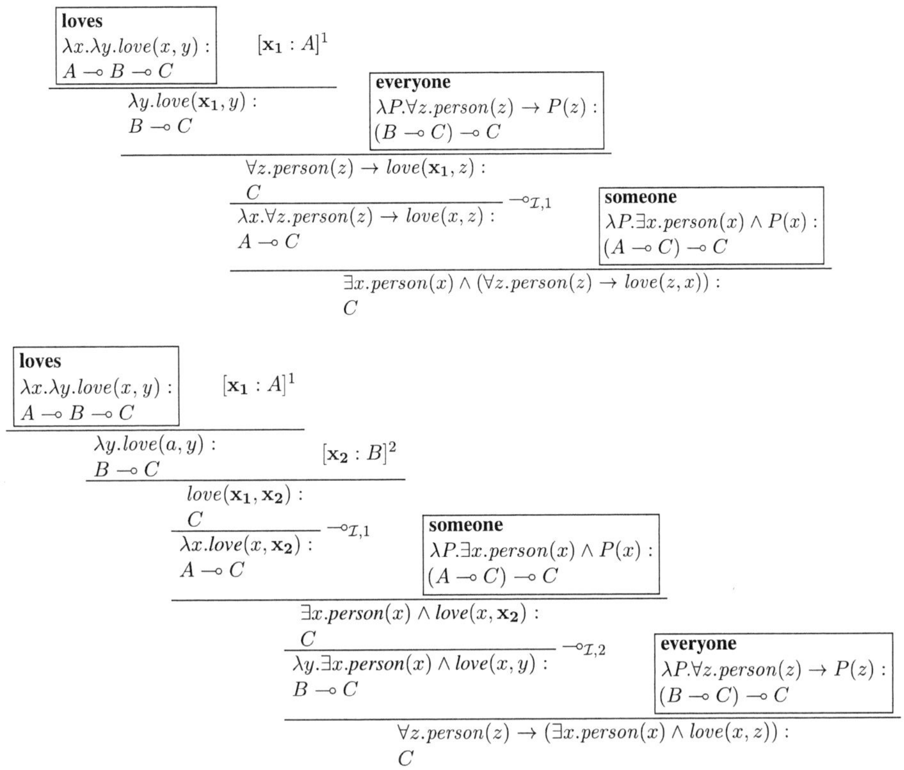

Figure 3: Glue proofs for the two readings of *Someone loves everyone*

node and constructs a linear logic type that corresponds to something of type e on the meaning side. The type of a noun, then, can be given as $E(\hat{*}) \multimap T(\hat{*})$, where $\hat{*}$ refers to the node that the noun occupies.

In order to make this work, it is not enough to be able to refer to the word's own node with $\hat{*}$; we must also be able to refer to the syntactic context to make sure that entries "fit together". Here we exploit the fact that sets of paths through the dependency tree can be expressed through regular expressions over the alphabet $\mathcal{L} \cup \{\uparrow\}$, where $\mathcal{L}$ is the set of syntactic labels and $\uparrow$ refers to the mother node. For convenience we also use $\hat{*}$ as a start symbol. For example, assuming standard labels, $\hat{*}$ SUBJ in a lexical entry refers to that node's subject daughter, $\hat{*}$ OBJ to the object daughter, $\hat{*}$ (SUBJ|OBJ) to the set of the subject and object daughter, and $\hat{*}$ COMP* SUBJ to the set of SUBJ daughters embedded under zero or more COMP daughters.

For the case of the transitive sentence involving quantifiers that we saw in Section 4, we can use the full lexical entries in Figure 4. The terms of the linear logic (i.e. the arguments to the type constructors E and T) are paths through the tree. Given a syntactic tree with numbered nodes, they can be *instantiated* to numbers. Assume that *someone*, *loves* and *everyone* are numbered 1, 2, 3 and that 1 and 3 are SUBJ and OBJ daughters of 2 respectively. Then the type of *someone* becomes $(E(1) \multimap T(2)) \multimap T(2)$, *loves* gets the type $E(1) \multimap E(2) \multimap T(2)$ and *everyone* $(E(3) \multimap T(2)) \multimap T(2)$. It is easily seen that these types are isomorphic to the atomic types we used in Figure 3 and so the same proofs go through.

This technique can be extended to deal with elements that are semantically active but not present in the syntactic structure. First, consider the case of pro-drop. Many dependency grammarians take the view that pro-dropped subjects should not be represented in the syntax, but they are obviously semantically active. To deal with this, we allow paths in lexical entries to be *constructive*, i.e. if a path does not lead to a node in the tree, we construct the path, making sure we pick unused numbers for the implicit nodes we need. If a second path references the same node that did not exist in the syntax, we use this number to reference it. To avoid infi-

someone	$\lambda P.\exists x.person(x) \wedge P(x)$	:	$(E(\hat{*}) \multimap T(\uparrow)) \multimap T(\uparrow)$
loves	$\lambda x.\lambda y.love(x, y)$	:	$E(\hat{*}\ \text{SUBJ}) \multimap E(\hat{*}\ \text{OBJ}) \multimap T(\hat{*})$
everyone	$\lambda P.\forall x.person(x) \rightarrow P(x)$	:	$(E(\hat{*}) \multimap T(\uparrow)) \multimap T(\uparrow)$

Figure 4: Lexical entries for *Someone loves everyone*

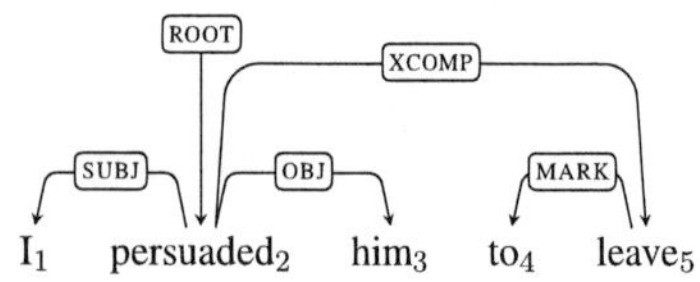

Figure 5: Control infinitive

nite trees, path parts under the Kleene star are not interpreted constructively.

When we allow constructive paths, we can deal with pro-dropped subjects by assuming that all verbs that require a subject also introduce a meaning constructor of type $E(\hat{*}\ \text{SUBJ})$ or its Montague lift $(E(\hat{*}\ \text{SUBJ}) \multimap T(\hat{*}\ \uparrow)) \multimap T(\hat{*}\ \uparrow)$.[2] The meaning side will depend on the semantics for anaphora that is adopted (if the pro-drop subject is anaphoric, as is usually the case).

Let us now look at the slightly more complicated example of control infinitives. These too have an implicit subject position which must be represented in the syntax, but which is often not made explicit in a dependency syntax tree. We will see how Glue Semantics makes it possible to nevertheless give a semantic analysis.

A sample syntactic structure is given in Figure 5, with lexical entries and the linear logic proof in Figures 6–7. The fact that the object of *persuade* is also interpreted as the subject of the infinitive is encoded in the meaning of *persuade* by the fact that the variable y occurs in both positions. Crucially, the constructive interpretation of paths allows us to identify $E(\hat{*}\ \text{SUBJ})$ in the meaning constructor of *leave* and $(E(\hat{*}\ \text{XCOMP SUBJ})$ in the constructor of *persuade*, even if *leave* has no subject in the syntactic representation.

Finally, let us look at the more complicated example of relative clauses. We first consider English relative clauses of the type *the dog that they thought we admired*. Figure 8 show two ways of analyzing such sentences that are found in the Dependency Grammar literature, differing in how *that* is attached. The two dashed lines show the main options: either it is attached as an object of *admire*, or it is attached to *think* as a subordinator.

The first type of annotation makes explicit where the gap inside the relative clause is. The second does not; and if *that* is left out, there is in any case no way of indicating where the gap is in a surface-oriented dependency analysis. In settings such as Gotham and Haug (2018), where no lexical information is assumed, it is crucial to know where the gap is, but in the present, theoretical Dependendcy Grammar setting, we can assume we have access to valency information telling us that *admire* takes an object and *think* does not; therefore there is no ambiguity in where the gap is.[3]

From a semantic point of view, the ordinary analysis of relative clauses in formal semantics, which we follow here, is that they denote properties or, extensionally speaking, sets. That is *dog* denotes the set of dogs, *that they thought we admired* denotes the set of things that they thought we admired, and *dog that they thought we admired* denotes the intersection of these sets, i.e. the entities that are dogs and that they thought we admired. The precise semantic analysis is not our agenda here, but a reasonable interpretation of *that they thought we admired* (simplifying away from tense and intensionality) would be $\lambda x.think(a_1, admire(s_+, x))$ where a_1 is a free variable representing the anaphor *they* and s_+ is a constant referring to a group including the speaker.

The lexical entries are given in Figure 9. Notice that *that* is semantically vacuous (whether analysed as a subordinator or an object). When these meanings are instantiated with the node numbers from Figure 8, we can construct the proof in Figure 10. To save space we do not show how *admire* and *think* combine with their subjects. Notice how node 9 is introduced, since the dependency tree has no object daughter of *admire*. This does not imply any commitment to an empty category in the syntax: the only role of this element is to provide abstraction over the gap in the relative clause. This

[2] This meaning constructor can be optional, since it will not be possible to construct a proof with it when there is also an overt subject. Alternatively, the meaning constructor can be introduced only when there is no overt subject.

[3] Although there can be ambiguity even with valency information in case of verbs with several frames.

I	s	:	$E(\hat{*})$
persuaded	$\lambda x.\lambda y.\lambda P.persuade(x, y, P(y))$	:	$E(\hat{*}\ \text{SUBJ}) \multimap E(\hat{*}\ \text{OBJ}) \multimap (E(\hat{*}\ \text{XCOMP SUBJ}) \multimap T(\hat{*}\ \text{XCOMP})) \multimap T(\hat{*})$
him	a_1	:	$E(\hat{*})$
leave	$\lambda x.admire(x)$	:	$E(\hat{*}\ \text{SUBJ}) \multimap T(\hat{*})$

Figure 6: Lexical entries for control infinitive

$$\dfrac{\dfrac{s : E(1) \quad a_1 : E(3) \quad \begin{array}{c}\lambda x.\lambda y.\lambda P.persuade(x, y, P(y)) :\\ E(1) \multimap E(3) \multimap (E(6) \multimap T(5)) \multimap T(2)\end{array}}{\begin{array}{c}\lambda P.persuade(s, a_1, P(a_1)) :\\ (E(6) \multimap T(5)) \multimap T(2)\end{array}} \quad \begin{array}{c}\lambda x.leave(x) :\\ E(6) \multimap T(5)\end{array}}{persuade(s, a_1, P(y)) : T(2)}$$

Figure 7: Proof for control infinitive structure

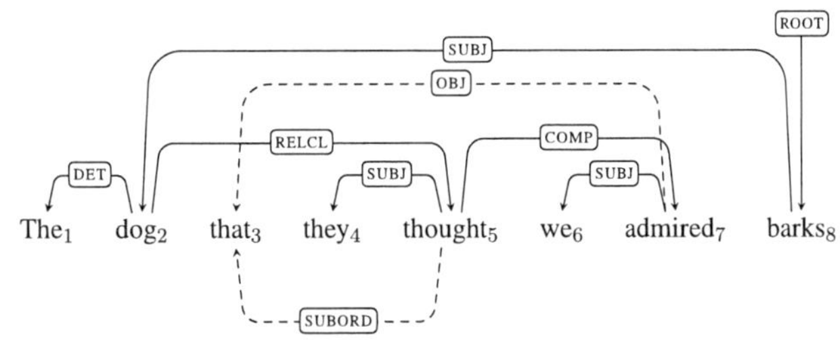

Figure 8: Two styles of relative clause annotation

they	a_1	:	$E(\hat{*})$
thought	$\lambda x.\lambda P.think(x, P)$	:	$E(\hat{*}\ \text{SUBJ}) \multimap T(\hat{*}\ \text{COMP}) \multimap T(\hat{*})$
we	s_+	:	$E(\hat{*})$
admired	$\lambda x.\lambda y.admire(x, y)$	:	$E(\hat{*}\ \text{SUBJ}) \multimap E(\hat{*}\ \text{OBJ}) \multimap T(\hat{*})$
thought-RELCL	$\lambda P.\lambda Q.\lambda x.P(x) \wedge Q(x)$	:	$\forall \xi.(E(\xi) \multimap T(\hat{*})) \multimap (E(\uparrow) \multimap T(\uparrow)) \multimap E(\uparrow) \multimap T(\uparrow)$

Figure 9: Lexical entries for sample relative clause

$$\dfrac{\dfrac{\dfrac{\lambda y.admire(s_+, y) : E(9) \multimap T(7) \quad [\mathbf{x_1} : E(9)]^1}{admire(s_+, \mathbf{x_1}) : T(7)} \quad \lambda P.think(a_1, P) : T(7) \multimap T(5)}{think(a_1, admire(s_+, \mathbf{x_1})) : T(5)}}{\lambda x.think(a_1, admire(s_+, x)) : E(9) \multimap T(5)} \multimap_{\mathcal{I},1}$$

Figure 10: Proof structure for the relative clause

is the crucial part of the proof in Figure 10: abstraction over the object of *admire* gives us the set of x such that they think we admire x as the meaning of the relative clause. The next step is to intersect this meaning with the meaning of *dog* which has the meaning constructor $\lambda x.dog(x) : E(2) \multimap T(2)$. The meaning constructor **thought-RELCL** from Figure 9 will do this, though we do not show it in the proof.

What we call **thought-RELCL** is different from other meaning constructors in several ways. First, it is a *constructional* meaning, i.e. it is not associated with a lexical item alone, but triggered by a syntactic configuration, in this case a verb that bears the RELCL relation. To interpret the paths correctly, it must still be associated with a node in the tree, in this case naturally the verb of the relative clause. However, we cannot simply precombine **thought-RELCL** and the meaning of **thought** because the verb must combine with its arguments first. Thus, Glue Semantics allows us to split the meaning contributions at the interface to semantics without giving up on lexical integrity in the syntax.

Second, we see that this meaning constructor uses quantification over possible gaps, i.e. it requires some type E resource to be missing in the relative clause: of course, we only get a successful proof if this is instantiated to the introduced index 9 of the actually missing element, the object of *admire*. In this way, we can construct a proper meaning for relative clauses without a commitment to empty categories in the syntax. Another virtue of this approach is that we can restrict relativization sites if needed. In Figure 9 we use universal quantification, which allows all kinds of gaps, but as we mentioned above, it is also possible to use regular expressions to express non-deterministic paths. For example, if the language we analyze only allows e.g. relativization on local subjects and objects, we can use $E(\hat{*}\ (\text{SUBJ}|\text{OBJ}))$, and if the language allows non-local relativization, but only on subjects and objects, we can use $E(\hat{*}\ \text{COMP}^{*}\ (\text{SUBJ}|\text{OBJ}))$. Whether such an interface restriction on relativization is preferrable to a purely syntactic one is an empirical question, but given the widespread avoidance of empty syntactic categories in Dependency Grammar, this approach at least offers an alternative.

6 Conclusion

We have seen how Glue Semantics lets us connect dependency syntax analyses to formal semantics by drawing on a framework that is quite close in spirit to Dependency Grammar, namely Lexical Functional Grammar. In particular, both frameworks reject the adoption of abstract syntactic analysis merely for the purpose of syntax-semantics homomorphism; and both frameworks assume lexical integrity and therefore reject decomposing lexical items in the syntax. Glue Semantics gives us fine-grained control over the syntax-semantics interface, allowing us to achieve the effects of empty categories and lexical decomposition there while preserving the surface-oriented syntactic analyses characteristic of both frameworks.

The most immediate advantage for Dependency Grammar is that this opens the door to the large literature in formal semantics. We have seen how we can analyse quantifier scope, control infinitives, and constructions with gaps, such as relative clauses. This is valuable in itself and can of course be extended to numerous other constructions.

But there is a reason why the interface to semantics is particularly important to Dependency Grammar. One way of motivating the surface-oriented structures that are often adopted in Dependency Grammar is by delegating to semantics the work that abstract syntax does in other frameworks. But if this is to go beyond mere hand-waving, it is important to accompany such claims with explicit analysis. We hope this paper has shown one way this can be done.

Acknowledgements

This research was funded by the Norwegian Research Council, project 300495 *Universal Natural Language Understanding*.

References

Ash Asudeh. 2012. *The logic of pronominal resumption*. Oxford University Press, Oxford.

Ash Asudeh. 2022. Glue Semantics. *Annual Review of Linguistics*, 8:321–341.

Laura Banarescu, Claire Bonial, Shu Cai, Madalina Georgescu, Kira Griffitt, Ulf Hermjakob, Kevin Knight, Philipp Koehn, Martha Palmer, and Nathan Schneider. 2013. Abstract Meaning Representation for sembanking. In *Proceedings of the 7th Linguistic Annotation Workshop and Interoperability with Discourse*, pages 178–186, Sofia, Bulgaria. Association for Computational Linguistics.

Joan Bresnan and Sam A Mchombo. 1995. The lexical integrity principle: Evidence from bantu. *Natural Language & Linguistic Theory*, 13(2):181–254.

Ann Copestake, Dan Flickinger, Carl Pollard, and Ivan A Sag. 2005. Minimal recursion semantics: An introduction. *Research on language and computation*, 3(2):281–332.

Richard Crouch and Aikaterini-Lida Kalouli. 2018. Named graphs for semantic representation. In *Proceedings of the Seventh Joint Conference on Lexical and Computational Semantics*, pages 113–118, New Orleans, Louisiana. Association for Computational Linguistics.

Haskell B. Curry and Robert Feys. 1958. *Combinatory logic: volume I*. North Holland, Amsterdam.

Mary Dalrymple, John Lamping, Fernando Pereira, and Vijay Saraswat. 1999. Overview and introduction. In Mary Dalrymple, editor, *Semantics and syntax in Lexical Functional Grammar: the resource logic approach*. MIT Press, Cambridge, MA.

Mary Dalrymple, John Lamping, and Vijay Saraswat. 1993. LFG semantics via constraints. In *Sixth Conference of the European Chapter of the Association for Computational Linguistics*, Utrecht, The Netherlands. Association for Computational Linguistics.

Mary Dalrymple, John J. Lowe, and Louise Mycock. 2019. *The Oxford Reference Guide to Lexical Functional Grammar*. Oxford University Press, Oxford.

Marie-Catherine de Marneffe, Christopher D. Manning, Joakim Nivre, and Daniel Zeman. 2021. Universal Dependencies. *Computational Linguistics*, 47(2):255–308.

B. Elan Dresher and Harry van der Hulst. 1998. Head–dependent asymmetries in phonology: complexity and visibility. *Phonology*, 15(3):317–352.

Jean-Yves Girard. 1987. Linear logic. *Theoretical Computer Science*, 50(1):1–102.

Matthew Gotham and Dag Trygve Truslew Haug. 2018. Glue semantics for universal dependencies. In *Proceedings of the LFG'18 Conference, University of Vienna*, pages 208–226, Stanford, CA. CSLI Publications.

Dag T. T. Haug. 2014. Partial Dynamic Semantics for Anaphora: Compositionality without Syntactic Coindexation. *Journal of Semantics*, 31(4):457–511.

Julia Hockenmaier and Mark Steedman. 2007. CCGbank: A corpus of CCG derivations and dependency structures extracted from the Penn Treebank. *Computational Linguistics*, 33(3):355–396.

William A. Howard. 1980. The formulae-as-types notion of construction. In *To H. B. Curry: essays on combinatory logic, lambda calculus, and formalism*, pages 479–490. Academic Press, London. Circulated in unpublished form from 1969.

Sylvain Kahane. 2003. The meaning-text theory. In *Dependency and Valency, Handbooks of Linguistics and Communication Sciences*. De Gruyter.

Sylvain Kahane. 2005. Structure des représentations logiques et interface sémantique-syntaxe. In *Actes de la 12ème conférence sur le Traitement Automatique des Langues Naturelles*, pages 153–162, Dourdan, France. Association pour le Traitement Automatique des Langues.

Aikaterini-Lida Kalouli and Richard Crouch. 2018. GKR: the graphical knowledge representation for semantic parsing. In *Proceedings of the Workshop on Computational Semantics beyond Events and Roles*, pages 27–37, New Orleans, Louisiana. Association for Computational Linguistics.

Hans Kamp and Uwe Reyle. 1993. *From Discourse to Logic: Introduction to Modeltheoretic Semantics of Natural Language, Formal Logic and Discourse Representation Theory*. Dordrecht: Kluwer Academic Publishers.

Ronald M. Kaplan and Joan Bresnan. 1982. Lexical-Functional Grammar: a formal system for grammatical representation. In Joan Bresnan, editor, *The mental representation of grammatical relations*, pages 173–281. MIT Press, Cambridge, MA.

Miltiadis Kokkonidis. 2007. First-order glue. *Journal of Logic, Language and Information*, 17:43–68.

Alexander Koller, Stephan Oepen, and Weiwei Sun. 2019. Graph-based meaning representations: Design and processing. In *Proceedings of the 57th Annual Meeting of the Association for Computational Linguistics: Tutorial Abstracts*, pages 6–11, Florence, Italy. Association for Computational Linguistics.

Richard Montague. 1973. The proper treatment of quantification in ordinary English. In K. Jaakko, J. Hintikka, Julius M. E. Moravcsik, and Patrick Suppes, editors, *Approaches to natural language: proceedings of the 1970 Stanford workshop on grammar and semantics*, number 49 in Synthese Library, pages 221–243. Reidel, Dordrecht.

Siva Reddy, Oscar Täckström, Slav Petrov, Mark Steedman, and Mirella Lapata. 2017. Universal semantic parsing. In *Proceedings of the 2017 Conference on Empirical Methods in Natural Language Processing*, pages 89–101, Copenhagen, Denmark. Association for Computational Linguistics.

Greg Restall. 2000. *An introduction to substructural logics*. Routledge, London.

Livio Robaldo. 2006. *Dependency Tree Semantics*. Ph.D. thesis, University of Turin.

Petr Sgall, Eva Hajičová, and Jarmila Panevová. 1986. *The meaning of the sentence in its semantic and pragmatic aspects*. Academia, Prague.

Daniel Zeman and Jan Hajic. 2020. FGD at MRP 2020: Prague tectogrammatical graphs. In *Proceedings of the CoNLL 2020 Shared Task: Cross-Framework Meaning Representation Parsing*, pages 33–39, Online. Association for Computational Linguistics.

Predicates and entities in Abstract Meaning Representation

Antoine Venant
OLST, Université de Montréal
antoine.venant@umontreal.ca

François Lareau
OLST, Université de Montréal
francois.lareau@umontreal.ca

Abstract

Nodes in Abstract Meaning Representation (AMR) are generally thought of as neo-Davidsonian entities. We review existing translation into neo-Davidsonian representations and show that these translations inconsistently handle copula sentences. We link the problem to an asymmetry arising from a problematic handling of words with no associated PropBank frames for the underlying predicate. We introduce a method to automatically and uniformly decompose AMR nodes into an entity-part and a predicative part, which offers a consistent treatment of copula sentences and quasi-predicates such as *brother* or *client*.

1 Introduction

Over the past decade, graph-based semantic representation formalisms have gained a lot of attention, with Abstract Meaning Representation (AMR) arguably leading the trend (Banarescu et al., 2013; Knight et al., 2021). AMR takes a dependency approach to meaning representation, using labeled directed acyclic graphs (incidentally called Abstract Meaning Representations). Labeled graph nodes represent *concepts*, while labeled directed edges represent the *roles* that concepts play in relation to others. For instance, in the sentence *A girl likes herself*, the entity concepts denoted by the noun *girl* plays two roles (agent and theme, Parsons, 1990) in the eventuality concept denoted by the verb *likes*, which is represented by the AMR in figure 1, both as (a) a graph and (b) a tree in PENMAN notation (Mann, 1983). The root of the graph is indicated by double boundaries. Note the use of co-indexed variables in the tree to express graph reentrance. AMR relies whenever possible on PropBank's frames (Palmer et al., 2005) for thematic role labeling (in this case, the frame *likes-01*), hence the use of arg0 and arg1 rather than *agent* and *theme*.

The root of an AMR serves as "a rudimentary representation of overall focus" (Banarescu et al., 2019). Following AMR guidelines, an existential sentence like *There is a girl who likes herself* or a phrase like *a girl who likes herself* would be associated the same representation, shown in figure 2, which differs from the one in figure 1 only by its root. Figure 2 also illustrates how inverse roles like arg0-of are used to unfold a directed graph as a tree from a designated root.

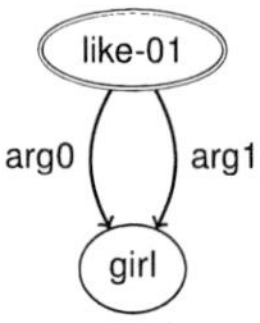

(a) Graph

```
(l/like-01
  :arg0 (x/girl)
  :arg1 x
)
```

(b) Tree

Figure 1: AMR for *A girl likes herself*

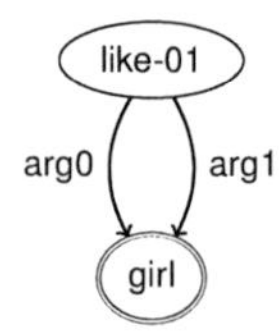

(a) Graph

```
(x/girl
  :arg0-of
    (l/like-01
      :arg1 x
    )
)
```

(b) Tree

Figure 2: AMR for *There is a girl who likes herself*

AMR, like other formalisms historically linked to natural language generation (*e.g.*, Meaning-Text Theory, Mel'čuk, 1973, 2016), departs from logical meaning representations insofar as it comes with no notion of bound variable or scope. The semantic treatment of determiners and adverbs closely mirrors their treatment in dependency syntax, as they simply introduce a polarity or quantity role in the concept denoted by the word they modify. Overall, AMR aims at a transparent representation of predicate-argument structure independent from syntactic contingencies[1] and leaves aside other as-

[1] For instance, referring to an event with a verb or a noun (possibly combined with a light verb).

Proceedings of the Seventh International Conference on Dependency Linguistics (Depling, GURT/SyntaxFest 2023), pages 32 - 41
March 9-12, 2023 ©2023 Association for Computational Linguistics

pects of logical structure, most notably scoping phenomena induced by quantification, negation or modality. As a result, AMR offers a simplified formal apparatus for meaning representation, yielding better consistency among annotators, and effective comparison metrics for comparing semantic annotations.[2] These operational and computational benefits however come at the cost of lacking a model-theory (or a proof-theory, for that matter). This might be unsatisfying empirically or theoretically: empirically, because a formalisation of entailment or equivalence between different AMRs might help downstream tasks or resolve annotation conflicts, and theoretically, because one might want semantic descriptions to describe the recursive relationship between semantic components and the world to count as more than paraphrases of the original sentences (Davidson, 1967). For these reasons, translations of large fragments of AMR into logic have been proposed (Bos, 2016; Lai et al., 2020).

While discussions of AMR's relationship to logical or model-theoretic approaches mostly revolve around questions of quantifier scope, in this paper, we are instead concerned with the **type** of object that AMR nodes denote. Our aim is to answer the following: do AMR nodes always denote entities (objects, events, or states), or do they sometimes denote properties or propositions? Do they denote several of these things at once? Can one **consistently** assign a denotation of a fixed type to a node?

We will argue that the answer to these questions is less clear-cut than AMR's general framing as a "simplified, standard neo-Davidsonian semantics" (Banarescu et al., 2019) or existing translations into logic might suggest. There is a potential difficulty which might prevent us from systematically thinking of AMR nodes as objects, events or states. AMR merges two distinct terms of classical logic into a single node (or rather, a single attachment point): predicate and variable symbols. The logical counterpart to a node labeled 'cat' involves intuitively a formula like $\mathsf{cat}(x)$, combining a predicate symbol cat and a variable x. By *merging*, we do not mean that AMR does not *display* these two components separately (in fact, it does, since the entity arguably corresponds to the node itself, and the predicate to its label).[3] What we mean, is that AMR merges the possibilities to further *refer* to the predicate, or the variable. In other words, a node features only one attachment point for two distinct components of meaning.[4] The situation is different in, say, Church's theory of simple types (commonly used in semantics, in conjunction with the neo-Davidsonian approach), where a term like $cat(x)$ results from the combination of two different terms in the lexicon, which nothing refrains from occurring separately as arguments of other terms. One is of type $\langle e,t\rangle$ ($\lambda x \mathsf{cat}(x)$, generally modeled as originating from the noun), and one of type e (x, generally modeled as originating from the determiner, jointly with a binding quantifier). We will assess whether this difference challenges a denotational semantics for AMR. We will base our investigation on two types of evidence: the logical translation proposed by Lai et al. (2020) and intuitions based on annotated sentences in AMR corpora and guidelines (Knight et al., 2021; Banarescu et al., 2019).

2 Graph nodes as entities

As mentioned above, AMR claims to implement a simplified neo-Davidsonian semantics, which naturally suggests interpreting nodes as individuals or eventualities: "We do not point to an element in an AMR and say 'that is a noun' or 'that is a verb'. Rather, we say 'that is an object' or 'that is an event'" (Banarescu et al., 2019). Bos (2016) and Lai et al. (2020) formalize the connection with systematic translations from AMR into symbolic logic. We will take the latter (which in many ways constitutes a refinement of the former) as a starting point to examine the denotation of AMR elements.

By definition, a *compositional* semantics for AMR needs syntactic composition rules to operate. Since the treatment of universal quantification or negation has no incidence on our discussion, we restrict ourselves to what Bos (2016) calls "basic" AMRs, the syntax of which is described by the BNF grammar below.

$$\mathbf{A} ::= c \mid x \mid (\mathbf{N})$$
$$\mathbf{N} ::= x/P \mid \mathbf{N}{:}r\,\mathbf{A} \mid \mathbf{N}{:}r^{-1}\,\mathbf{A}$$

Non-terminals are in bold sans. x, c, P and r are meta-variables. x ranges over variable

[2]Importantly, metrics such as SMATCH approximating graph homomorphism through comparison of ⟨start node, label, end node⟩ triples.

[3]AMR authors also introduce an alternative logical notation $\exists x \mathsf{instance}(x, \mathsf{cat})$ employing an *instance* relation, which they claim to be equivalent to the graph.

[4]This seems true even under the *instance*-based representations because no other role than *instance* ever attach to the target node of an *instance* edge, to our knowledge.

symbols $\{x, y, \ldots\}$, c over constant sequences {"M. Krupps", "Obama",...}, P over node labels {like-01, girl,...}, and r over (non-inverse) roles {arg0, arg1, domain,...}. r^{-1} describes the inverse of role r (arg0^{-1} = arg0-of, domain^{-1} = mod, ...). Finally, ε denotes the empty sequence. Both Bos (2016) and Lai et al. (2020) syntactically distinguish "projective" and "assertive" nodes to provide a sound treatment of reentrance. We simplify this by systematically interpreting arguments to an inverse role as assertive and arguments to a standard role as projective without additional syntax.[5]

Lai et al. (2020) provide a continuation-style compositional semantics for AMR. The semantic composition rules are given below.

$$[\![c]\!] = \lambda f\, f(c)$$
$$[\![x]\!] = \lambda f\, f(x)$$
$$[\![(\mathbf{N})]\!] = [\![\mathbf{N}]\!]$$
$$[\![x/P]\!] = \lambda f\, \exists x P(x) \wedge f(x)$$
$$[\![\mathbf{N} \text{:} r\, \mathbf{A}]\!] = \lambda f\, [\![\mathbf{A}]\!](\lambda m\, [\![\mathbf{N}]\!](\lambda n\, r(n,m) \wedge f(n)))$$
$$[\![\mathbf{N} \text{:} r^{-1}\, \mathbf{A}]\!] = \lambda f\, [\![\mathbf{N}]\!](\lambda n\, [\![\mathbf{A}]\!](\lambda m\, r(m,n) \wedge f(n)))$$

Figure 4 illustrates the syntax of the AMR of figure 2 (*There is a girl who likes herself*). Figure 3 shows how the semantics of this example unpacks.

$$[\![x]\!] = \lambda f\, f(x)$$
$$[\![a/\text{like-01}]\!] = \lambda f\, \exists a\, \text{like-01}(a) \wedge f(a)$$
$$[\![x/\text{girl}]\!] = \lambda f\, \exists x\, \text{girl}(x) \wedge f(x)$$
$$[\![[a/\text{like-01}]_{\mathbf{N}} \text{ :arg1 } [x]_{\mathbf{A}}]\!]$$
$$= \lambda f\, [\![x]\!](\lambda m\, [\![\text{a/like-01}]\!](\lambda n\, \text{arg1}(n,m) \wedge f(n)))$$
$$= \lambda f\, \exists a\, \text{like-01}(a) \wedge \text{arg1}(a,x) \wedge f(a)$$
$$[\![[x/\text{girl}]_{\mathbf{N}} \text{ :arg0-of } [(\text{a/like-01 :arg1 } x)]_{\mathbf{A}}]\!]$$
$$= \lambda f [\![x/\text{girl}]\!]($$
$$\lambda n\, [\![(\text{a/like-01 :arg1 } x)]\!](\lambda m\, \text{arg0}(m,n) \wedge f(n)))$$
$$= \lambda f\, \exists x\, \text{girl}(x) \wedge \exists a\, \text{like-01}(a) \wedge \text{arg1}(a,x)$$
$$\wedge\, \text{arg0}(a,x) \wedge f(x)$$

Figure 3: Logical interpretation of (x/girl :arg0-of (a/like-01 :arg1 x))

The above rules interpret AMR as trees rather

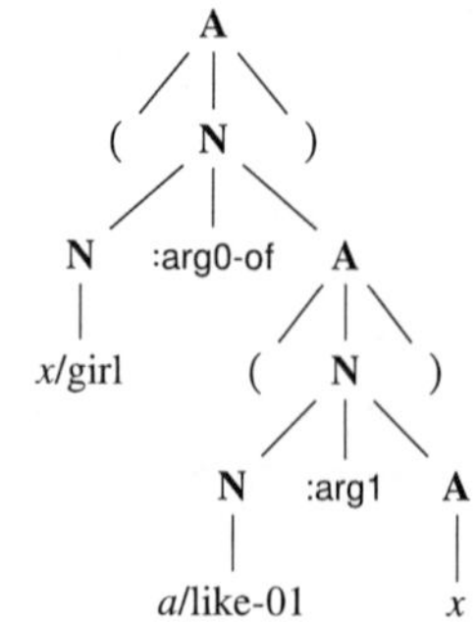

Figure 4: Syntax of (x/girl :arg0-of (a/like-01 :arg1 x))

than graphs. Two AMRs differing only by their root will generally receive distinct denotations. For instance the AMRs from figures 1 and 2 contribute equivalent propositions, but they would pass on different entities as argument to incoming roles (respectively, the girl and the liking). This also means that graph nodes have a dual denotation, because they generally assume two different forms in the corresponding tree. For each node x in the graph, the tree must contain exactly once an *instance* description x/P, and it can additionally contain an arbitrary number of additional references to x as a standalone variable (as many times as the node is argument to a re-entrant role). While both cases have distinct denotations, these denotations are all of the same *type*, namely that of a generalized quantifier $\langle\langle e,t\rangle,t\rangle$.[6] We can thus safely say that a node denotes a set of properties. While this obviously differs from denoting objects or events, it comes very close given that logical representations bear the extra burden of explicitly binding entities to some quantifier and domain of restriction. In the above translation, this binding is built into the denotation of the instance description x/P, which is why x/P does not denote an entity. In contrast, any other reference to the node as a variable x denotes $\lambda f\, f(x)$, which is exactly the standard lifting of an **entity** x to the type $\langle\langle e,t\rangle,t\rangle$. Hence, nodes are seen as plain entity when used as argument to re-entrant roles. In the same order of ideas, note that AMR does not express any distinction between indefinite and definite entities. Thus the AMR in figure 2 is also associated with the phrase "It's the girl who likes herself". To make this reading available, one could for instance non-deterministically switch to a rule like $[\![x/P]\!] = \lambda f\, f(\iota x P(x))$, which,

[5]It offers less control over the relative scoping of quantifiers, but it is sufficient to handle reentrance. Also, it yields semantically equivalent interpretations for all examples discussed by Lai et al. (2020), including donkey sentences.

[6]Assuming that type e is a supertype of all entities, including objects, events and states.

again, makes (x/P) denote a type-lifted entity.[7]

Bos (2016) and Lai et al. (2020) thus clarify the relationship between AMR nodes and entities. Their translations show that, while labeled nodes systematically introduce three distinct components of meaning from a logical perspective (a variable entity, a predicate restricting the domain of this entity, and a binding quantifier), nodes can be thought of as entities, in the sense that the AMR roles linking nodes to one another logically express relations between entities.

3 Copula sentences

Some copula sentences represent a challenge for the view developed in the previous section. AMR guidelines (section *Main verb "be"*), state that copula sentences are represented using the :domain role most of the time. They associate the sentence *The man is a lawyer* with the AMR below:

AMR 1: *The man is a lawyer*

```
(l/lawyer :domain (m/man))
```

Accordingly, we should have the following sentence-AMR association:

AMR 2: *The man who sings is a lawyer*

```
(l/lawyer :domain
  (m/man :arg0-of (s/sing-01)))
```

Applying the translation from section 2 yields the following term:

$$\lambda f\, \exists m\, \mathsf{man}(m) \wedge \exists s\, \mathsf{sing\text{-}01}(s) \wedge \mathsf{arg0}(s,m) \wedge \exists l\, \mathsf{lawyer}(l) \wedge \mathsf{domain}(l,m) \wedge f(l). \quad (\phi)$$

One of the motivations for relating AMR to logic is to model entailment.[8] Another is to specify the denotation of AMR elements. However, as it stands, ϕ fails at both of these tasks. To see why, consider the sentence *A lawyer sings*, which is entailed by *The man who sings is a lawyer*, and its AMR:

AMR 3: *A lawyer sings*

```
(s/sings :arg0 (l/lawyer))
```

The latter logically translates as:

$$\lambda f\, \exists l\, \mathsf{lawyer}(l) \wedge \exists s\, \mathsf{sing\text{-}01}(s) \wedge \mathsf{arg0}(s,l) \wedge f(s) \quad (\psi)$$

[7]Moreover, an equivalent treatment of indefinite is likely achievable using Hilbert's epsilon calculus.

[8]Provided of course that we uniformly resolve parts left underspecified by AMR in the putative premise and consequent.

In order to discuss actual propositions rather than sets of continuations, let us define $\mathsf{cls}(\Gamma)$ as $\Gamma(\lambda n\, \top)$ (the closure of Γ under a continuation trivially true of anything). The problem is that $\mathsf{cls}(\psi)$ is not entailed by $\mathsf{cls}(\phi)$, because $\mathsf{lawyer}(m)$ is not entailed by $\mathsf{lawyer}(l) \wedge \mathsf{domain}(l,m)$. Hence, we fail to capture even simple entailments. Comparing ϕ and ψ also leaves us unsure about the denotation of l (and, consequently, lawyer) in these examples. Does it denote a person in both, or a person in the first and a state/property in the second?

Importantly, we are not trying to decide whether copula constructions (or other kinds of predications) systematically introduce states (on this matter, see for instance Asher, 1993; Maienborn, 2005), only whether we can interpret an element like (l/lawyer) **consistently** accross different AMRs assuming either option. If Lai et al. (2020)'s semantics is to achieve this, then we should be able to explain the link between ϕ and ψ without making distinct assumptions about the domain of quantification for l, or the denotation of lawyer in interpreting one or the other.

One way to satisfy this requirement, and solve the entailment issue, is to assume that l denotes a person in both AMRs and interpret the :domain as equating two entities. This makes $\mathsf{lawyer}(l) \wedge \mathsf{domain}(l,m)$ equivalent to $\mathsf{lawyer}(l) \wedge l = m$ which entails $\mathsf{lawyer}(m)$. Unfortunately, this solution is inconsistent with cases of copula constructions with adjectives, because the latter are also handled with :domain. Let us illustrate this with another sentence from the guidelines: *The marble is small.* The annotated AMR is (s/small :domain (m/marble)). If :domain expresses equality of entities, then the logical translation (after closure) of this AMR is equivalent to:

$$\exists m\, \mathsf{marble}(m) \wedge \exists s\, \mathsf{small}(s) \wedge s = m$$

which we can informally paraphrase as: *The marble = a small thing*. This analysis seems dubious. If the sentence hid quantification over the domain of the adjective, one should expect semantic ambiguities, which are not observed for adjective copula constructions. For instance, *Lila believes that the marble is small* does not have the *de re* reading *There is a small thing which Lila believes to be = to the marble.* But crucially, we can also reject it from more AMR-centered considerations. For instance, the AMR for *The marble is very small* is:

```
(s/small :domain (m/marble)
         :degree (v/very)).
```

Interpreting :domain as equality between entities in the latter is nonsensical, since it would let *very* modify an object, and would therefore amount to reading the sentence as *The marble = a small thing which is very*.

We thus reject an interpretation of :domain as equality on the basis that its two arguments are generally of incompatible *types*. In the example above, *(m/marble)* denotes an object, but *(s/small)* must denote something of a more abstract nature, which supports degree modification. Potential candidates for the denotation of *(s/small)* are the property of being small, or a neo-Davidsonian entity representing a "state" of having this property. This is backed up by cases of copula sentences which are not handled with :domain in AMR. We provide two examples below, respectively taken from the guidelines and proxy files of the AMR corpus (Knight et al., 2021), and suitably truncated for the sake of space ([...] indicates truncated roles):

AMR 4: *The boy is a hard worker* (isi_0001.25)

```
(w/work-01 :arg0 (b/boy)
           :manner (h/hard-02))
```

AMR 5: *Iftikhar Ahmed is a Pakistani interior ministry official* (PROXY_AFP_ENG_20020115_0320.13)

```
(p2 / person [...]
  :arg0-of (h/have-org-role-91
              :arg1 (m/ministry [...])
              :arg2 (o/official)))
```

There is arguably no reason to think that these two sentences would relate different types of objects from the ":domain" kind of copula sentences above. AMR 4 relates a person to a work that he performs, and AMR 5 relates a person to an institutional position that he occupies.[9] In both cases, a concrete object is related to a more abstract object akin to a property that the former can have, or a state that it can be in. We take this as evidence that :domain should behave similarly and relate an entity to some property or state.

If these conclusions are correct, then Lai et al. (2020)'s proposal cannot consistently handle AMR representations of copula constructions like AMR 2, because they switch the denotation of an element like $(l/lawyer)$ to a type of object (a property or a state) different from their "standard" denotation in other AMRs like AMR 3. We will now show how to amend the compositional interpretation rules to resolve this inconsistency.

[9]We think that the focus on *p2* is an annotation mistake and should rather be on *h*, but this does not change our point.

4 Default entity decomposition

In the previous section, we have discussed a problem with the denotation of *(l/lawyer)* in sentences with the noun *lawyer*. This problem only generalizes to nouns giving rise to :domain edges in copula constructions. It does not occur with nouns that invoke Propbank frames, such as *worker*, or AMR role frames such as *president*. Consider the two AMRs below:

AMR 6: *The man who sings is a worker*

```
(work-01
   :arg0 (m/man :arg0-of (sing-01)))
```

AMR 7: *The worker sings*

```
(s/sing-01
   :arg0 (p/person
            :arg0-of (work-01)))
```

The (closure) of their logical interpretation is given below, respective of the order:

$$\exists m\,\mathsf{man}(m) \wedge \exists s\,\mathsf{sing\text{-}01}(s) \wedge \mathsf{arg0}(s,m) \wedge \exists w\,\mathsf{work\text{-}01}(w) \wedge \mathsf{arg0}(w,m)$$

$$\exists p\,\mathsf{person}(p) \wedge \exists w\,\mathsf{work\text{-}01}(w) \wedge \mathsf{arg0}(w,p) \wedge \exists s\,\mathsf{sing\text{-}01}(s) \wedge \mathsf{arg0}(s,p)$$

Assuming $\models \forall x\, man(x) \rightarrow person(x)$ as a meaning postulate, we predict the entailment from AMR 6 to AMR 7 without further difficulties.

Surely, the difference between *worker* and *lawyer* does not stem from a difference between :arg0 and :domain. Rather, it stems from a difference of focus (in the AMR sense). In the *worker* case, the focus of AMR 6 (*(w/work-01)*) is not an instance of the same concept as the focus of the arg0 role of *(s/sing-01)* in AMR 7. In contrast, in the lawyer case, the focus of AMR 2 and the focus of the arg0 role of *(s/sing-01)* in AMR 3 are instances of the same concept. The ability of the word *worker* to invoke two concepts, a person and a "working", solves the issue because both concepts can claim the focus depending on the use of *worker* in a sentence. In its "standard" use, the focus is on the person, but when used as object of a copula, the focus switches to the "working". This is not possible for *lawyer* basically because there is no PropBank frame corresponding to the activity of "lawing", simply because there is no such word in English.

In order to offer a consistent treatment for all copula sentences, we should therefore try to unify the treatment of "lucky" words which decompose along some PropBank frame, and "unlucky" ones which do not. An appealing idea to this effect is to provide a default decomposition for every node, *e.g.*, consider (x/P) as syntactic sugar for (x/E :mod (x_p/P)), where E is a vacuous "entity" predicate. However, two obstacles are in the way: 1) without further restrictions, node decomposition would yield infinite AMRs through recursive rewriting. For instance (x/P) would be understood as syntactic sugar for (x/E :mod (x_p/P)), which itself would rewrite as (x/E :mod (x_p/E :mod (x_{p_p}/P))) and so forth and so on. 2) applying the decomposition rule to **both** occurences of (l/lawyer), in 3 and 2 respectively, would leave us with the very same problem regarding the type of (l_p/lawyer) instead of (l_p/lawyer).

Essentially, the solution to both problems is to forbid decomposing the origin of a :domain role (or the target of a :mod role), in order to implement the focus-switching mechanism described above. The idea is to let 'normal' nodes decompose into an AMR (x/E :mod (x_p/P)) focusing the fresh entity node, while leaving nodes with a domain role unaltered and thus keep focus on the original node in the latter case. We let τ denote the resulting "default decomposition" transformation. τ decomposes every node of an AMR tree into an entity modified by a predicate, except when it has a :domain role. It is informally schematized below:

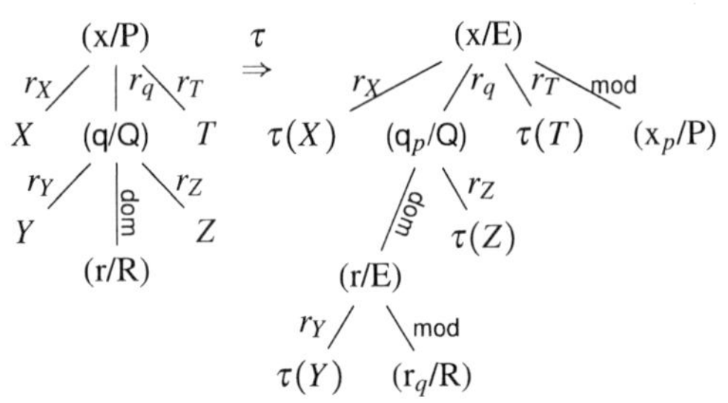

For instance, in AMR 2 both (m/man) and $(s/sing-01)$ receive a default decomposition into an entity (m for *man*, s for *sing-01*) and a state (m_p for being a man, s_p for being a singing), but $(l/lawyer)$ does **not**, because it has a domain edge. The result is the AMR below:

```
(l_p/lawyer
  :domain (m/E :mod (m_p/man)
              :arg0-of (s/E :mod
                          (s_p/sing-01))))
```

In fact, altering the original AMR is not even necessary, since we can directly implement the default decomposition into the denotational semantics. To this extent, let us assume that $V_p = \{x_p, y_p, \dots\}$ is a set of variable symbols disjoint from the one used in AMR trees, such that each AMR variable x can be injectively mapped to a variable x_p in V_p. We introduce a second interpretation function $[\![\cdot]\!]^D$ which is triggered for nodes with an outgoing :domain edge. In all of the following, r ranges over all roles except domain and mod. We abbreviate domain as dom. The "standard" interpretation rules are:

$$[\![c]\!] = \lambda f f(c)$$
$$[\![x]\!] = \lambda f f(x)$$
$$[\![(\mathbf{N})]\!] = [\![\mathbf{N}]\!]$$
$$[\![x/P]\!] = \lambda f \exists x \exists x_P P(x_P) \wedge \mathrm{dom}(x_p, x) \wedge f(x)$$
$$[\![\mathbf{N}\,{:}r\,\mathbf{A}]\!] = \lambda f [\![\mathbf{A}]\!](\lambda m [\![\mathbf{N}]\!](\lambda n\, r(n,m) \wedge f(n)))$$
$$[\![\mathbf{N}\,{:}r^{-1}\,\mathbf{A}]\!] = \lambda f [\![\mathbf{N}]\!](\lambda n [\![\mathbf{A}]\!](\lambda m\, r(m,n) \wedge f(n)))$$
$$[\![\mathbf{N}\,{:}\mathrm{dom}\,\mathbf{A}]\!] = \lambda f [\![\mathbf{A}]\!](\lambda m [\![\mathbf{N}]\!]^D(m)(\lambda n\, \mathrm{dom}(n,m) \wedge f(n)))$$
$$[\![\mathbf{N}\,{:}\mathrm{mod}\,\mathbf{A}]\!] = \lambda f [\![\mathbf{N}]\!](\lambda n [\![\mathbf{A}]\!]^D(n)(\lambda m\, \mathrm{dom}(m,n) \wedge f(n)))$$

and for nodes with a :domain role:

$$[\![c]\!]^D = \lambda e \lambda f f(c)$$
$$[\![x]\!]^D = \lambda e \lambda f f(x_P)$$
$$[\![(\mathbf{N})]\!]^D = [\![\mathbf{N}]\!]^D$$
$$[\![x/P]\!]^D = \lambda e \lambda f \exists x_P P(x_P) \wedge f(x_P)$$
$$[\![\mathbf{N}\,{:}r\,\mathbf{A}]\!]^D = \lambda e \lambda f [\![\mathbf{A}]\!](\lambda m [\![\mathbf{N}]\!]^D(e)(\lambda n\, r(e,m) \wedge f(n)))$$
$$[\![\mathbf{N}\,{:}r^{-1}\,\mathbf{A}]\!]^D = \lambda e \lambda f [\![\mathbf{N}]\!]^D(e)(\lambda n [\![\mathbf{A}]\!](\lambda m\, r(m,e) \wedge f(n)))$$
$$[\![\mathbf{N}\,{:}\mathrm{dom}\,\mathbf{A}]\!]^D = \lambda e \lambda f [\![\mathbf{A}]\!](\lambda m [\![\mathbf{N}]\!]^D(e)(\lambda n\, \mathrm{dom}(e,m) \wedge f(n)))$$
$$[\![\mathbf{N}\,{:}\mathrm{mod}\,\mathbf{A}]\!]^D = \lambda e \lambda f [\![\mathbf{N}]\!]^D(e)(\lambda n [\![\mathbf{A}^D]\!](e)(\lambda m\, \mathrm{dom}(m,e) \wedge f(n)))$$

Figure 5 shows how the semantics unpacks for AMR 2. One easily verifies that the result entails AMR 3: the latter interprets as $\exists l \exists l_p\, \mathrm{lawyer}(l_p) \wedge \mathrm{dom}(l_p, l) \wedge \exists s \exists s_p\, \text{sing-01}(s_p) \wedge \mathrm{dom}(s_p, s) \wedge \mathrm{arg0}(s, l)$ (since 3 does not have any :domain role, each of its nodes is decomposed). To check the entailment, notice that, up to renaming of the quantified variable l to m, every conjunct in the formula above also appears as a conjuct of the interpretation of AMR 2 in figure 5.

To conclude this section, let us discuss some of the properties, benefits and limitations of the proposed default entity decomposition approach. While the target logical interpretations are undoubtedly less readable, they are obtained from the (unaltered) original AMR. So what we have achieved is an improved notion of entailment between AMRs,

$$
\begin{aligned}
&[\![\text{(m/man :arg0-of (s/sing-01))}]\!] \\
&= \lambda f \exists m \exists m_p \, \text{man}(m_p) \wedge \text{dom}(m_p, m) \\
&\quad \wedge \exists s \exists s_p \text{sing-01}(s_p) \wedge \text{dom}(s_p, s) \\
&\quad \wedge \text{arg0}(s, m) \wedge f(m) \\
&[\![\text{l/lawyer}]\!]^D = \lambda e \lambda f \exists l_p \, \text{lawyer}(l_p) \wedge f(l_p) \\
&[\![\text{(l/lawyer :domain (m/ man :arg0-of (s/sing-01)))}]\!] \\
&= \lambda f \, [\![\text{(m/man :arg0-of (s/sing-01))}]\!] (\\
&\quad \lambda m \, [\![\text{l/lawyer}]\!]^D (m)(\lambda n \, \text{dom}(n, m) \wedge f(n))) \\
&= \lambda f \exists m \exists m_p \, \text{man}(m_p) \wedge \text{dom}(m_p, m) \\
&\quad \wedge \exists s \exists s_p \text{sing-01}(s_p) \wedge \text{dom}(s_p, s) \\
&\quad \wedge \text{arg0}(s, m) \\
&\quad \wedge \exists l_p \, \text{lawyer}(l_p) \wedge \text{dom}(l_p, m) \wedge f(l_p)
\end{aligned}
$$

Figure 5: Interpretation of AMR 2 with default entity decomposition

and a better understanding on the denotation of AMR nodes in copula sentences, at no cost for the annotation capabilities of the formalism.

The attentive reader might have noticed that nodes with a :domain role have an interpretation of type $\langle e, \langle e,t \rangle, t \rangle$ differing from "regular" nodes whose interpretation is of type $\langle \langle e,t \rangle, t \rangle$. While the additional entity-type argument might seem vacuous at first, it is in fact essential to handle (rather frequent) cases of nominal copula constructions where the noun following the copula is itself modified. Consider, as an exemple, the following sentence from the AMR corpus: *Teikovo is a small town in the Ivanovo region about 250 kilometers or 155 miles northeast of Moscow.* The full AMR is given in annex. For our present purpose, we only need to consider the following partial AMR: (t/town :mod (s/small) :domain (c2/city)). Our semantics, ensures that in this context the subtree (t/town :mod (s/small)) denotes the complex property of being a town which is small, and that, as a result, Teikovo (the city) is attributed both properties of being a town and being small. Importantly, the property of being small is not attributed to the *predicate* town, but to the same entity that the latter ends up attributed to, whichever it might be.

Put another way, our semantics implements an intersective treatment of chains of modifiers. Hence, (c/cat :mod (r/grey :mod (f/fierce))) denotes a cat which is both grey and fierce. Of course, adjectival modification is not always intersective, and roles such as degree or time will require a separate treatment. However, the intersective semantics appears necessary to reconciliate some observed variations in annotations, as displayed by the examples below.

The revised interpretation can help us assess some difficult annotation choices. Consider the two sentences *Only if Ron Paul doesn't become president then there will be war* and *And, that is something needed to become President.* Both sentences are from the AMR corpus, and their AMRs are provided in annex. Annotators have made different choices for these two sentences: the first involves (b/become-01 :arg2 (p2/president)) whereas the second involves (b/become-01 :arg2 (p2/person :arg1-of (h/have-org-role-91 :arg2 (p3/president)))). Are these two treatments of *become president* equivalent or incompatible? We can answer this question, at least if we admit that *becomes* is akin to a kind of copula construction[10] and that have-org-role-91 is also akin to :domain in that respect; it is the (reified) relation used to express *e.g.*, *Ron Paul is president.*[11] Under these assumptions, the question amounts to spotting the difference (if any) between (p/president :domain (r/Ron_Paul)) and (x/person :mod (p/president) :domain (r/Ron_Paul)) (ignoring AMR decomposition of named entity, for simplicity). Our semantics associates the former with the proposition $\exists r \exists r_p \, \text{Ron\_Paul}(r_p) \wedge \text{dom}(r_p, r) \wedge \exists p_p \, \text{president}(p_p) \wedge \text{dom}(p_p, r)$ and the latter with the proposition $\exists r \exists r_p \, \text{Ron\_Paul}(r_p) \wedge \text{dom}(r_p, r) \wedge \exists x_p \text{person}(x_p) \wedge \exists p_p \, \text{president}(p_p) \wedge \text{dom}(p_p, r) \wedge \text{dom}(x_p, r)$. If a president must always be a person, then the two are clearly logically equivalent.

The approach, however, yields arguably puzzling scoping when *e.g.* attitude verbs have copula sentences as objects. While the two AMRs discussed in the previous paragraph have equivalent **closures**, their different focus yield different propositions when embedded. Consider, under the same modeling hypotheses, the sentence *I believe that Ron Paul is president.* The AMR

```
(believe-01 :arg0 (i/I)
            :arg1 (p/president :domain
                  (r/Ron_Paul)))
```

[10] *X becomes Y* is commonly seen as *asserting* that *X* is *Y* and *presupposing* that *X* was not *Y* before. In this view, *XbecomesY* can be thought of as a paraphrase of *X starts to be Y*.

[11] become-01 and have-org-role-91 are similar to domain at least regarding the type of objects that they relate, and dealing with them as such would require that we extends our semantics to account for this fact.

could arguably be paraphrased as *I believe that a state of being president obtains which has Ron Paul as theme*, whereas

```
(believe-01 :arg0 (i/I)
  :arg1 (x/person
          :mod (p/president)
          :domain (r/Ron_Paul)))
```

would rather be paraphrased as *Ron Paul is president, and I believe that a state obtains of being a person which has Ron Paul as theme.* We do not commit on whether this is a bug or a feature of the approach. However, we note that we have voluntarily stuck with an approach producing pure first-order target Davidsonian propositions. To render the the two AMRs above fully equivalent (if deemed desirable), one probably needs to allow roles' participants to be higher-order objects like propositions, because as things stand, we are able to express states of 'being a person' or 'being president', but not of 'being a person who is president'.

5 Quasi-predicates

We now turn to a different problem, which originates from the same discrepancy between the words of english which invoke PropBank frames, and those which do not.

The phenomenon at stake is the treatment of what Meaning-Text Theory (MTT) calls quasi-predicates. Mel'čuk and Polguère (2008); Polguère (2012) define predicates as those lexical meanings that have two properties: 1) they denote situations (in a broad sense including events and facts), and 2) they involve a number of semantic participants whose value is contingent, but whose participation is necessary. Polguère notes that predicate are commonly put in opposition to *semantic names*, like the meanings 'rock' or 'star'. Semantic names denote entities rather than situations and they can be defined without reference to participants. Yet, Polguère observes that there is a vast class of meanings, like those of *brother*, *consumer* or *therapist* which denote entities (like semantic names), but cannot denote without accounting for a certain number of participants, due to the presence of a predicate with unbound arguments in their semantic decomposition. These meanings are called quasi-predicates (henceforth, QP).

In essence, a QP can be assimilated to a pair made of an entity and a defining predicate, with focus generally put on the entity (though Polguère (2012) remarks that this is challenged in some constructions, typically copula). For instance, the meaning of *brother* is an entity X (a man), combined with a predicate (X having a common parent with Y). Sometimes, the structure of a QP is displayed explicitly in AMR, *i.e.*, the entity and the defining predicate give rise to different nodes. Consider for instance the example below:

AMR 8: *My brother*

```
(p/person
  :arg0-of (h/have-rel-role-91
    :arg1 (i/I)
    :arg2 (b/brother)))))
```

But this is not always the case:

AMR 9: *Our clients*

```
(c/client :poss (w/we))
```

In this case, the entity *client* itself is linked to the other participant, there is no separation between entity and defining predicate.

While in and of itself these differences are not a problem, they have no other basis than the peculiarities of the English lexicon. The verb *to client* does not exist, and consequently, there is no PropBank frame to decompose the meaning of *client*. The asymmetry between *client* and *brother* is therefore the same as noted in the previous section between *worker* and *lawyer*. What is new however, is that AMR suffers expressive limitations when representing QPs because of this. For instance, we cannot represent the meaning of *The therapist thanks his client* in a way that makes explicit both the fact that the client is the client of the therapist, and that the therapist is the therapist of the client, for we would end up with the cyclic AMR below.

```
(t/thanks-01 :arg0 (t2/therapist :poss
    (c/client :poss t2)) :arg1 c)
```

Interestingly however, reifying (Banarescu et al., 2019) :poss with own-01 removes the cycle:

AMR 10: Reified :poss

```
(t/thank-01
  :arg0 (t2/therapist
    :arg0-of (o1/own-01
      :arg1 (c/client
        :arg0-of (o2/own-01 :arg1 t2))))
    :arg1 c)
```

Reification is introduced in AMR as a mechanism needed to focus a role. But in this case, it is not what it achieves. Rather, reification "borrows" the frame own-01 and uses it as a default to decompose *therapist* and *client*. Indeed, the problem disappears for words which invoke PropBank frames, for instance *The seller thanks the buyer* has an AMR isomorphic to AMR 10.

The default decomposition approach from previous section generalizes this solution, by systematically providing an additional abstract attachment point (the *predicate*) for any outgoing role of the defining predicate of a QP:

AMR 11: Default decomposition

```
(t/E :mod (t_p/thank-01)
 :arg0 (t2/E
  :mod (t2_p/therapist
   :arg1 (c/E
    :mod (c_p/client :arg1 t2)))):arg1 c)
```

Importantly, the approach allows to handle any kind of QP, even if the relationship to their participants is not expressible as a reifiable non-core role like :poss.

6 Conclusion

Whereas seeing AMR nodes as Davidsonian entities seems overall very sound from a logical perspective, we have shown that copula sentences pose an important challenge to this view. The challenge arises because they require to isolate the predicative part of a node from the entity it denotes. We have proposed a unifying mechanism of default decomposition, which systematically entangles the two notions. We have implemented it in a denotational semantics for AMR which does not require any addition to the original AMR annotation. We have shown that this approach generally resolves linguistically unjustified asymmetries depending on the existence of PropBank frames, in particular regarding the representation of quasi-predicates.

References

Nicholas Asher. 1993. *Reference to Abstract Objects in Discourse*. Dordrecht, Boston, and London: Kluwer.

Laura Banarescu, Claire Bonial, Shu Cai, Madalina Georgescu, Kira Griffitt, Ulf Hermjakob, Kevin Knight, Philipp Koehn, Martha Palmer, and Nathan Schneider. 2013. Abstract meaning representation for sembanking. In *LAW@ACL*, pages 178–186. The Association for Computer Linguistics.

Laura Banarescu, Claire Bonial, Shu Cai, Madalina Georgescu, Kira Griffitt, Ulf Hermjakob, Kevin Knight, Philipp Koehn, Martha Palmer, and Nathan Schneider. 2019. Abstract meaning representation (AMR) 1.2.6 specification. `https://github.com/amrisi/amr-guidelines/blob/master/amr.md#focus-1`. Accessed 2022-11-12.

Johan Bos. 2016. Squib: Expressive power of Abstract Meaning Representations. *Computational Linguistics*, 42(3):527–535.

Donald Davidson. 1967. Truth and meaning. *Synthese*, 17(1):304–323.

Kevin Knight, Bianca Badarau, Laura Baranescu, Claire Bonial, Madalina Bardocz, Kira Griffitt, Ulf Hermjakob, Daniel Marcu, Martha Palmer, Tim O'Gorman, and Nathan Schneider. 2021. Abstract Meaning Representation (AMR) Annotation Release 3.0.

Kenneth Lai, Lucia Donatelli, and James Pustejovsky. 2020. A continuation semantics for Abstract Meaning Representation. In *Proceedings of the Second International Workshop on Designing Meaning Representations*, pages 1–12, Barcelona Spain (online). Association for Computational Linguistics.

Claudia Maienborn. 2005. On the limits of the davidsonian approach: The case of copula sentences. *Theoretical Linguistics*, 31:275–316.

William C. Mann. 1983. An overview of the penman text generation system. In *Proceedings of the Third AAAI Conference on Artificial Intelligence*, AAAI'83, page 261–265. AAAI Press.

Igor A. Mel'čuk. 1973. Towards a linguistic "Meaning-Text" model. In Ferenc Kiefer, editor, *Trends in Soviet Theoretical Linguistics*, pages 33–57. Reidel, Dordrecht.

Igor A. Mel'čuk. 2016. *Language: From Meaning to Text*. Ars Rossica, Moscow/Boston.

Igor A. Mel'čuk and Alain Polguère. 2008. Prédicats et quasi-prédicats sémantiques dans une perspective lexicographique. *Revue de linguistique et de didactique des langues*, 37:99–114.

Martha Palmer, Daniel Gildea, and Paul Kingsbury. 2005. The proposition bank: An annotated corpus of semantic roles. *Computational Linguistics*, 31(1):71–106.

Terrence Parsons. 1990. *Events in the semantics of English: a study in subatomic semantics*. MIT Press, Cambridge, MA / London.

Alain Polguère. 2012. Propriétés sémantiques et combinatoires des quasi-prédicats sémantiques. *SCOLIA*, 26:131–152.

7 Annex

We reproduce below the annotations for sentences *Only if Ron Paul doesn't become president then there will be war* and *And, that is something needed to become President* discussed in section 4.

```
# ::id DF-200-192451-579_6417.3
# ::tok Only if Ron Paul doesnt become
    president then there will be war .
(w / war-01~e.11
    :condition~e.1 (b / become-01~e.5
        :polarity -
        :ARG1 (p / person :wiki "Ron_Paul"
            :name (n / name
                :op1 "Ron"~e.2
                :op2 "Paul"~e.3))
        :ARG2 (p2 / president~e.6)
        :mod (o / only~e.0))
    :time (t / then~e.7))
```

```
# ::id bolt-eng-DF-170-181103-8886306_0011.6
# ::tok And , that is something needed to
    become President .
(a / and~e.0
    :op2 (n / need-01~e.5
        :ARG0 (b / become-01~e.7
            :ARG2 (p2 / person
                :ARG1-of (h / have-org-role-91
                :ARG2 (p3 / president~e.8))))
        :ARG1 (s / something~e.4)))
```

```
# ::id PROXY_APW_ENG_20080515_0931.17
# ::snt Teikovo is a small town in the Ivanovo
    region about 250 kilometers or 155 miles
    northeast of Moscow.
(t / town
    :mod (s / small)
    :location (p / province :wiki "Ivanovo"
        :name (n / name :op1 "Ivanovo"))
    :location (r / relative-position
        :op1 (c / city :wiki "Moscow"
            :name (n2 / name :op1 "Moscow"))
        :direction (n3 / northeast)
        :quant (a / about
            :op1 (d / distance-quantity
                :quant 250
                :unit (k / kilometer))))
    :domain (c2 / city :wiki "Teykovo"
        :name (n4 / name :op1 "Teikovo")))
```

Character-level Dependency Annotation of Chinese

Li Yixuan
Université Paris3 - Sorbonne Nouvelle
LPP (CNRS)
yixuan.li@sorbonne-nouvelle.fr

Abstract

In this paper, we propose a new model for annotating dependency relations at the Mandarin character level with the aim of building treebanks to cope with the unsatisfactory performance of existing word segmentation and syntactic analysis models in specific scientific domains, such as Chinese patent texts. The result is a treebank of 100 sentences annotated according to our scheme, which also serves as a training corpus that facilitates the subsequent development of a joint word segmenter and dependency analyzer that enables downstream tasks in Chinese to be separated from the non-standardized pre-processing step of word segmentation.

1 Introduction

Word segmentation has long been a chicken-and-egg problem in Chinese. The notion of distinct words with spaces as natural boundaries in languages using the Latin alphabet has never been widely agreed upon in Chinese. In the absence of both natural delimiters and inflection marks, two main indicators of wordhood (Magistry et al., 2012), the distinction between words and larger lexical units in Chinese has been an unfamiliar and confusing concept since it was introduced by Zhang Shizhao in 1907. This has resulted in a low agreement rate of 76% on lexicality among native Chinese speakers (Sproat et al., 1997).

All existing Mandarin treebanks and syntactic annotation schemes for Mandarin Chinese employ word segmentation as the first step in the annotation. However, their segmentation criteria are far different without a clear unified standard. At the same time, dependency analyzers trained on these treebanks end up with inconsistent results with each other, especially on corpora containing a large number of domain-specific new terms, such as patent texts (Li et al.)

It is in this context that we decided to explore the idea of developing a character-based Chinese annotation schema. A treebank annotated with additional internal relations of words can be used as a resource to train a joint segmenter-parser, combining the two steps into one. Moreover, (Li et al., 2019) also showed that character-level annotations, even coarse ones, can help improve the results of dependency analysis for Chinese of different text types.

In the most widely accepted morphological theory of Chinese (Feng, 1997; Zhang, 2003; Dong, 2011), complex words are derivative words or compound words. The second group includes five types: modifier-head type, coordinative type, predicate-object type, predicate-complement type, and subject-predicate type. He (He et al., 2012) and Chi (Chi et al., 2019) suggest in their work that there is a parallelism between compound word structure and syntactic structure in Chinese, from which from which it is feasible to build a new dependency model that unifies the character level with the current word level relationship. Some previous works have also discussed the possibility of the joint dependency parsing and multi-word expression recognition on other languages (Candito et al., 2014; Nasr et al., 2015).

From this perspective, it is important to integrate the new word internal relations of the new words into dependency trees built on the basis of similar distributional criteria. This is why this work chose to base itself on a variant of UD (Gerdes et al., 2018), Surface-Syntactic Universal Dependencies (SUD), which is a near-isomorphic but more surface syntactic alternative schema of UD with a more classical word distribution-based dependency structure that favors functional heads. And to obtain the relationships between these roles, we applied syntactic tests that allowed us to

Proceedings of the Seventh International Conference on Dependency Linguistics (Depling, GURT/SyntaxFest 2023), pages 42 - 53
March 9-12, 2023 ©2023 Association for Computational Linguistics

Word internal structure	Examples			SUD
Coordination compounds	价值	*jià zhí*	'price_N' + 'value_N' = 'value_N/V'	conj
	国家	*guó jiā*	'country_N' + 'family_N' = 'country_N'	
	查封	*chá fēng*	'examine_V' + 'close_V' = 'seize_V'	
	始终	*shǐ zhōng*	'begin_V' + 'finish_V' = 'all along_ADV'	
	明亮	*míng liàng*	'bright_ADJ' + 'bright_ADJ' = 'bright_ADJ'	
	高矮	*gāo ǎi*	'tall_ADJ' + 'short_ADJ' = 'height_N'	
Modifier compounds	蜂巢	*fēng cháo*	'bee_N' + 'nest_N' = 'beehive_N'	mod
	汉字	*hàn zì*	'Chinese_ADJ' + 'character_N' = 'Chinese character_N'	
	飞机	*fēi jī*	'fly_V' + 'machine_N' = 'plane_N'	
	火红	*huǒ hóng*	'fire_N' + 'red_ADJ' = 'red as fire_ADJ'	
	深蓝	*shēn lán*	'dark_ADJ' + 'blue_ADJ' = 'dark blue_ADJ'	
	滚烫	*gǔn tàng*	'roll(ing)_V' + 'hot_ADJ' = 'boiling hot_ADJ'	
	迟到	*chí dào*	'late_ADJ' + 'arrive_V' = 'be late_V'	
	鼠窜	*shǔ cuàn*	'rat_N' + 'flee_V' = 'scamper off like a rat_V'	
	夜游	*yè yóu*	'night_N' +' tour_V' = 'noctivagation_N/V'	
Subject-predicate compounds	目睹	*mù dǔ*	'eye_N' + 'see_V' = 'witness_V'	subj
	性急	*xìng jí*	'temper_N' + 'impatient_ADJ' = 'impatient_ADJ'	
	海啸	*hǎi xiào*	'sea_N' + 'howl_V' = 'tsunami_N/V'	
Predicate-object compounds	结果	*jié guǒ*	'bear_V' + 'fruit_N' = 'bear fruit_V'/ 'result_N'	comp:obj
	睡觉	*shuì jiào*	'sleep_V' + 'sleep_N' = 'sleep_V'	
	喝水	*hē shuǐ*	'drink_V' + 'water_N' = 'drink water_V'	
Predicate-complement compounds	请教	*qǐng jiào*	'ask_V' + 'teach_V' = 'ask (obj) to teach/consult_V'	comp:obl, comp:pred, comp:aux
	推动	*tuī dòng*	'push_V' + 'move_V' = 'push (obj) to move_V'	
	说明	*shuō míng*	'speak_V' + 'clear_ADJ' = 'explain_V'	
	来自	*lái zì*	'come_V' + 'from_ADJ' = 'come from_V'	
	可变	*kě biàn*	'can_AUX' + 'change_V' = 'changeable_ADJ'	
	书本	*shū běn*	'book_N' + "Classifier" = 'book_N'	
	雪花	*xuě huā*	'snow_N' + 'flower_N' = 'snowflakes_N'	
Simple words	车	*chē*	'car_N'	flat
- transliterated words	咖啡	*kā fēi*	'coffee_N'	
- onomatopoeia	叮咚	*dīng dōng*	'ding-dong_Onomatopoeia'	
- reduplicated words	侃侃	*kǎn kǎn*	'eloquently_ADV'	

Table 1: List of Chinese word internal structures with examples and English translation.

identify the head and internal structure of the composite based on distributional criteria.

After discussing Chinese morphology and syntactic theory, the parallelism between Chinese compound word structure and syntactic structure is discussed especially in sections 2 and 3. The next two sections explain the complete annotation process, including two sub-steps. (1) automatic tokenization, POS tagging and dependency parsing using existing NLP pipelines (Section 4.1); and (2) manual correction and annotation follo-wing our SUD-based character-level annotation schema (Section 4.2). Then, Section 4.3 describes the conversion of the character-level treebank to a standard word-level UD treebank and the evaluation of the automatically converted treebank.

2 The Annotation Schema for Chinese Word Internal Relations

Instead of the conventional first step of word segmentation in Chinese treebank annotation, the annotation of character-based treebanks starts with the analysis of the relations between individual characters. Such relations can be typical syntactic relations, internal relations of words that do not conform to any syntactic relations in modern Chinese, or the third between the two kinds of relations mentioned above, which are more frozen than independent syntactic constituents but still largely corresponds to certain syntactic structures

In this section, we explain the criteria for wordhood and parts-of-speech. Our model annotates these relations between characters at all three levels of granularity simultaneously. Without the word segmentation process, all characters of a sentence are separated. Moreover, the word level is distinguished from the syntactic level by the sub-relation ":m", instead of the blank. The criteria for this distinction are described in Section 2.1, and the next Section 2.2 explains the choice of part-of-speech labels, especially at the character level.

2.1 Wordhood and word boundaries

One of the most widely used Chinese word segmentation standards is the Penn Chinese

Treebank (3.0) Segmentation Guidelines (Xia, 2000a). The guidelines introduced the concept of "word" based on the smallest syntactic unit, which was largely followed by the later UD Chinese Hong Kong Treebank (Poiret et al., 2021). The guidelines provided for Bakeoff 2005 is another applicable standard and includes a table summarizing decisions for a range of difficult cases. Magistry (2017) summarizes all the different segmentation guidelines to discuss wordhood in Chinese and defines a word as "the smallest sequence of autonomous characters to which we can attribute at least one word class". Kratochvíl (1967) first proposed a more syntactic definition-based approach, which was later developed by (Huang, 1984; Duanmu, 1998; Packard, 2000; Nguyen, 2006). This approach proposes a set of widely applicable linguistic criteria to test whether a sequence of characters can be considered as a word: (1) Conjunction Reduction, (2) Freedom of Parts (3) Semantic Composition, (4) Exocentric Structure, (5) Adverbial Modification, (6) XP Substitution, (7) Productivity Criterion, (8) Syllable Count and (9) Insertion.

In this work, we mainly follow the provided test set, focusing on the independence criterion, the productivity criterion, and the presence of part-of-speech variation when the expression is used as a word (see Section 4.2 for a detailed analysis).

(1)	喝了。	给我水。
	hē le	*gěi wǒ shuǐ*
	'(I) drank.'	'Give me water.'

Taking the three predicate-object compounds in Table 1 as an example, both 结果 (*jié guǒ* 'result') and 睡觉 (*shuì jiào* 'sleep') are considered as words, while 喝水 (*hē shuǐ* 'drink') is a syntactic unit, since all characters in the latter can be used independently as a word, as follows. Therefore, in our work, structures considered as words are annotated as purely syntactic relations, such as A-not-A (e.g., 来不来 *lái bù lái* 'come or not come').

2.2 Choices for parts-of-speech tags

Whether the parts-of-speech are based on meaning or syntactic distribution has long been a central issue in POS tagging (Xia, 2000b). Since almost all Chinese characters have multiple parts of speech and have neither delimiters nor inflection marks, which are the two main indicators of languages using the Latin alphabet (Magistry et al., 2012), the distinction between different parts-of-speech is mainly indicated by the distribution position. Therefore, instead of considering semantics, we placed the choice of part-of-speech labels on distributional position in both word-level and character-level annotations.

Open class words	Closed class words	Other
ADJ	ADP	PUNCT
ADV	AUX	SYM
INTJ	CCONJ	X
NOUN	DET	
PROPN	NUM	
VERB	PART	
	PRON	
	SCONJ	

Table 3: List of UD POS tags.

Based on an automatic POS tagging described in Section 3.1, we manually correct the results referring to the Part-Of-Speech Tagging Guidelines for the Penn Chinese Treebank (3.0) (Xia, 2000b) for the word-level and to Xinhua Dictionary for the character-level. Especially, as the choices for POS tags and for the word internal relation labels on characters are being made simultaneously, the relation type has a heavy influence on the POS choice, which is discussed in Section 3.

Based on the automatic POS tagging described in Section 3.1, we manually corrected the results on word-level by referring to the Part-Of-Speech Tagging Guidelines for the Penn Chinese Treebank (3.0) (Xia, 2000b) and the character-level by referring to the Xinhua Dictionary. In particular, since the selection of POS tags and internal relation labels of words is going to be done simultaneously, the type of relationship has a great influence on the selection of POS, which will be discussed in Section 3.

And one method often used to identify its POS during annotation is to test whether a character can be combined with a functional character specifically reserved for a particular POS (see Table 2 for details).

This schema retains all 17 part-of-speech (UDPOS) tags of UD[1] (Nivre et al., 2016) in Table 3.

3 Correspondence between Chinese word internal structures and dependency relations in SUD

The annotation of syntactic relations is based on the Surface-Syntactic Universal Dependency (SUD) model proposed by (Gerdes et al., 2018). And based on this, we added our own character-level annotation labels by analogy with the surface-syntactic relations of SUD.

In this section, we introduce six categories of character-level relations in modern Chinese vocabulary. For each category, we describe the definition of a category, and its correspondence with the syntactic relations in SUD, and give some criteria to test whether a compound belongs to a certain category (see the full decision tree in Appendix A).

3.1 Coordination compounds

Coordinated compounds are composed of two or more morphemes that are usually synonymous, antonymic, or semantically related. The meaning of a compound can be a combination of its morphemes, completely independent of the meaning of its components, or inclined to one of its characters.

In terms of POS, a coordinating complex can consist of the following components:

(1) Two nouns characters: N1 + N2

In Table 1, 价值 (*jià zhí* 'value') and 国家 (*guó jiā* 'country') are two examples of this subcategory. In 价值 the two characters are synonyms and the meaning of the compound is the their synthesis, while in 国家 (*guó jiā* 'country') the meaning is inclined to 国 (*guó* 'country').

(2) Two verbs characters: V1 + V2

Among examples of this subcategory, 查封 (*chá fēng* 'to seize'), which consists of a sequence of two verbs is itself a verb and 始终 (*shǐ zhōng* 'all along'), which consists of a pair of antonyms is usually used as an adverb.

(3) Two adjectives characters: A1 + A2

Similar to subcategories (1) and (2), the external POS of the compound can be the same as (e.g. 明亮 *míng liàng* 'bright' is an adjective) or different to (e.g. 高矮 *gāo ǎi* 'height', the external POS of the word as a whole is a noun while both characters are adjectives).

All coordination structures are considered as "conj" relations in SUD, with the edges oriented from left to right. Which means the first character of a coordination compound is always the head in its internal relation.

We proposed a set of tests to decide whether a compound word "AB" can be assigned to each of the three subcategories of coordination: whether "AB" can be extended[2] into a "先 A 后 B (*xiān A hòu B* 'first A and then B')" structure or "边 A 边 B (*biān A biān B* 'A while B')" structure for subcategory (2), and into a "A 而不 B (*A ér bù B* 'is A but not B')" structure or "又 A 又 B (*yòu A yòu B* 'not only A but also B')" structure for subcategory (3). As for subcategory (1), the two noun characters can usually be extended into "A 和 B (*A hé B* 'A and B')".

3.2 Modifier compounds

A common modifier compound may consist of two or three characters. In the first case, a term AB, where A (or the modifier) modifies B (the head, which can be a noun, an adjective or a verb). In the example of Table 1:

- 蜂巢 (*fēng cháo* 'beehive'), 汉字 (*hàn zì* 'Chinese character') and 飞机 (*fēi jī* 'plane') all have a nominative center character. However, the modifier can also be a noun (as in the first word 蜂巢), an adjective (as in the second word 汉字) or a verb (as in the third word 飞机).

- Modifier compounds with an adjective center like the noun-centered compounds above. The modifier can be a noun (e.g. 火红 *huǒ hóng* 'red as fire'), an adjective (e.g. 深蓝

[1] In regard to the specificity of the patent writing style, INTJ dose not actually appear in the final treebank.

[2] The notion "expend" here allows to add extra characters if necessary (examples are given in following subsections) , considering the disyllabification in modern Chinese. In this case, the single character can be seen as a shortened form of the disyllabic term.

shēn lán 'dark blue') or a verb (e.g. 滚烫 *gǔn tàng* 'boiling hot').

- 迟到 (*chí dào* 'be late') is an example with a verbal center character and an adjective/adverb modifier, while noun characters can also be used as a modifier of a verbal character as shortened forms of oblique structures such as "V as N", "V with N", "V towards N", etc.

And in the second case, a term ABC, where AB together modifies C (the center character). In contrast to the variety of POS of bisyllabic modifier compounds, most trisyllabic modifier compounds are nouns, where the central character is also considered as a suffix in some works, according to its productivity.

The syntactic head (center character) of a modifier compound is always its last character, and the external POS of the entire term is always the same as the POS of its head character. Compound words in this group are annotated with a "mod" label and the direction of the edge runs from right to left..

For modifier compounds, the tests set includes a check for presence or absence of the following deformations (example (2)):

1. Possible expansion with 的/地/得 *de* [3], e.g. 蜂巢 (*fēng cháo* 'beehive') can be extend-ed into 蜜蜂的巢 (*mì fēng de cháo* 'hive of bee'), where 蜂 (*fēng* 'bee') stands for 蜜蜂 (*mì fēng* "honeybee", which is itself a modifier-head compound with 蜂 *fēng* 'bee' as its head).
2. Paradigm of the head character, such as the productive character 巢 (*cháo* 'nest') can combine with 蜂 and 鸟 (*niǎo* 'bird').
3. Possible expansion into a corresponding phrase for those with a verbal center character, e.g. 鼠窜 (*shǔ cuàn* 'scamper off like a rat') is expended into 像鼠一样窜 (*xiàng shǔ yī yàng cuàn* 'scamper off like a rat'); 夜游 (*yè yóu* 'noctivagation') is expended into 在夜里游 (*zài yè lǐ yóu* 'tour in the night').

(2) 蜂巢	鸟巢
fēng cháo	*niǎo cháo*
'beehive'	'bird nest'

3.3 Subject-predicate compounds

In subject-predicate compounds, similar to modifier compounds, the head character is always the last character, which is either a verb (e.g. 目睹 *mù dǔ* 'wittiness', 海啸 *hǎi xiào* 'tsunami') or an adjective (e.g. 性急 *xìng jí* 'impatient'), while the first character is a noun, which serves as the subject of the head character. Unlike modifier compounds, the external POS of a subject-predicate compound does not always correspond to the POS of the head character.

The subject-predicate structure is annotated as "subj", with the marginal direction running from right to left.

Together with the predicate-object compounds and predicate-complement compounds, the test for the latter three types is that at least one character in the compound can have one of the aspect markers 了 (*le*) /着 (*zhe*) /过 (*guo*) without changing the meaning. This means that the character can only be a verbal character. The subject-predicate compounds differ from the other two in that they have only one verbal character in the second position, and their first character can be modified by the noun modifying particle '的 (*de*)' without a change of meaning, which means that this first character is a nominal character. In the example of 海啸 (*hǎi xiào* 'tsunami'), it is possible to say 啸着 (*xiào zhe* 'is howling') and ADJ 的海 (*ADJ de hǎi* 'ADJ sea').

3.4 Predicate-object compounds

In contrast to the subject-predicate structure, the first character in a predicate-object compound is the head character and the second character is the direct object of the verbal head character on the first position. This second character is usually a noun character (e.g. 结果 *jié guǒ* 'result', 睡觉 *shuì jiào* 'sleep', 喝水 *hē shuǐ* 'drink water').

The predicate-object structure is considered equivalent to the "comp:obj" relationship in SUD with a left-to-right edge.

[3] 的 / 地 / 得 *DE* are noun modifier particle, adjective modifier particle and verb modifier particle in Chinese.

Unlike the subject-predicate compounds, the predicate-object and predicate-complement compounds have a verbal head character in the first position. Although they are both annotated as "comp", the predicate-object compounds always have a noun character on the second position, while there is usually no nominal character in the second position of the predicate-complement compounds.

3.5 Predicate-complement compounds

There are two types of predicate-complement compounds. The first type can be compared to predicate-complement structure at the syntactic level: the first character of predicate-complement compounds is a verbal head character, which is similar to the predicate-complement structure, and its second character is a verbal or adjective character that acts as a resultative or directional complement of the head character in the first position.

A predicate-complement compound is always a verb and has a "comp"-like internal relationship marked as different types of sub-relations in SUD, such as "comp:obl" (for oblique arguments of verbs, adjectives, adverbs, nouns or pronouns, e.g. 来自 *lái zì* 'come from'), "comp:pred" (for predicative arguments of verbs, e.g. 请教 *qǐng jiào* 'consult', 推动 *tuī dòng* 'push (obj) to move') and "comp:aux" (for the argument of auxiliaries, e.g. 可变(*kě biàn* 'variable'), and corresponds to the "aux" relationship defined by UD). In this version of annotation, all sub-relations of predicate-complement are simply annotated as "comp".

The second type has a noun head character in its first position and in its second position a classifier (e.g. 书本 *shū běn* 'books') or a second noun character indicating the category or form of the first noun character (e.g. 雪花 *xuě huā* 'snowflakes'). The external POS of a compound of this type is always noun. This type can be easily identified by the presence of a classifier as the character in the second position.

3.6 Non-compound words and terms with unclear internal structures

In addition to the compound words in modern Chinese, there are also words that contain multiple characters but whose internal structure does not directly correspond to the syntactic relationships in modern Chinese, such as polysyllabic monograms, transliterated words, and onomatopoeic words. We borrowed the tag "flat"[4] from the UD/SUD schema, and established the corresponding character-level relationship "flat:m" for them.

Note that the subclass ":m" is specifically designed for relationships between Chinese characters. Thus, transliterated words using Chinese characters are marked as "flat:m", but foreign words are always marked as "flat".

Another point is that our annotation schema no longer contains the confusing label "compound". In the original UD schema, "compound" relations contained noun-noun compounds, verb and verb-object compounds (subdivided into "compound: dir", "compound:ext", "compound:vo" and "compound:vv"), and their boundaries with "nmod", "scomp", "xcomp" and their word segmentation boundaries are not very clear.

4 Construction and annotation of the Character-based Chinese Patent Tree-bank

To apply this annotation schema in a real corpus, we chose patents, one of the most challenging genres for syntactic parsing tasks due to their syntactic complexity and frequent use of uncommon domain-specific terms.

4.1 Collection of the data and automatic an-notation

We built the Chinese patent treebank by randomly selecting 100 sentences of patent claims from November 2017 to September 2018[5], which have been segmented to reduce the length of the sentences[6] In addition to line breaks, the ";" and ":" are also segmented. The shortened sentences were then split on individual characters as shown in Figure 1.

The obtained character-level treebanks were first automatically annotated with (1) word segmentation[7], (2) POS tags and (3) dependency analysis, based on votes from three state-of-the-

[4] The label "flat" is used to link names without internal structure in UD and SUD annotation.

[5] All patents are collected from the official site of CNIPA (China National Intellectual Property Administration, former SIPO): http://patdata1.cnipa.gov.cn/

[6] A Chinese patent claim sentence contain between 50 and 70 characters in average, which is extremely long compared to general texts, and even harder to parse.

[7] The results of word segmentation are present by ":m" on the relation labels.

art language processing pipelines. spaCy[8], Stanza[9] and Trankit[10].

Like the automatic annotation method for characters, the automatic POS tagging at the word level is based on a poll of three language processing pipelines. Unlike character-level annotation, the one single label we reserve for word-level annotation is the part of speech for each single character, which is saved as an external POS ("ExtPos") for the character combination.

These automatically annotated sub-relations ":m" and POS tags are later manually corrected according to the criteria described in Section 2.

4.2 Problematic cases

Cases of disagreement among annotators in annotated patent claim sentences can be divided into three main types: (1) compounds containing functional characters, (2) compounds involving resultative complements, and (3) compounds with obscure internal relation.

- Functional characters

Compound words containing functional characters or classic Chinese structures are usually highly frozen terms. However, many of them have a large paradigm.

(3) 之前 *zhī qián* 'before' — 之后 *zhī hòu* 'after'

之间 *zhī jiān* 'between' — 之内 *zhī nèi* 'within'

(4) 以前 *yǐ qián* 'before' — 以后 *yǐ hòu* 'after'

以来 *yǐ lái* 'since' — 以内 *yǐ nèi* 'within'

As a literal replacement for 的 (*de* 'PART indicating pre-modification') in Chinese, 之 (*zhī* 'PART') is usually combined with a positional word, such as in the example (3) below. These words containing 之 (*zhī* 'PART') are considered as a single word in the Penn Segmentation guidelines. Taking the change of part-of-speech we also annotated the relations in the terms 之前 (*zhī qián* 'before') and 之后 (*zhī hòu* 'after') as internal relations of words labeled as "mod:m", although each character is independent,. While 之间 (*zhī jiān* 'between') and 之内 (*zhī nèi* 'within') are annotated as the syntactic relation "mod".

(5) 其中 *qí zhōng* 'among (them)' — 其间 *qí jiān* 'between (them)'

其实 *qí shí* 'in fact'

The other two problematic function words 以 (*yǐ* 'ADP') and 其 (*qí* 'PRON') can also be combined with positional words such as 之 (*zhī* 'PART'). Under the same criteria, all four expressions in example (4) are annotated as word internal relations "comp:m", in which 以 is the head. And 其中 (*qí zhōng* 'among (them)'), 其间 (*qí jiān* 'between (them)') and 其实 (*qí shí* 'in fact') in example (5) are labeled as "det:m", in which 其 (*qí* 'PRON') as the dependent character.

所 *(suo3* 'PART') is a extremely productive character used in the "所+VERB" structure and often found in patent claims, can 所 *(suo3* 'PART') can be seen as a function word capable of converting VERB into an ADJ-liked unit. Evolving from the ancient 所 structure, 所 *(suo3* 'PART') is sometimes omitted in modern Chinese (especially in

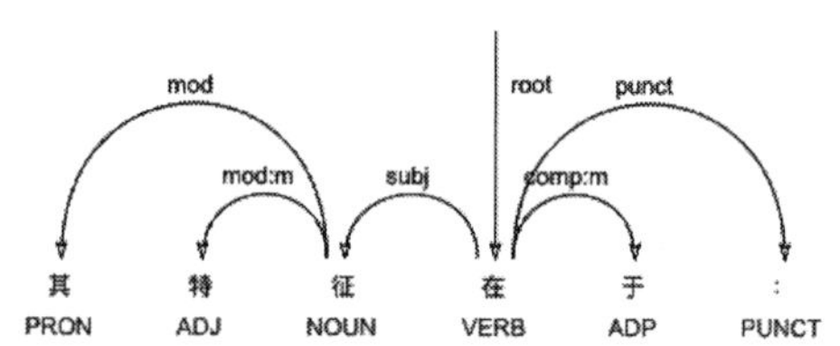

Figure 1: An example of character-based SUD Chinese Patent treebank.

8 https://spacy.io/

9 https://stanfordnlp.github.io/stanza/

10 https://trankit.readthedocs.io/en/latest/

spoken language). In our schema, 所 *(suo3* 'PART') is considered as the head character of the structure and the relation is systematically annotated as "comp:m" relation in the Chinese patent treebank.

(6) 所述 所以
suǒ shù *suǒ yǐ*
'said' 'because'

第一 章 中 (所) 描述 的 方法
dì yī zhāng zhōng (suǒ) miáo shù de fāng fǎ
'The method described in chapter 1'

The last remarkable problematic function word is 自 *(zi4* 'self'). As with 所 *(suo3* 'PART'), 自 *(zi4* 'self') is always combined with VERB to form a self-reflexive verbal expression, in which the pronoun 自 *(zi4* 'self') acts as the subject and the object at the same time, e.g. 自测 *(zì cè* 'self-evaluate') in example (7) is equivalent to 自己测试自己 *(zì jǐ cè shì zì jǐ* 'one evaluate himself'). This structure is annotated as "subj:m" with 自 as the dependent. A special case is the word 自由 *(zì yóu* 'free; freedom'), which is too frozen that it is difficult to observe the syntactic-liked structure, and is thus annotated as "flat:m" like compounds with obscure internal relation.

(7) 自测 自由
zì cè *zì yóu*
'self-evaluate' 'free; freedom'

- Resultative complements

The resultative complements can be seen as a single word by itself or as part of a VERB-complement compound (Xia, 2000a), depending on the segmentation criteria.

We adopt the test proposed by Xia based on syllable count in and segment it only if the verb or the complement have more than 2 syllables or the complement is the finished aspect mark 完 *(wán* 'finish'). In (8) only 浸没 *(jìn mò* 'submerged') is remained unsegmented and is annotated as "comp:m" structure, while 连接至 *(lián jiē zhì* 'connected to') is segmented into 连接 *(lián jiē* 'connect') and the adposition 至 *(zhì* 'ADP'), 配置有 *(pèi zhì yǒu* 'configured with') is segmented into 配置 *(pèi zhì* 'configure; configuration') and 有 *(yǒu* 'have') and 清干净 *(qīng gān jìng* 'clean up') into 清 *(qīng* 'clean_V') and 干净 *(gān jìng* 'clean_ADJ') with the syntactic label "comp".

(8) 浸没 连接 至
jìn mò *lián jiē zhì*
'submerged' 'connected to'

配置 有 清 干净
pèi zhì yǒu *qīng gān jìng*
'configured with' 'clean up'

- Obscure internal relation

This type involves those compounds usually highly frozen and whose internal structure is not obvious anymore, just like the example of 自由 discussed above.

Other examples in (9) are 根据 *(gēn jù* 'according to; proof') and 作用 *(zuò yòng* 'effect; function'). 根据 is hard to label due to the ambiguity: the structure can be interpreted as "root proof" or "root occupies". According to the preference to distributional standards of the annotation schema, the first structure is chosen so that the external POS is same to that of the head character 据 *(ju4* 'occupy; proof '). As for 作用 *(zuo4 yong4* 'effect; function'), the choice of relation label is between "comp:m" and "conj:m" as it dose not correspond to any of the tests of them. It is simply annotated "flat:m" instead to avoid a tedious study on the etymology.

(9) 根 据 作 用
gēn jù *zuò yòng*
root occupy; proof compose use
'according to; proof' 'effect; function'

4.3 Convertibility

The character-based Chinese treebank can be easily converted to a standard word-based treebank by simply combining all relations with the sub-relation ":m". The part-of-speech of the merged words is used as the external POS annotated on the head characters of the compound words.

The conversion from the SUD schema to the original UD schema is performed by Grew Match following the method proposed in (Gerdes et al., 2018).

The UD version of the treebank is released on https://github.com/UniversalDependencies/UD_Chinese-PatentChar.

5 Conclusion and Future Works

In this paper, we propose a new character-based Chinese annotation model. Instead of starting with non-standardized, information-wasting word segmentation, we analyze the word internal structures and distribute syntactic-liked labels based on the parallelism between compound word structure and syntactic structure in Chinese. Finally, we annotated the first character-level tree database consisting of 100 patent claim sentences.

Based on this character-level treebank, we have the possibility to train a character-based dependency analyzer by bootstrapping that can handle both word segmentation and syntactic analysis simultaneously.

In future work, we are also interested in developing a premoderne Chinese treebank containing a richer character-level structure[11].

Acknowledgments

I gratefully acknowledge the financial support for my doctoral study provided by the China Scholarship Council (csc).

[11] The word-level UD premoderne Chinese treebank is released on Removed for anonymous submission

References

Marie Candito and Matthieu Constant. 2014. Strategies for Contiguous Multiword Expression Analysis and Dependency Parsing. 52nd Annual Meeting of the Association for Computational Linguistics, ACL 2014 - Proceedings of the Conference.

Kang Chen, Xiaotie Deng, and Weimin Zheng. 2004. Accessor Variety Criteria For Chinese Word Extraction. Computational Linguistics, 30:75–93.

Chi Changhai and Lin Zhiyong. A New Discussion on the Parallelism Between Compound Word Structure and Syntactic Structure in Chinese [J]. Journal Of Zhejiang University (Hu-Manties And Social Sciences), 2019, 49(5): 210-223

Chen Gong, Zhenghua Li, Min Zhang, and Xinzhou Jiang. 2017. Multi-grained Chinese Word Segmentation. In Proceedings of the 2017 Conference on Empirical Methods in Natural Language Processing, pages 692–703, Copenhagen, Denmark. Association Computational Linguistics.

Kim Gerdes, Bruno Guillaume, Sylvain Kahane, and Guy Perrier. 2018. SUD or Surface-Syntactic Universal Dependencies: An Annotation Scheme Near-isomorphic to UD. In Proceedings of the Second Workshop on Universal Dependencies (UDW 2018), pages 66–74, Brussels, Belgium. Association for Computational Linguistics.

Kim Gerdes and Sylvain Kahane. 2016. Dependency Annotation Choices: Assessing Theoretical and Practical Issues of Universal Dependencies. In Proceedings of the 10th Linguistic Annotation Workshop held in conjunction with ACL 2016 (LAW-X 2016), pages 131–140, Berlin, Germany. Association for Computational Linguistics.

Chen Gong, Zhenghua Li, Min Zhang, and Xinzhou Jiang. 2017. Multi-grained Chinese Word Segmentation. In Proceedings of the 2017 Conference on Empirical Methods in Natural Language Processing, pages 692–703, Copenhagen, Denmark. Association for Computational Linguistics.

Chen Gong, Zhenghua Li, Bowei Zou, and Min Zhang. 2020. Multi-Grained Chinese Word Segmentation with Weakly Labeled Data. In Proceedings of the 28th International Conference on Computational Linguistics, pages 2026–2036, Barcelona, Spain (Online). International Committee on Computational Linguistics

Xia Fei. 2000a. The Segmentation Guideliens for the Penn Chinese Treebank (3.0). University of Pennsylvania Institute for Research in Cognitive

Science Technical Report No. IRCS-00-06, http://repository.upenn.edu/ircs_reports/37/

Xia Fei. 2000b. The Part-of-Speech Tagging Guidelines for the Penn Chinese Treebank (3.0). University of Pennsylvania Institute for Research in Cognitive Science Technical Report No. IRCS-00-07, http://repository.upenn.edu/ircs_reports/38/

Harbin Institute of Technology Research Center for Social Computing and Information Retrieval (哈尔滨工业大学信息检索研究中心) [HIT-SCIR]. 2010. HIT-CIR Chinese Dependency Treebank Annotation Guideline (HITCIR 汉语依存树库标注规范).

Yang He and Yanlei Cui. The Similarities and Differences of Chinese Compound Word Structure and Syntactic Structure and Their Roots [J] (汉语复合词结构与句法结构的异同及其根源). Language Studies, 2012 (1): 6

Paul Kratochvíl. 1967. On The Phonology Of Peking Stress. Transactions of the Philological Society, 66(1):154–178.186

Herman Leung, Rafaël Poiret, Tak-sum Wong, Xinying Chen, Kim Gerdes, and John Lee. 2016. Developing Universal Dependencies for Mandarin Chinese. In Proceedings of the 12th Workshop on Asian Language Resources (ALR12), pages 20–29, Osaka, Japan. The COLING 2016 Organizing Committee.

Yixuan Li, Chuanming Dong, and Kim Gerdes. 2019. Character-level Annotation for Chinese Surface-Syntactic Universal Dependencies. In Depling 2019 - International Conference on Dependency Linguistics, Paris, France.

Pierre Magistry. 2013. Unsupervised Word Segmentation and Wordhood Assessment.

Pierre Magistry and Benoît Sagot. 2012. Unsupervized word segmentation: the case for Mandarin Chinese. In Proceedings of the 50th Annual Meeting of the Association for Computational Linguistics (Volume 2: Short Papers), pages 383–387, Jeju Island, Korea. Association for Computational Linguistics. 200

Alexis Nasr, Carlos Ramisch, José Deulofeu and André Valli. 2015. Joint Dependency Parsing and Multiword Expression Tokenisation.

Étienne Van Tien Nguyen. 2006. Unité lexicale et morphologie en chinois mandarin: vers l'élaboration d'un dictionnaire explicatif et combinatoire du chinois.

Jerome Lee Packard. 2000. The Morphology of Chinese: A Linguistic and Cognitive Approach. Cambridge University Press, United Kingdom.

Richard Sproat. 1990. A Statistical Method For Finding Word Boundaries in Chinese Text. International Journal of Computer Processing of Languages, 4:336–351.

Richard Sproat and Thomas Emerson. 2003. The first international Chinese word segmentation bakeoff. In Proceedings of the Second SIGHAN Workshop on Chinese Language Processing, pages 133–143, Sapporo, Japan. Association for Computational Linguistics.

Richard Sproat, Chilin Shih, William Gale, and Nancy Chang. 1994. A Stochastic Finite-State Word- Segmentation Algorithm for Chinese.

Andi Wu. 2003. Customizable Segmentation Of Morphologically Derived Words in Chinese. Int. J. Comput. Linguistics Chin. Lang. Process., 8.

Nainwen Xue, Xia Fei, Fu-Dong Chiou, and Marta Palmer. 2005. The Penn Chinese Treebank: Phrase Structure Annotation of a Large Corpus. Natural Language Engineering, 11(2):207–238.

Nianwen Xue, Xiuhong Zhang, Zixin Jiang, Martha Palmer, Fei Xia, Fu-Dong Chiou, and Meiyu Chang. 2013. Chinese Treebank 8.0 LDC2013T21. Linguistic Data Consortium, Philadelphia, https://catalog.ldc.upenn.edu/ldc2013t21

A Decision Tree for Word Internal Rela-tion Labeling

Figure 2 shows the complete decision tree for word internal relation annotation. The criteria are mostly distributional with some semantic test in addition, such as whether the two character are synonym/antonyms. The synonym/antonyms here are strictly limited to polar antonyms (大 *da4* 'big' and 小 *xiao3* 'small') and coordinated structure like 春夏秋冬 (*shun1 xia4 qiu1 dong1* "four seasons").

B Comparison of the character-level Chinese treebank to the SUD and UD word-level treebank

And here is a comparison between the character-based treebank (Figure 3), the SUD word-based treebank (Figure 4) and the UD word-based tree-bank (Figure 5) of the same sentence in Chinese.

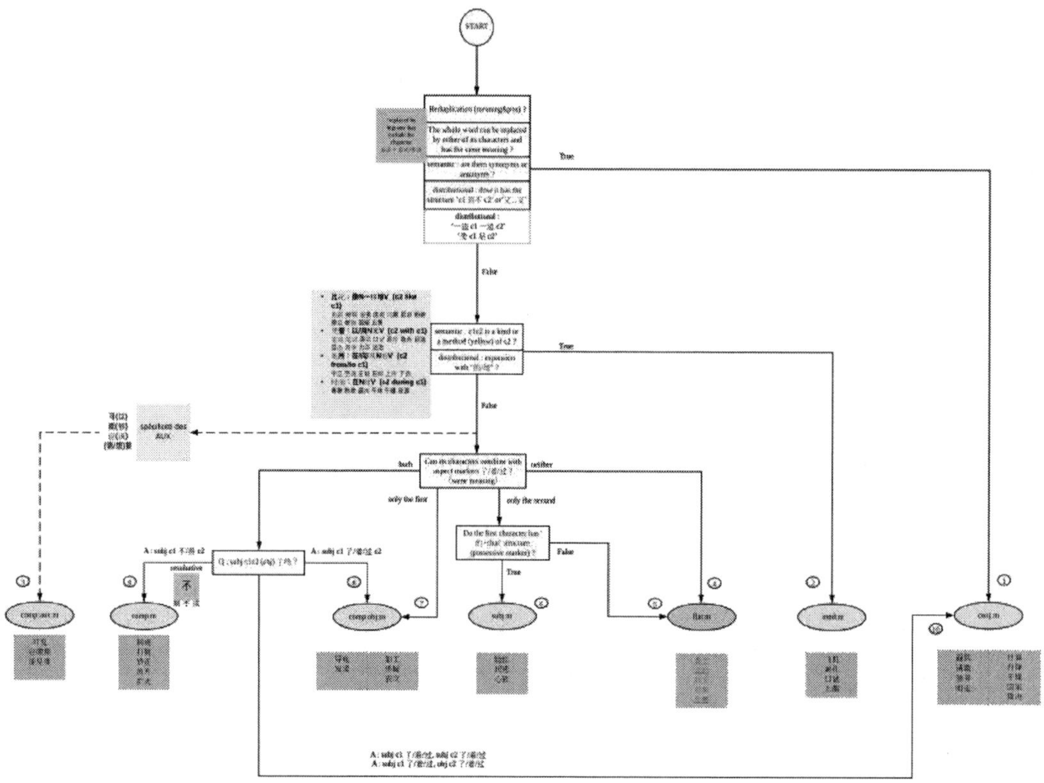

Figure 2: Decision tree for word internal relation annotation.

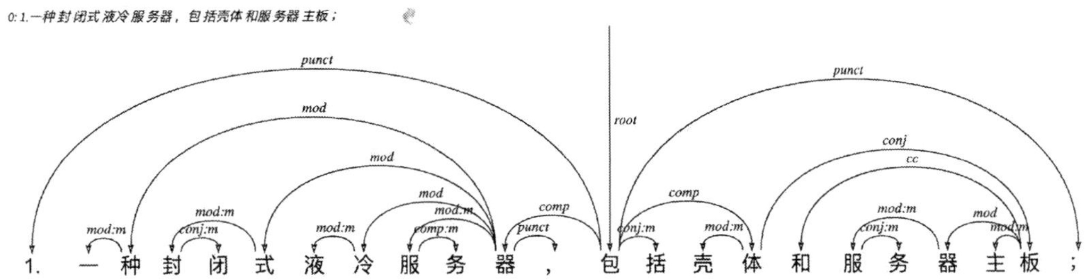

Figure 3: SUD character-based treebank.

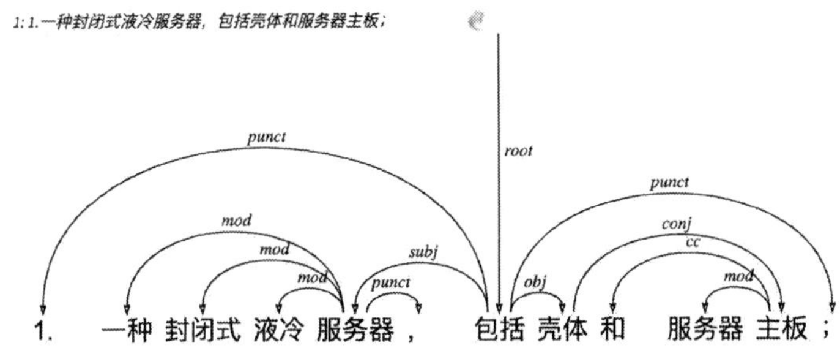

Figure 4: SUD word-based treebank.

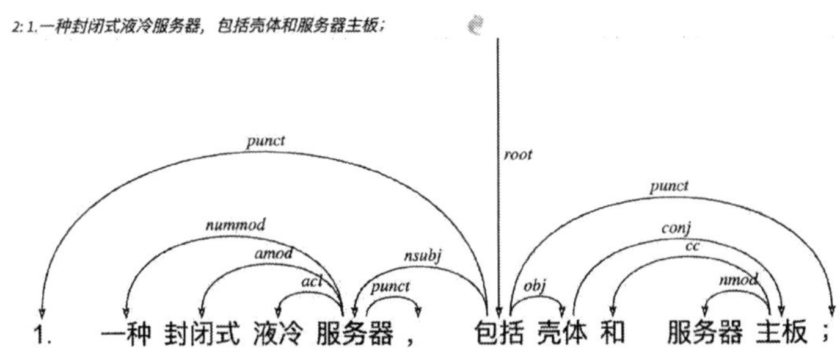

Figure 5: UD word-based treebank.

What quantifying word order freedom can tell us about dependency corpora

Maja Buljan
University of Oslo / Language Technologies Group
majabu@ifi.uio.no

Abstract

Building upon existing work on word order freedom and syntactic annotation, this paper investigates whether we can differentiate between findings that reveal inherent properties of natural languages and their syntax, and features dependent on annotations used in computing the measures. An existing quantifiable and linguistically interpretable measure of word order freedom in language is applied to take a closer look at the robustness of the basic measure (word order entropy) to variations in dependency corpora used in the analysis. Measures are compared at three levels of generality, applied to corpora annotated according to the Universal Dependencies v1 and v2 annotation guidelines, selecting 31 languages for analysis. Preliminary results show that certain measures, such as subject-object relation order freedom, are sensitive to slight changes in annotation guidelines, while simpler measures are more robust, highlighting aspects of these metrics that should be taken into consideration when using dependency corpora for linguistic analysis and generalisation.

1 Introduction

With the breadth of existing resources and research into developing dependency treebanks, cross-linguistic research has expanded to large-scale comparative work, formalising and computing quantifiable properties of natural language. The use of morphological and syntactic annotations, to name a few, has enabled typological research to move from type-based—treating languages as individual data points with a categorical value—to token-based—making generalisations and comparative analyses by using corpora to observe linguistic units in language use and express their behaviour using aggregate measures (Levshina, 2019).

In this work, the focus is on word order freedom, a property of natural language syntax, extensively covered in previous work that makes use of dependency treebanks (Liu, 2010; Futrell et al., 2015; Naranjo and Becker, 2018). The main point of interest is word order freedom expressed by the measure of Word Order Entropy (WOE), as defined by Futrell et al. (2015).

The cited work expands on methodological issues, aiming to find a balance between linguistic interpretability, robustness independent of corpus size, and cross-lingual applicability. The defined measure also enables quantitative verification of hypotheses on the relation between case marking and word order freedom (Kiparsky, 1997); word order freedom and patterns across languages with respect to head direction; and the positions of subject and object in the main clause (Greenberg et al., 1963).

However, in applying this measure to different corpus domains and sources, several issues arise and require further addressing—mainly, when expressing word order freedom with measures based on dependency annotations, does the measure reveal more about the language itself, or the annotation used as a layer between the raw text and the computable data? Further, and in line with the question raised in the original study, is this measure consistent across corpus sizes, and different text samples?

These questions are investigated through a replication of the methodology on the same set of languages covered by the original study (with minor exceptions). The aim is to compare two generations of Universal Dependency annotation styles (Nivre et al., 2016b, 2020), using the latest releases of Universal Dependencies v1 (Nivre et al., 2016a) and v2 (Zeman et al., 2021). The analysis is focused on three levels—(1) comparing scores obtained over the full corpus with multiple random samples, to verify whether the measure is robust to sample size; (2) comparing scores across two versions of annotation guidelines in the same style, to test whether

Proceedings of the Seventh International Conference on Dependency Linguistics (Depling, GURT/SyntaxFest 2023), pages 54 - 67
March 9-12, 2023 ©2023 Association for Computational Linguistics

the measure remains consistent through alterations in annotation guidelines and treebank development; and (3) comparing this replication study to the original findings, partially overlapping in corpora, to further verify consistency.

Section 2 gives a brief summary of the key methodological points of Futrell et al. (2015) (further also referred to as "the original study"). Section 3 highlights the specifics of the experimental setup. Results and findings are presented in Section 4, and Section 5 concludes the paper.

2 Background

Futrell et al. (2015) define *word order freedom* as "the extent to which the same word or constituent in the same form can appear in multiple positions while retaining the same propositional meaning and preserving grammaticality." The cited study aims to employ dependency treebanks in computing quantitative properties of natural language syntax—specifically, word order freedom—and develop linguistically interpretable measures.

The degree of word order freedom is quantified through the unordered dependency graph of a sentence, using conditional entropy:

$$H(X|C) = \sum_{c \in C} p_C(c) \sum_{x \in X} p_{x|c}(x|c) \log p_{X|C}(x|c) \tag{1}$$

where X is the dependent variable, conditioned on C, the conditioning variable. Since directly measuring the conditional entropy of sequences of words is intractable, the authors decide on three entropy measures over partial information about dependency trees, considering three parameters: (1) estimating H from joint counts of X and C (further discussed in 3.2); (2) information contained in X; and (3) information contained in C. The goal is to balance the need to avoid data sparsity against the preference to retain linguistic interpretability.

To avoid the issue of sparsity, entropy is computed only on local subtrees—consisting of a head and its immediate dependents. To avoid issues with misrepresented variability in certain word order phenomena, this means preferring annotation styles with content-head dependency. This requirement is satisfied in Universal Dependencies annotations.

Futrell et al. (2015) introduce three measures of word order entropy (WOE):

Relation Order Entropy (ROE) Conditioning on the unordered local subtree structure (C being the set of dependency relations and part-of-speech (POS) tags of constituents), the dependent variable X is the linear order of relation types expressed in the local subtree.

Subject-Object Relation Order Entropy (SOE) Assuming that ROE will result in some data sparsity issues despite limiting the search to local subtrees, SOE narrows the criteria to local subtrees containing relations of type *nsubj* and *dobj* (UDv1) or *obj* (UDv2), conditioned on the POS of these dependents.

Head Direction Entropy (HDE) The most narrowly defined of these measures, HDE is conditioned only on a dependent and its head, for all relation types; the dependent variable denotes whether the head is to the left or right of the dependent.

3 Experimental setup

This study follows the methodology of Futrell et al. (2015) as closely as possible, with three exceptions: omitting three languages from the original study due to data limitations, adjusting entropy estimation due to technical limitations, and performing computations over multiple random subcorpora samples to perform a more robust evaluation of the effects of sampling and data sparsity. The experimental setup is further detailed in subsequent paragraphs.

3.1 Treebank matching

In order to compare WOE scores between UDv1 and UDv2 annotations of the same text, it is first necessary to consolidate the available treebanks across the 34 languages of the original study. The aim is to retain the maximum number of sentences with both UDv1- and UDv2-style annotations.

The last release of UDv1 is used: version 1.4 (Nivre et al., 2016a); and the latest release of UDv2 at the time when the experiments were carried out: version 2.8 (Zeman et al., 2021).

Two of the languages featured in the original study—Bengali and Telugu—do not have a UDv1 release; the original study used HamleDT annotations (Zeman et al., 2012). For this reason, they cannot be featured in the analysis, so the total number of languages is reduced to 32, with a total of 52 available treebanks.

	UD1 vs. UD2		
	$<$	$=$	$>$
no. of treebanks	17	24	11

Table 1: Breakdown of available treebanks and their UD1 vs. UD2 coverage, by treebank count, for 32 languages featured in the original study.

Despite the continuous growth of both the number of languages featured in UD, as well as the respective treebanks (Nivre et al., 2020), the data is limited to the intersection of treebanks (or, in certain cases, individual sentences) between UDv1.4 and UDv2.8. Table 1 breaks down the treebank coverage between releases for the 32 languages group. The majority of treebanks either have an exact match between the two releases, or UDv2 expands the treebanks featured in UDv1, in terms of sentence count. For a fifth of the cases, there is a reduction in the number of sentences going from the UDv1 to the UDv2 version of the treebank.

To ensure a truly "parallel" corpus of UDv1 and UDv2 annotations, those treebank sentences that do not feature in either of the two latest releases need to be removed. Given that the releases followed no set sentence identifier standard before UDv2.0, this means resorting to heuristic matching methods.

The heuristic matching raised unexpected challenges in equating sentences that a human reader would consider superficially identical. Most of these challenges stemmed from increased annotator experience and refined annotation guidelines—resulting in, e.g., altered dependency relations between constituents, and different annotation conventions for multi-word expressions and complex names—or were the result of updated tokenisation, lemmatisation, and treatment of abbreviations. Due to this, the features taken into consideration in the matching process were wordform and lemma comparisons, POS tags and dependency relations, and the Levensthein distance of sentence surface forms.

During the matching process, Japanese was also removed from the pool of languages, due to a negligibly small (roughly 200) number of sentences identified as matches in the only treebank featured both in the UDv1.4 and UDv2.8 release.

Finally, Figure 1 visualises the total size of the annotated corpora[1] per language, from the smallest treebank (Tamil, 600 sentences) to the largest

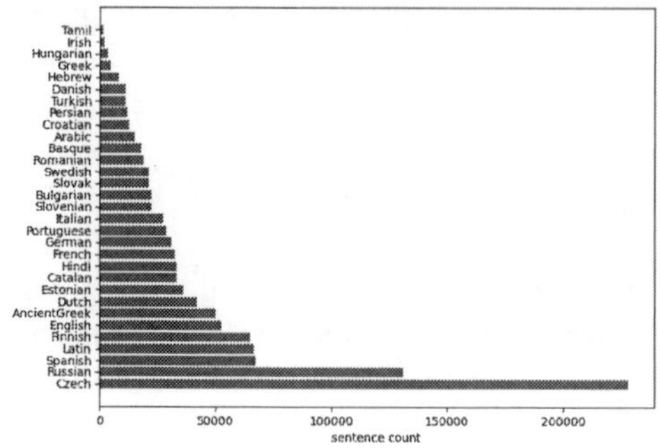

Figure 1: Total corpus size in number of sentences.

collection of treebanks (Czech, 113 682 sentences).

Due to the large variation in corpus sizes, and in line with Futrell et al. (2015), the experiments are performed both on the full corpora for each language, and on 10 randomly sampled subcorpora of 1000 sentences for each language. Note that, while the 1000 sentences are picked randomly, the samples are matched between the UDv1 and the UDv2 versions of the corpus—maintaining the "same sentence, two annotations" setup.

3.2 Entropy estimation

Apart from the equally sized subcorpora, Futrell et al. (2015) address the issue of sample size by applying the bootstrap entropy estimator of DeDeo et al. (2013), arguing that entropy is otherwise underestimated. However, due to backward compatibility issues with the implementation of the bootstrap estimator in the original study, this study resorts to using the naive estimator (Cover et al., 1991), assuming that the analysis performed is not sensitive to the order of magnitude of absolute entropy scores, as its internal consistency allows for forming and comparing rankings between languages. This is further discussed in Section 4.3.

3.3 Variables

In line with the approach of Futrell et al. (2015), conditional entropy is computed on local subtrees: a head and its immediate dependents. The conditioning variable is the unordered set of dependency relations between the head and its dependent(s), and the POS tags of all constituents.

In the case of relation order entropy, the dependent variable is the linear order of relation types in the subtree. For subject-object entropy, the dependent variable is the linear order of the subject and

[1]Detailed statistics are given in Appendix A.

object in subtrees whose predicate head has both a subject and an object in its dependents. Finally, head direction entropy is computed over all head-and-dependent pairs, where the dependent variable notes whether the head is to the left or right of its dependent.

4 Analysis

The aim of the analysis is threefold: (1) comparing the scores obtained on the full corpora against the random samples, to evaluate the effects of sampling and data sparsity, as well as comparing the random samples to estimate variance; (2) comparing UDv1 scores to UDv2 scores, to evaluate the effect of annotation; and (3) comparing the results of the original study to the rankings obtained on UDv1 and UDv2.

4.1 Full corpus vs. random sample

Figures 2 through 4 present the entropy estimates over the full corpora[2] and randomly sampled subcorpora, for UDv1 and UDv2, over the three metrics described in Section 2.

In the case of Relation Order Entropy (Figure 2), there is a clear difference between the full-corpus entropy estimates and the random-sample scores, which would also affect the rankings of the featured languages on a scale from "least-" to "most word order freedom", if the WOE score was used as the main quantifying metric. As mentioned in Section 3.2, Futrell et al. (2015) argue that the entropy estimator plays a role in under- or overestimating the entropy score, considering data sparsity and the long-tailed frequency distribution of words in natural language. However, with the naive estimator, this difference between the full corpus and the 1000-sentence samples is not nearly as striking for the other two metrics, SOE (Figure 3) and HDE (Figure 4); nor do the full-corpus rankings correlate, at a glance, with the corpus sizes shown in Figure 1. An observed explanation for this discrepancy is the fact that ROE—the least narrowly defined metric—allows for an explosion in the number of possible values for the conditioning variable when computing over the full corpus, compared to the relatively limited set of values available in the subcorpora.

Subject-Object Relation Order Entropy (Figure 3) shows less of a discrepancy between full-corpus entropy and that of subcorpora, in line with the SOE metric being more limited in the number and type of constituents forming the values for the conditioning variable. However, there is more of a variance between the entropy scores of different subcorpora (represented with red dots in the figures) than seen with the other two metrics. Furthermore, the different subcorpora scores again have the potential to dramatically alter the rankings. In the case of a relatively narrow definition of word-order metric, where the dependent variable values are permutations of (subject, object, predicate) paired with POS tags, this brings into question the reliability of random samples to give an accurate WOE score according to which languages may consistently be compared as more or less rigid in word order freedom.

Finally, Head Direction Entropy (Figure 4) demonstrates the highest (visual) match between full-corpus and subcorpora scores. Intuitively, this is in line with expectations, considering the narrow definition of HDE and the binary value of the dependent variable—a small random sample will likely have a similar distribution to the full corpus.

The figures alone imply that random samples may be less reliable than full-corpus scores if the WOE metric is less narrowly defined. However, in an attempt to not rely on visualisations alone, these differences are also quantified by calculating the Kendall rank correlation coefficient between rankings obtained from the full-corpus entropy scores, and those based on random-sample scores. Table 2 presents these coefficients, comparing the UDv1 and UDv2 computations, as well as the rankings from the original study for comparison.

The correlation between random samples and full-corpus scores expressed in Kendall τ (Table 2, top) is rather low—and in most cases not significant. The only metric that shows a weak correlation is HDE. Table 3 presents the correlation score between WOE rankings and rankings according to corpus size. No correlation is found between corpus size and WOE ranking, which seems to support the decision to use naive entropy estimations to formulate rankings.

4.2 UDv1 vs. UDv2

Figures 2 through 4 also allow for comparison between scores and rankings computed over the UDv1 and UDv2 annotations.

Figure 2, ROE, apart from a shift in rankings,

[2]Note that, for all metrics, entropy estimates for the full Tamil corpus match all random samples—as the full corpus comprises 600 sentences in total.

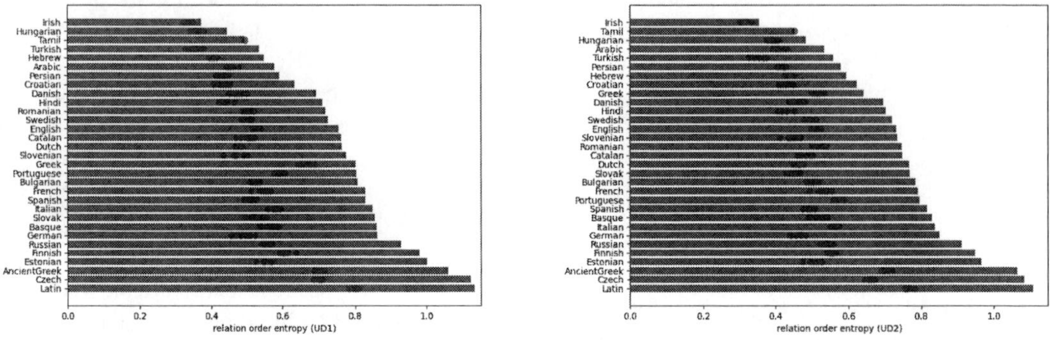

Figure 2: ROE; UDv1 (left) vs. UDv2 (right). The bar represents the relation order entropy estimated from the full corpora; the red dots represent entropies estimated from ten random samples of 1000-sentence subcorpora. Languages are ranked according to the full-corpus ROE estimate.

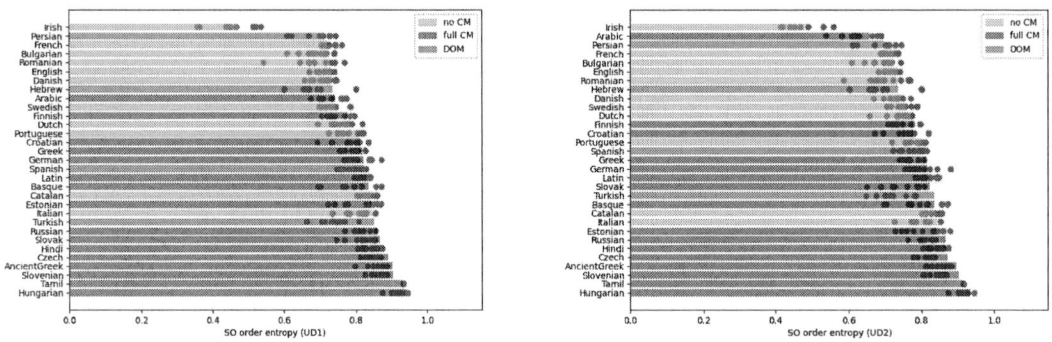

Figure 3: SOE; UDv1 (left) vs. UDv2 (right). The bar represents the relation order entropy estimated from the full corpora; the red dots represent entropies estimated from ten random samples of 1000-sentence subcorpora. Languages are ranked according to the full-corpus SOE estimate. Bars are coloured in line with Futrell et al. (2015), denoting the nominative-accusative case marking system type: "full" means fully present case marking; "DOM" means Differential Object Marking (Aissen, 2003).

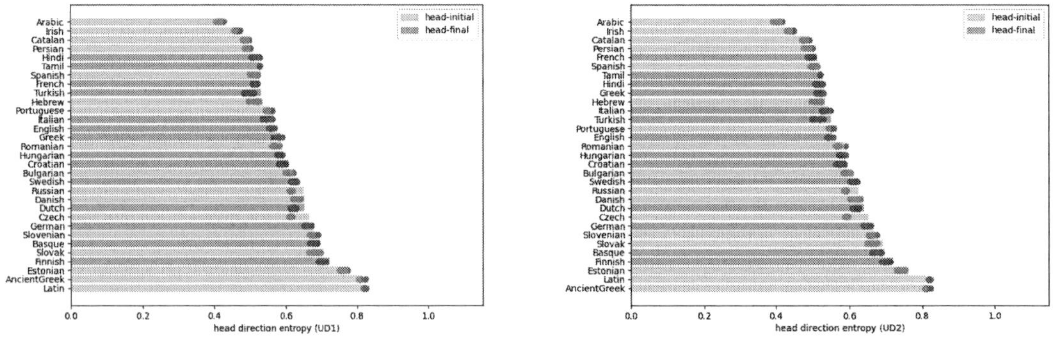

Figure 4: HDE; UDv1 (left) vs. UDv2 (right). The bar represents the relation order entropy estimated from the full corpora; the red dots represent entropies estimated from ten random samples of 1000-sentence subcorpora. Languages are ranked according to the full-corpus HDE estimate.

	ori	UDv1	UDv2
ROE	.161 $_{p=0.210}$	.165 $_{p=0.259}$	.098 $_{p=0.484}$
SOE	.449 $_{p=0.001}$	.068 $_{p=0.584}$	.187 $_{p=0.215}$
HDE	.372 $_{p=0.003}$	.297 $_{p=0.071}$	.200 $_{p=0.176}$

Table 2: Kendall τ entropy estimate rank correlation (averaged in the case of UDv1 and UDv2), comparing full corpus vs. random sample rankings. "ori" denotes rank correlation between full corpus and random sample rankings for data from the original study—note that these scores are based on rankings obtained from visualisations (as absolute entropy estimates were not available), and using only a single data point for each language's random samples.

	full	sample	
ROE	.027 $_{p=0.839}$	.027 $_{p=0.839}$	UDv1
	-0.07 $_{p=0.566}$	.006 $_{p=0.973}$	UDv2
SOE	.002 $_{p=1.0}$	.088 $_{p=0.499}$	UDv1
	.062 $_{p=0.636}$	.118 $_{p=0.361}$	UDv2
HDE	-0.17 $_{p=0.164}$	-0.16 $_{p=0.198}$	UDv1
	-0.01 $_{p=0.919}$	-0.18 $_{p=0.144}$	UDv2

Table 3: Kendall τ scores for WOE vs. corpus size rankings.

also shows different discrepancies between full-corpus scores and random-sample scores for particular languages, as well as different "outliers" in this sense.

The differences are even more notable in the case of SOE (Figure 3). Futrell et al. (2015) make observations on word order freedom implying the presence of case marking, as in the highest-scoring third of languages according to Figure 3. However, certain outliers demonstrate different behaviour between annotation versions. While superficial changes in labelling, e.g., direct objects and passive subjects from UDv1 to UDv2 are accounted for in the computing process, these results imply a non-negligible effect of annotation guidelines or annotator choices on results quantifying word order freedom. In fact, looking into differences between the "parallel" UD corpora reveals nearly universal discrepancies in the number of annotated *nsubj* and *(d)obj* relations, resulting in the more severely affected languages changing their relative positions in the rankings.

As in the previous section, HDE (Figure 4) is the most consistent between annotation versions, with the same group of head-initial languages ranking most- and least-rigid with respect to word order, and variations in rank mostly being pairwise switching. This again confirms the most narrowly-defined

	full	sample
ROE	.105 $_{p=0.417}$	.273 $_{p=0.089}$
SOE	.088 $_{p=0.499}$	.110 $_{p=0.465}$
HDE	.397 $_{p=0.001}$	.380 $_{p=0.013}$

Table 4: Kendall τ entropy estimate rank correlation, comparing UDv1 vs. UDv2 rankings, for full corpus scores and random samples.

	full	sample
ROE	.225 $_{p=0.076}$	.051 $_{p=0.525}$
SOE	.075 $_{p=0.566}$	.052 $_{p=0.612}$
HDE	.075 $_{p=0.566}$	.025 $_{p=0.555}$

Table 5: Kendall τ entropy estimate rank correlation, original study vs. newly obtained rankings; UDv1 only.

measure to be the most robust.

Again, Table 4, top shows an attempt to quantify the differences between UDv1 and UDv2 scores through the Kendall τ of rankings. Again, the scores are mostly insignificant, with HDE being the least unstable measure across annotation versions.

4.3 Comparing across studies

Finally, WOE rankings obtained on UDv1 data are compared[3] with those retrieved from the Futrell et al. (2015) study. Rank correlations, again expressed in Kendall τ only, are given in Table 5.

No correlation is found between the rankings obtained on random samples for any of the metrics. Further work is needed to determine how much this is influenced by differences in the corpus content and annotations, or possibly different methods of entropy estimation—especially in the case of ROE, the only notable outlier in this case.

5 Conclusion

This paper has taken a deeper look into an existing methodology of quantifying word order freedom in dependency corpora. The study attempted to determine whether this methodology and measure allows for draw reliable conclusions about word order freedom, or whether it depends to a relevant extent on the underlying dependency annotations—both in terms of annotation guidelines, and in the quality of annotation depending on annotator experience and consistency. The study identified diffi-

[3]In the interest of space, visual comparisons between the scores provided in the original study and those obtained through these computations are not included in the main body of this work; however, they are available in Appendix C.

culties in finding a definition of measure that would be robust enough to avoid noise and misrepresentation, yet fine-grained enough to give meaningful linguistic insight. The analysis shows that changes in annotation styles can alter the results of estimates and change the comparative presentation of word order freedom across languages. Furthermore, it has shown that the observed measures may be susceptible to differences between samples, and that random sampling as defined by this methodology is selectively unreliable, depending on measure complexity. In conclusion, there is merit in cross-testing treebank-based metrics on different versions of treebanks, considering changes in annotation guidelines or even annotator teams, as well as on random subsamples of treebanks. Future work may also investigate the optimal size for these samples—currently fixed on an arbitrary count.

Building on existing work on Universal Dependencies, the question that next arises concerns what potential levels of complexity using Enhanced Universal Dependencies would introduce to this method of quantifying word order freedom. Future work may also focus on similar comparisons between manually annotated (gold-standard) and automatically generated dependency annotations, as well as possible differences between domains (e.g., newswire vs. literary text; written vs. spoken corpora), as well as across different annotation styles.

Acknowledgements

I would like to thank Stephan Oepen, Lilja Øvrelid, Joakim Nivre, and Paola Merlo for valuable discussions and comments on this work. I also thank the anonymous reviewers for their comments.

References

Judith Aissen. 2003. Differential object marking: Iconicity vs. economy. *Natural Language & Linguistic Theory*, 21(3):435–483.

Thomas M Cover, Joy A Thomas, et al. 1991. Entropy, relative entropy and mutual information. *Elements of information theory*, 2(1):12–13.

Simon DeDeo, Robert XD Hawkins, Sara Klingenstein, and Tim Hitchcock. 2013. Bootstrap methods for the empirical study of decision-making and information flows in social systems. *Entropy*, 15(6):2246–2276.

Richard Futrell, Kyle Mahowald, and Edward Gibson. 2015. Quantifying word order freedom in dependency corpora. In *Proceedings of the third international conference on dependency linguistics (Depling 2015)*, pages 91–100.

Joseph H Greenberg et al. 1963. Some universals of grammar with particular reference to the order of meaningful elements. *Universals of language*, 2:73–113.

Paul Kiparsky. 1997. The rise of positional licensing. *Parameters of morphosyntactic change*, 460:494.

Natalia Levshina. 2019. Token-based typology and word order entropy: A study based on universal dependencies. *Linguistic Typology*, 23(3):533–572.

Haitao Liu. 2010. Dependency direction as a means of word-order typology: A method based on dependency treebanks. *Lingua*, 120(6):1567–1578.

Matías Guzmán Naranjo and Laura Becker. 2018. Quantitative word order typology with ud. In *Proceedings of the 17th International Workshop on Treebanks and Linguistic Theories (TLT 2018), December 13–14, 2018, Oslo University, Norway*, 155, pages 91–104. Linköping University Electronic Press.

Joakim Nivre, Željko Agić, Lars Ahrenberg, Maria Jesus Aranzabe, Masayuki Asahara, Aitziber Atutxa, Miguel Ballesteros, John Bauer, Kepa Bengoetxea, Yevgeni Berzak, Riyaz Ahmad Bhat, Eckhard Bick, Carl Börstell, Cristina Bosco, Gosse Bouma, Sam Bowman, Gülşen Cebiroğlu Eryiğit, Giuseppe G. A. Celano, Fabricio Chalub, Çağrı Çöltekin, Miriam Connor, Elizabeth Davidson, Marie-Catherine de Marneffe, Arantza Diaz de Ilarraza, Kaja Dobrovoljc, Timothy Dozat, Kira Droganova, Puneet Dwivedi, Marhaba Eli, Tomaž Erjavec, Richárd Farkas, Jennifer Foster, Claudia Freitas, Katarína Gajdošová, Daniel Galbraith, Marcos Garcia, Moa Gärdenfors, Sebastian Garza, Filip Ginter, Iakes Goenaga, Koldo Gojenola, Memduh Gökırmak, Yoav Goldberg, Xavier Gómez Guinovart, Berta Gonzáles Saavedra, Matias Grioni, Normunds Grūzītis, Bruno Guillaume, Jan Hajič, Linh Hà Mỹ, Dag Haug, Barbora Hladká, Radu Ion, Elena Irimia, Anders Johannsen, Fredrik Jørgensen, Hüner Kaşıkara, Hiroshi Kanayama, Jenna Kanerva, Boris Katz, Jessica Kenney, Natalia Kotsyba, Simon Krek, Veronika Laippala, Lucia Lam, Phng Lê Hồng, Alessandro Lenci, Nikola Ljubešić, Olga Lyashevskaya, Teresa Lynn, Aibek Makazhanov, Christopher Manning, Cătălina Mărănduc, David Mareček, Héctor Martínez Alonso, André Martins, Jan Mašek, Yuji Matsumoto, Ryan McDonald, Anna Missilä, Verginica Mititelu, Yusuke Miyao, Simonetta Montemagni, Keiko Sophie Mori, Shunsuke Mori, Bohdan Moskalevskyi, Kadri Muischnek, Nina Mustafina, Kaili Müürisep, Lng Nguyễn Thị, Huyền Nguyễn Thị Minh, Vitaly Nikolaev, Hanna Nurmi, Petya Osenova, Robert Östling, Lilja Øvrelid, Valeria Paiva, Elena Pascual, Marco Passarotti, Cenel-Augusto Perez, Slav Petrov, Jussi Piitulainen, Barbara Plank, Martin Popel, Lauma Pretkalniņa, Prokopis Prokopidis, Tiina Puolakainen, Sampo Pyysalo, Alexandre Rademaker, Loganathan Ramasamy, Livy Real,

Laura Rituma, Rudolf Rosa, Shadi Saleh, Baiba Saulīte, Sebastian Schuster, Wolfgang Seeker, Mojgan Seraji, Lena Shakurova, Mo Shen, Natalia Silveira, Maria Simi, Radu Simionescu, Katalin Simkó, Mária Šimková, Kiril Simov, Aaron Smith, Carolyn Spadine, Alane Suhr, Umut Sulubacak, Zsolt Szántó, Takaaki Tanaka, Reut Tsarfaty, Francis Tyers, Sumire Uematsu, Larraitz Uria, Gertjan van Noord, Viktor Varga, Veronika Vincze, Lars Wallin, Jing Xian Wang, Jonathan North Washington, Mats Wirén, Zdeněk Žabokrtský, Amir Zeldes, Daniel Zeman, and Hanzhi Zhu. 2016a. Universal dependencies 1.4. LINDAT/CLARIAH-CZ digital library at the Institute of Formal and Applied Linguistics (ÚFAL), Faculty of Mathematics and Physics, Charles University.

Joakim Nivre, Marie-Catherine De Marneffe, Filip Ginter, Yoav Goldberg, Jan Hajic, Christopher D Manning, Ryan McDonald, Slav Petrov, Sampo Pyysalo, Natalia Silveira, et al. 2016b. Universal dependencies v1: A multilingual treebank collection. In *Proceedings of the Tenth International Conference on Language Resources and Evaluation (LREC'16)*, pages 1659–1666.

Joakim Nivre, Marie-Catherine de Marneffe, Filip Ginter, Jan Hajič, Christopher D Manning, Sampo Pyysalo, Sebastian Schuster, Francis Tyers, and Daniel Zeman. 2020. Universal dependencies v2: An evergrowing multilingual treebank collection. *arXiv preprint arXiv:2004.10643*.

Daniel Zeman, David Marecek, Martin Popel, Loganathan Ramasamy, Jan Stepánek, Zdenek Zabokrtskỳ, and Jan Hajic. 2012. Hamledt: To parse or not to parse? In *LREC*, pages 2735–2741.

Daniel Zeman, Joakim Nivre, Mitchell Abrams, Elia Ackermann, Noëmi Aepli, Hamid Aghaei, Željko Agić, Amir Ahmadi, Lars Ahrenberg, Chika Kennedy Ajede, Gabrielė Aleksandravičiūtė, Ika Alfina, Lene Antonsen, Katya Aplonova, Angelina Aquino, Carolina Aragon, Maria Jesus Aranzabe, Bilge Nas Arıcan, H̄órunn Arnardóttir, Gashaw Arutie, Jessica Naraiswari Arwidarasti, Masayuki Asahara, Deniz Baran Aslan, Luma Ateyah, Furkan Atmaca, Mohammed Attia, Aitziber Atutxa, Liesbeth Augustinus, Elena Badmaeva, Keerthana Balasubramani, Miguel Ballesteros, Esha Banerjee, Sebastian Bank, Verginica Barbu Mititelu, Starkaður Barkarson, Victoria Basmov, Colin Batchelor, John Bauer, Seyyit Talha Bedir, Kepa Bengoetxea, Gözde Berk, Yevgeni Berzak, Irshad Ahmad Bhat, Riyaz Ahmad Bhat, Erica Biagetti, Eckhard Bick, Agnė Bielinskienė, Kristín Bjarnadóttir, Rogier Blokland, Victoria Bobicev, Loïc Boizou, Emanuel Borges Völker, Carl Börstell, Cristina Bosco, Gosse Bouma, Sam Bowman, Adriane Boyd, Anouck Braggaar, Kristina Brokaitė, Aljoscha Burchardt, Marie Candito, Bernard Caron, Gauthier Caron, Lauren Cassidy, Tatiana Cavalcanti, Gülşen Cebiroğlu Eryiğit, Flavio Massimiliano Cecchini, Giuseppe G. A. Celano, Slavomír Čéplö, Neslihan Cesur, Savas Cetin, Özlem Çetinoğlu, Fabricio Chalub, Shweta Chauhan, Ethan Chi, Taishi Chika, Yongseok Cho, Jinho Choi, Jayeol Chun, Alessandra T. Cignarella, Silvie Cinková, Aurélie Collomb, Çağrı Çöltekin, Miriam Connor, Marine Courtin, Mihaela Cristescu, Philemon. Daniel, Elizabeth Davidson, Marie-Catherine de Marneffe, Valeria de Paiva, Mehmet Oguz Derin, Elvis de Souza, Arantza Diaz de Ilarraza, Carly Dickerson, Arawinda Dinakaramani, Elisa Di Nuovo, Bamba Dione, Peter Dirix, Kaja Dobrovoljc, Timothy Dozat, Kira Droganova, Puneet Dwivedi, Hanne Eckhoff, Sandra Eiche, Marhaba Eli, Ali Elkahky, Binyam Ephrem, Olga Erina, Tomaž Erjavec, Aline Etienne, Wograine Evelyn, Sidney Facundes, Richárd Farkas, Marília Fernanda, Hector Fernandez Alcalde, Jennifer Foster, Cláudia Freitas, Kazunori Fujita, Katarína Gajdošová, Daniel Galbraith, Marcos Garcia, Moa Gärdenfors, Sebastian Garza, Fabrício Ferraz Gerardi, Kim Gerdes, Filip Ginter, Gustavo Godoy, Iakes Goenaga, Koldo Gojenola, Memduh Gökırmak, Yoav Goldberg, Xavier Gómez Guinovart, Berta González Saavedra, Bernadeta Griciūtė, Matias Grioni, Loïc Grobol, Normunds Grūzītis, Bruno Guillaume, Céline Guillot-Barbance, Tunga Güngör, Nizar Habash, Hinrik Hafsteinsson, Jan Hajič, Jan Hajič jr., Mika Hämäläinen, Linh Hà Mỹ, Na-Rae Han, Muhammad Yudistira Hanifmuti, Sam Hardwick, Kim Harris, Dag Haug, Johannes Heinecke, Oliver Hellwig, Felix Hennig, Barbora Hladká, Jaroslava Hlaváčová, Florinel Hociung, Petter Hohle, Eva Huber, Jena Hwang, Takumi Ikeda, Anton Karl Ingason, Radu Ion, Elena Irimia, Ọlájídé Ishola, Kaoru Ito, Tomáš Jelínek, Apoorva Jha, Anders Johannsen, Hildur Jónsdóttir, Fredrik Jørgensen, Markus Juutinen, Sarveswaran K, Hüner Kaşıkara, Andre Kaasen, Nadezhda Kabaeva, Sylvain Kahane, Hiroshi Kanayama, Jenna Kanerva, Neslihan Kara, Boris Katz, Tolga Kayadelen, Jessica Kenney, Václava Kettnerová, Jesse Kirchner, Elena Klementieva, Arne Köhn, Abdullatif Köksal, Kamil Kopacewicz, Timo Korkiakangas, Natalia Kotsyba, Jolanta Kovalevskaitė, Simon Krek, Parameswari Krishnamurthy, Oğuzhan Kuyrukçu, Aslı Kuzgun, Sookyoung Kwak, Veronika Laippala, Lucia Lam, Lorenzo Lambertino, Tatiana Lando, Septina Dian Larasati, Alexei Lavrentiev, John Lee, Phng Lê Hồng, Alessandro Lenci, Saran Lertpradit, Herman Leung, Maria Levina, Cheuk Ying Li, Josie Li, Keying Li, Yuan Li, KyungTae Lim, Bruna Lima Padovani, Krister Lindén, Nikola Ljubešić, Olga Loginova, Andry Luthfi, Mikko Luukko, Olga Lyashevskaya, Teresa Lynn, Vivien Macketanz, Aibek Makazhanov, Michael Mandl, Christopher Manning, Ruli Manurung, Büşra Marşan, Cătălina Mărănduc, David Mareček, Katrin Marheinecke, Héctor Martínez Alonso, André Martins, Jan Mašek, Hiroshi Matsuda, Yuji Matsumoto, Alessandro Mazzei, Ryan McDonald, Sarah McGuinness, Gustavo Mendonça, Niko Miekka, Karina Mischenkova, Margarita Misirpashayeva, Anna Missilä, Cătălin Mititelu, Maria Mitrofan, Yusuke Miyao, AmirHossein Mojiri Foroushani, Judit Molnár, Amirsaeid Moloodi, Simonetta Montemagni, Amir More, Laura

Moreno Romero, Giovanni Moretti, Keiko Sophie Mori, Shinsuke Mori, Tomohiko Morioka, Shigeki Moro, Bjartur Mortensen, Bohdan Moskalevskyi, Kadri Muischnek, Robert Munro, Yugo Murawaki, Kaili Müürisep, Pinkey Nainwani, Mariam Nakhlé, Juan Ignacio Navarro Horñiacek, Anna Nedoluzhko, Gunta Nešpore-Bērzkalne, Manuela Nevaci, Lng Nguyễn Thị, Huyền Nguyễn Thị Minh, Yoshihiro Nikaido, Vitaly Nikolaev, Rattima Nitisaroj, Alireza Nourian, Hanna Nurmi, Stina Ojala, Atul Kr. Ojha, Adédayọ Olúòkun, Mai Omura, Emeka Onwuegbuzia, Petya Osenova, Robert Östling, Lilja Øvrelid, Şaziye Betül Özateş, Merve Özçelik, Arzucan Özgür, Balkız Öztürk Başaran, Hyunji Hayley Park, Niko Partanen, Elena Pascual, Marco Passarotti, Agnieszka Patejuk, Guilherme Paulino-Passos, Angelika Peljak-Łapińska, Siyao Peng, Cenel-Augusto Perez, Natalia Perkova, Guy Perrier, Slav Petrov, Daria Petrova, Jason Phelan, Jussi Piitulainen, Tommi A Pirinen, Emily Pitler, Barbara Plank, Thierry Poibeau, Larisa Ponomareva, Martin Popel, Lauma Pretkalniņa, Sophie Prévost, Prokopis Prokopidis, Adam Przepiórkowski, Tiina Puolakainen, Sampo Pyysalo, Peng Qi, Andriela Rääbis, Alexandre Rademaker, Taraka Rama, Loganathan Ramasamy, Carlos Ramisch, Fam Rashel, Mohammad Sadegh Rasooli, Vinit Ravishankar, Livy Real, Petru Rebeja, Siva Reddy, Georg Rehm, Ivan Riabov, Michael Rießler, Erika Rimkutė, Larissa Rinaldi, Laura Rituma, Luisa Rocha, Eiríkur Rögnvaldsson, Mykhailo Romanenko, Rudolf Rosa, Valentin Roșca, Davide Rovati, Olga Rudina, Jack Rueter, Kristján Rúnarsson, Shoval Sadde, Pegah Safari, Benoît Sagot, Aleksi Sahala, Shadi Saleh, Alessio Salomoni, Tanja Samardžić, Stephanie Samson, Manuela Sanguinetti, Ezgi Sanıyar, Dage Särg, Baiba Saulīte, Yanin Sawanakunanon, Shefali Saxena, Kevin Scannell, Salvatore Scarlata, Nathan Schneider, Sebastian Schuster, Lane Schwartz, Djamé Seddah, Wolfgang Seeker, Mojgan Seraji, Mo Shen, Atsuko Shimada, Hiroyuki Shirasu, Yana Shishkina, Muh Shohibussirri, Dmitry Sichinava, Janine Siewert, Einar Freyr Sigurðsson, Aline Silveira, Natalia Silveira, Maria Simi, Radu Simionescu, Katalin Simkó, Mária Šimková, Kiril Simov, Maria Skachedubova, Aaron Smith, Isabela Soares-Bastos, Carolyn Spadine, Rachele Sprugnoli, Steinh͡ór Steingrímsson, Antonio Stella, Milan Straka, Emmett Strickland, Jana Strnadová, Alane Suhr, Yogi Lesmana Sulestio, Umut Sulubacak, Shingo Suzuki, Zsolt Szántó, Dima Taji, Yuta Takahashi, Fabio Tamburini, Mary Ann C. Tan, Takaaki Tanaka, Samson Tella, Isabelle Tellier, Marinella Testori, Guillaume Thomas, Liisi Torga, Marsida Toska, Trond Trosterud, Anna Trukhina, Reut Tsarfaty, Utku Türk, Francis Tyers, Sumire Uematsu, Roman Untilov, Zdeňka Urešová, Larraitz Uria, Hans Uszkoreit, Andrius Utka, Sowmya Vajjala, Rob van der Goot, Martine Vanhove, Daniel van Niekerk, Gertjan van Noord, Viktor Varga, Eric Villemonte de la Clergerie, Veronika Vincze, Natalia Vlasova, Aya Wakasa, Joel C. Wallenberg, Lars Wallin, Abigail Walsh, Jing Xian Wang, Jonathan North Washington, Maximilan Wendt, Paul Widmer, Seyi Williams, Mats Wirén, Christian Wittern, Tsegay Woldemariam, Tak-sum Wong, Alina Wróblewska, Mary Yako, Kayo Yamashita, Naoki Yamazaki, Chunxiao Yan, Koichi Yasuoka, Marat M. Yavrumyan, Arife Betül Yenice, Olcay Taner Yıldız, Zhuoran Yu, Zdeněk Žabokrtský, Shorouq Zahra, Amir Zeldes, Hanzhi Zhu, Anna Zhuravleva, and Rayan Ziane. 2021. Universal dependencies 2.8.1. LINDAT/CLARIAH-CZ digital library at the Institute of Formal and Applied Linguistics (ÚFAL), Faculty of Mathematics and Physics, Charles University.

A Corpus statistics

Table 6: Comprehensive list of corpus statistics; sentence count, subtree count, number of subtrees with noun subject and direct object, total count of noun subjects, *nsubj* of which passive, total count of direct objects; per language, and per annotation guidelines version, sorted by total corpus size (ascending).

TBs	UDv	sen	st	has(ns,do)	mult(ns)	nsubj	(o. w. passive)	(d)obj
Tamil	1	600	3901	205	1	665	1	12705
	2	600	3937	167	0	664	1	10492
Irish	1	1010	8762	298	1	1600	0	35252
	2	1010	9052	307	1	1562	0	34987
Hungarian	1	1800	16213	849	0	2614	0	44215
	2	1800	16252	850	1	2621	0	44298
Greek	1	2302	20713	1139	6	3299	0	68570
	2	2302	20106	1011	0	2499	711	62047
Hebrew	1	4198	36479	896	8	5447	0	67334
	2	4198	37177	896	8	5447	0	67371
Danish	1	5509	33106	3257	129	8402	683	110374
	2	5509	33943	3282	95	9085	0	110304
Turkish	1	5619	23750	1027	14	3588	0	58166
	2	5619	23440	976	14	3730	0	54963
Persian	1	5997	62226	1786	22	8861	149	128609
	2	5997	63611	1786	22	8861	149	128609
Croatian	1	6283	51595	2500	2	7798	818	128826
	2	6283	52995	3194	20	9944	0	137521
Arabic	1	7651	123462	7865	35	15732	562	1101114
	2	7651	128242	5246	448	17815	774	494711
Basque	1	8993	45923	2473	4	8716	0	102881
	2	8993	46946	2473	4	8716	0	102881
Romanian	1	9519	83019	3180	7	10178	1857	182848
	2	9519	84178	3183	0	10090	1928	177917
Swedish	1	10589	59962	5564	16	28792	3756	180440
	2	10589	61477	5871	4	29880	3888	182691
Slovak	1	10601	36869	2884	0	7120	220	80395
	2	10601	37791	2003	0	7121	220	57701
Bulgarian	1	11137	56582	3721	1	10209	1240	109351
	2	11137	57622	3354	0	10066	1434	99099
Slovenian	1	11168	56792	2745	0	17496	0	160994
	2	11168	58212	2747	0	17494	0	160187
Italian	1	13779	100170	4458	1	12401	2280	297825
	2	13779	101065	4478	2	12425	2275	296198
Portuguese	1	14400	106352	6431	8	33456	1416	305249
	2	14400	108011	6270	1	31196	3230	338361
German	1	15590	95538	6699	9	17346	3191	176865
	2	15590	97725	6468	10	17412	3192	171913
French	1	16334	136590	9666	24	21005	2716	423183
	2	16334	141126	7232	0	19689	3114	359869
Hindi	1	16611	134715	9020	8	21023	562	410484
	2	16611	128192	9021	8	21023	562	410484
Catalan	1	16677	187178	16818	223	27523	0	1405814
	2	16677	192623	16500	74	27431	25	1408426

(cont. on next page)

TBs	UDv	sen	st	has(ns,do)	mult(ns)	nsubj	(o. w. passive)	(d)obj
Estonian	1	18009	81927	5277	0	20099	0	181768
	2	18009	83159	5226	0	20201	0	181212
Dutch	1	20906	104414	6809	20	40866	0	309076
	2	20906	101450	6838	11	41118	5802	170403
AncientGreek	1	24929	126503	7193	27	42958	4578	428714
	2	24929	125374	6646	15	42610	3788	402153
English	1	26298	142986	12266	37	111537	7005	475591
	2	26298	145774	12320	26	111255	7245	482468
Finnish	1	32302	122859	7206	11	60748	0	256977
	2	32302	125952	7237	12	61190	0	257568
Latin	1	33309	172925	11014	30	96978	29253	503707
	2	33309	176146	7583	29	101202	24639	359377
Spanish	1	33693	346221	20607	205	45537	1182	1803269
	2	33693	355407	17591	30	45460	1234	1604446
Russian	1	65378	438671	14965	4	166572	11406	699931
	2	65378	451072	15224	2	150972	16170	709338
Czech	1	113682	761586	48833	8	334719	34563	2278743
	2	113682	780840	33216	3	334953	34563	1482098

B Corpus statistics, visualised

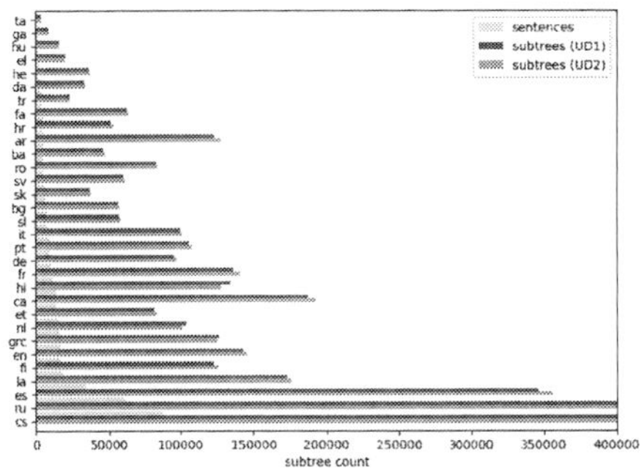

Figure 5: Number of subtrees, per language, across annotation gudeline versions.

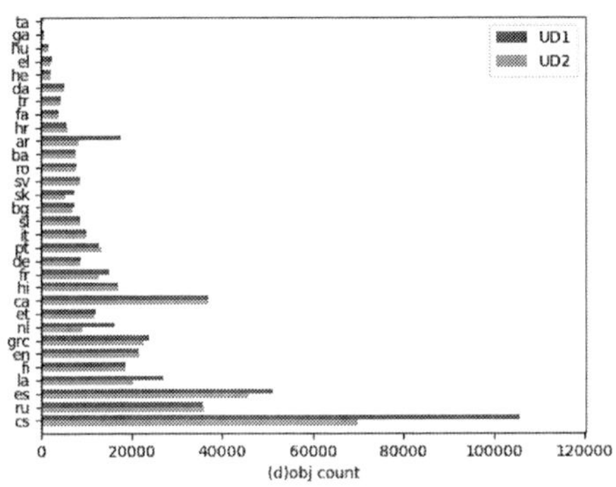

Figure 6: Number of (D)OBJ relation heads, per language, across annotation guideline versions.

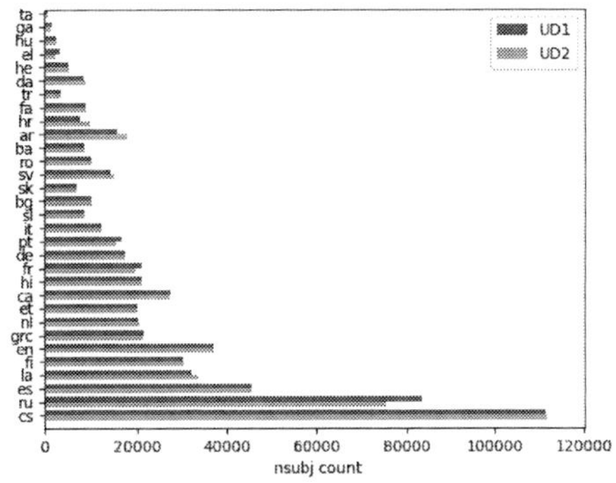

Figure 7: Number of NSUBJ relation heads, per language, across annotation guideline versions.

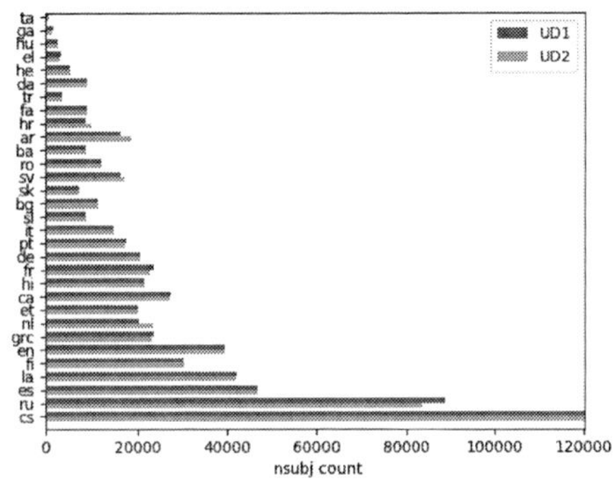

Figure 8: Number of NSUBJ relation heads, incl. variations of PASS, per language, across annotation guideline versions.

C Additional comparisons

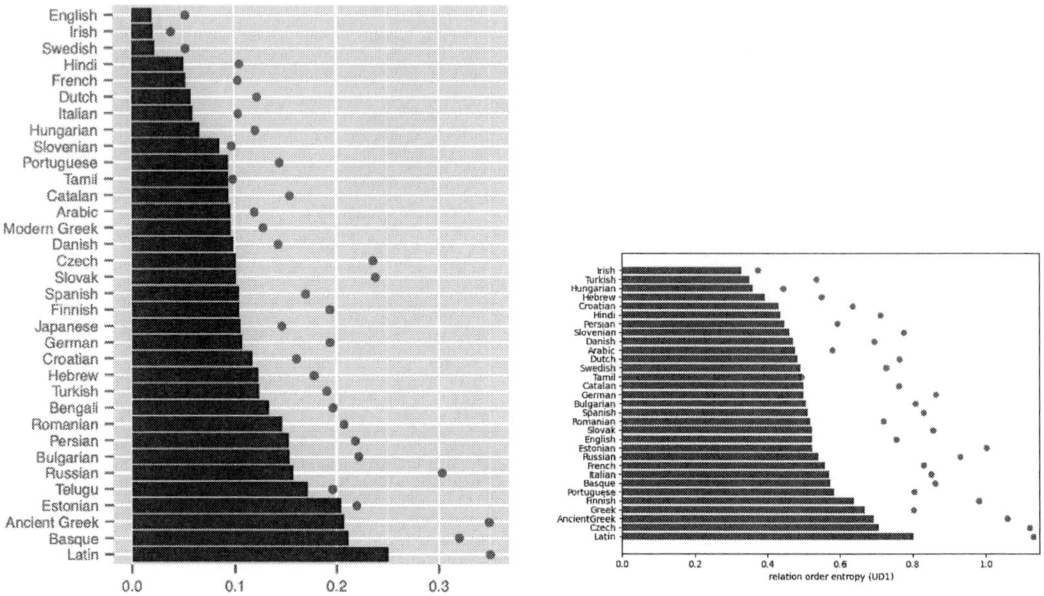

Figure 9: ROE; original study vs. UD1 rerun (random sample vs. full treebank)

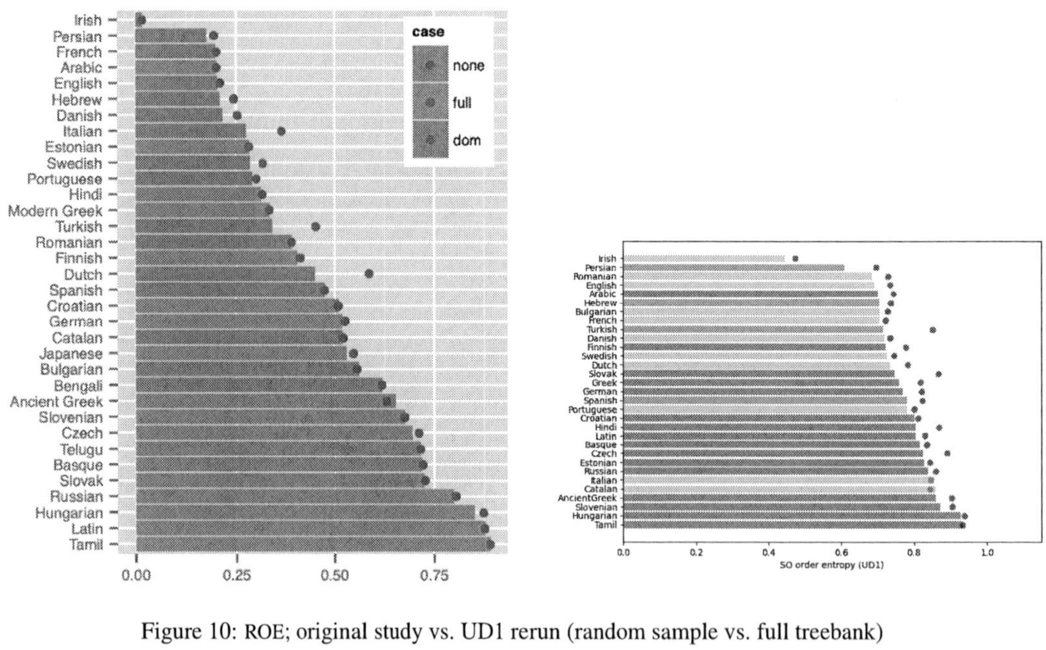

Figure 10: ROE; original study vs. UD1 rerun (random sample vs. full treebank)

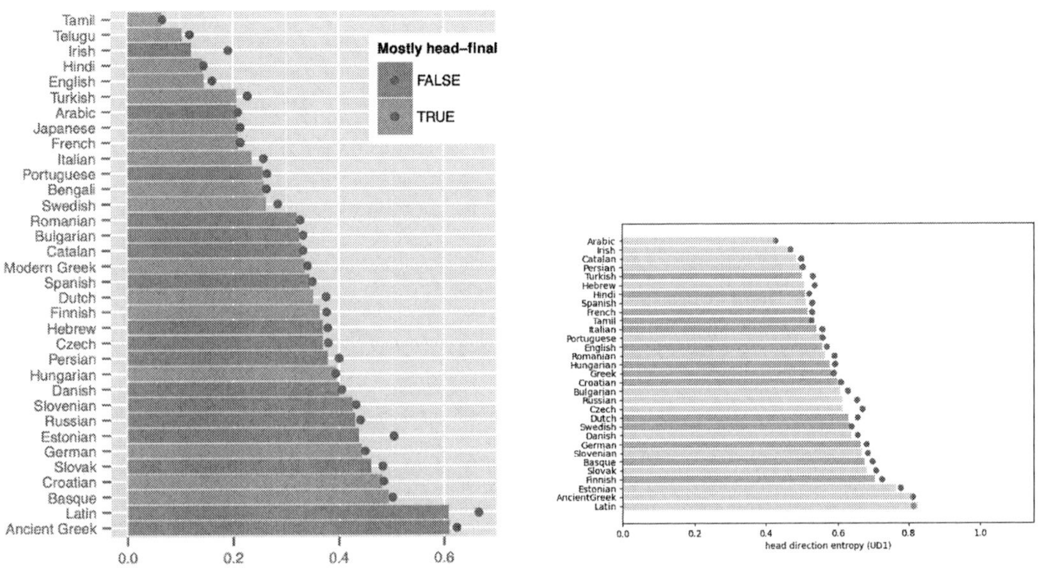

Figure 11: ROE; original study vs. UD1 rerun (random sample vs. full treebank)

Word order flexibility: a typometric study

Sylvain Kahane[1], Ziqian Peng[2], Kim Gerdes[2]

[1] Université Paris Nanterre, Modyco (CNRS)
[2] Université Paris-Saclay, Lisn (CNRS)

sylvain@kahane.fr

{ziqian.peng,kim.gerdes}@universite-paris-saclay.fr

Abstract

This paper introduces a typometric measure of flexibility, which quantifies the variability of head-dependent word order on the whole set of treebanks of a language or on specific constructions. The measure is based on the notion of head-initiality and we show that it can be computed for all of languages of the Universal Dependency treebank set, that it does not require ad-hoc thresholds to categorize languages or constructions, and that it can be applied with any granularity of constructions and languages. We compare our results with Bakker's (1998) categorical flexibility index. Typometric flexibility is shown to be a good measure for characterizing the language distribution with respect to word order for a given construction, and for estimating whether a construction predicts the global word order behavior of a language.

1 Introduction

For half a century, research in typology centers on the discussion of word order parameters, pioneered by Greenberg (1963, 1966), and elaborated by such authors as Hawkins (1983), Dryer (1992) and Nichols (1992). Bakker (1998) proposes a seminal study on *word order flexibility*, which we pursue here. First off, it is clear that languages differ in the flexibility of word order: Greek or Russian are more flexible than English or Chinese. Secondly, constructions differ in their flexibility across the diversity of languages: The relation between an adposition and its complement is less flexible than the relation between a verb and its direct object.

To give a first idea how this can be seen on a typometric scatter plot, consider Fig. 1 where each point corresponds to a language, with its x-value indicating the percentage of nominal dependents of adpositions on the right of the adposition and its y-value indicating the percentage of nominal object dependents of verbs to the right of the verb.

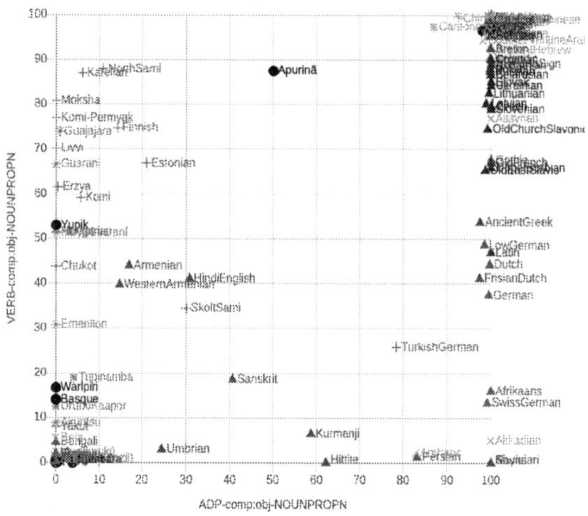

Figure 1: Two-dimensional scatter plot with ADP-comp:obj-NOUN/PROPN in the x-axis and VERB-comp:obj-NOUN/PROPN in the y-axis.

As a first observation, note that a large majority of languages have x=0 or x=100, leaving a rather empty space in the middle of the scatter plot. This shows that most languages have almost only prepositions or almost only postpositions; languages that mix prepositions and postpositions equally are rare.[1] However, many more languages accept both pre-verbal and post-verbal direct objects (Guzmán Naranjo & Becker 2018, Gerdes et

[1]The scatter plot view understates the fact that many languages cluster around the bottom left (0,0) and the top right (100,100) of the plot: Many strictly postpositional languages also have their nominal objects on the left, and, inversely, many strictly prepositional languages also have their nominal objects to the right of their verbal governor. This is a well-established observation in typology since Greenberg (1963), and is at the base of our choice of SUD treebanks (see Section 2 for details).

Proceedings of the Seventh International Conference on Dependency Linguistics (Depling, GURT/SyntaxFest 2023), pages 68 - 80
March 9-12, 2023 ©2023 Association for Computational Linguistics

al. 2021). Nonetheless, the postpositional languages on the left appear to be less strictly postpositional than the prepositional languages on the right are prepositional. This motivates the definition of flexibility in Section 4. See Section 3 for more details on how to compute and understand these plots.

How can we measure the flexibility of languages and constructions? What are the properties of flexibility across languages and constructions? We will try to give answers to these questions in Section 6.

Most classical approaches to typology, including Bakker (1998) and previous works, are categorical in the sense that languages are grouped into categories based on their order constraints, and often only one basic word order is assumed per language from which other word orders are derived by movement, dislocation, or similar operations.

We propose a *typometric* approach (also called *token-based typology* by Levshina 2019): With the availability of a wide range of uniformly annotated treebanks in the Universal Dependencies (UD) project, it has become possible to approach these questions empirically. Syntactic typology outgrows the need for ad hoc categories and measures of distribution of languages across empirical observations become the center of interest (Futtrell et al. 2020, Levshina 2022). In Gerdes et al. (2021), quantitative universals describe empty or sparsely populated spaces in unidimensional or multidimensional spaces instead of qualitative universals that are claiming rare or impossible combinations of language features based on categories.

Tesnière (1959) proposed a classification of languages based on the dependency direction referring to Steinthal (1850) and Schmidt (1926). He opposes strict word order, when head-daughter relations mostly go in one direction, to *mitigated* when the head is amidst its dependents going out in both directions. Among languages with mitigated word order, there are languages with free order, as well as languages with mixed word order, where word order is quite strict in most constructions but inconsistent between constructions. This is what flexibility measures.

In this paper we propose measures of flexibility that can be applied to dependency treebanks and discuss the distributions of these measures compared to other observations on dependency treebanks. Similar measures have been first introduced by Futrell (2015) under the name of *word-order entropy* and have been studied by Levshina (2019).

In this paper, we try to characterize the distribution of all languages of our sample in terms of word order direction for each construction C: We compute for each language L, the number of head-initial realization of the construction C in L, what we call the head-initiality of language L under C (Section 3). We deduce from head-initiality a second measure we call flexibility and study the relation between head-initiality and flexibility for all languages in our sample, distinguishing flexible languages from mixed word order languages (Section 4). The typometric measure of flexibility we introduce is compared with Bakker's (1998) categorical measure of flexibility, as well as a more typometric measure à la Bakker (Section 5). We show that the distribution of head-initiality for every construction C can be characterized by the average head-initiality of C and the flexibility of C (Section 6). In Section 7, we explore the question of the predictability of word order distribution from one construction to another.

2 Dependency syntax and word order

Dependency syntax encodes constructions by relations between words representing combinations between larger units (Tesnière 1959, Hudson 1984). A dependency relation goes from one word to another, from governor to dependent. There is no a priori assumption on locality of a relation, and a long distance dependency, for example, does not need any special encoding in a dependency tree, which makes dependency treebanks the obvious choice when attempting to measure tendencies in word order across languages (Liu 2008).

A syntactic relation is a class of combinations of the same type, having similar properties. Dependency syntax makes the assumption that most constructions are asymmetric, with a head element controlling the distribution of the combination. In some languages, constructions are very rigid and combinations of a certain type tend to always have the same word order between the governor and the dependent. Examples of such rigid relations are the *subject* and the *object* relation in English.[2] Subject and Object are different

[2]Widely discussed exceptions to the rigidity of subject and object in English include the relative pronoun (*a person who I never met*) and marginal cases of dislocation such as *Chocolate I adore!* As

constructions and therefore are annotated as different relations.

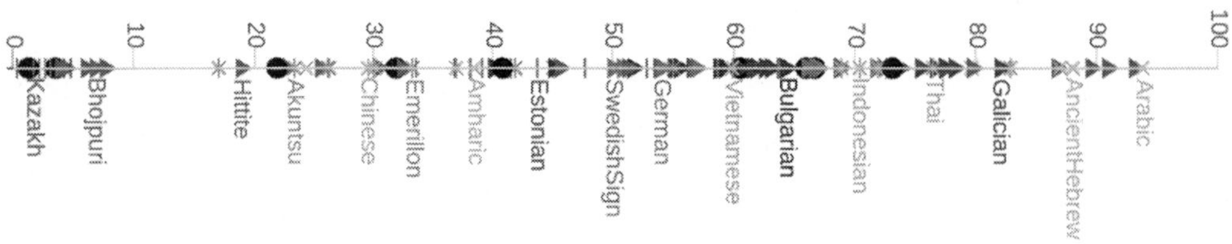

Figure 2: Head-initiality of core relations across SUD 2.11

Although the main criteria of distinguishing one relation from another is valency and morphology (for example an accusative case can be the main criterion for delimiting the direct object relation), in some cases the definition of a dependency relation relies on the word order itself and thus the relations have by definition a strict word order.[3]

Just as in the initial typometrics paper Gerdes et al. (2021), we rely for our measures on the Surface Syntactic Dependency (SUD) version of UD (Gerdes et al. 2018), in order to make our work comparable with previous work on word order typology, thus preserving "cross-category harmony" (Hawkings 1983) and avoiding complications in particular concerning adpositions and auxiliary verbs that are analyzed in an unusual manner in the original UD annotation scheme.[4]

Choosing SUD rather than UD has very little impact on the computation of the flexibility measures introduced in this paper.[5]

in other typological studies, we restrict our object measures to nominal objects, thus excluding the first case. Clearly, the measures we end up with will always depend on the annotation choices of each treebank.

[3]As an example, consider the annotation choices for Cantonese and Mandarin reported in Wong et al. (2017): Any element to the left of the verb is considered as "dislocated" even if it fills the verb's object slot.

[4]Guzmán Naranjo and Becker (2018), for example, find that UD's *case* relation stands out in their directional correlation measures.

[5]As SUD is obtained by a conversion of UD without any addition of information, the granularity remains similar, see Section 4. It only impacts locally some relations such as the subject, which, in SUD, is attached to the auxiliary rather than the content verb and whose direction can change in some cases (for instance, in German, where the subject can be between the auxiliary and the verb).

SUD's *comp* relation corresponds to UD's *aux, ccomp, iobj, obj, obl:arg, xcomp, cop, mark*, and *case*; *mod* corresponds to UD's *advcl, acl, advmod, amod, nmod, nummod,* and *obl:mod.* SUD's *subj* combines UD's *csubj* and *nsubj.* The relations *dislocated, det,* and *clf* remain unchanged between SUD and UD.

We base our work on the latest SUD version 2.11 which includes 243 treebanks in 138 languages in total. For our study, treebanks of the same language are combined and taken as one data point. 65 UD languages cover Indo-European languages. Afro-Asiatic, Uralic, and Tupian languages have 11 languages each. Turkic covers another 6 languages. Of the remaining languages only Basque, Chinese, Classical Chinese, Indonesian, Japanese, Korean, and Naija have more than 100k tokens. 21 of the UD languages are very small (less than 1000 tokens), which falls beneath our threshold for most of our measures.

3 Typometrics and scatter plots

A typometric analysis does not assume a basic word order or any threshold for categorizing languages or construction. Our basic observation is the measure of *head- initiality* defined for a language L and a construction C involving a unique dependency as follows:[6]

head_initiality(L, C) =

% of occurrences of C in L that are head-initial (governor < dependent)

In most cases the construction C limited to a dependency is defined as a *gov-rel-dep* triple (governor's POS, dependency relation, dependent's POS). In some cases the construction is defined as the sum of a series of gov-rel-*dep* triples. Note that any variable of the triplet (*gov, rel,* or *dep*) can be equal to *all,* denoting no restriction on this variable.

[6]Head-initiality is introduced in Gerdes et al. (2019, 2021), where it is called *direction*.

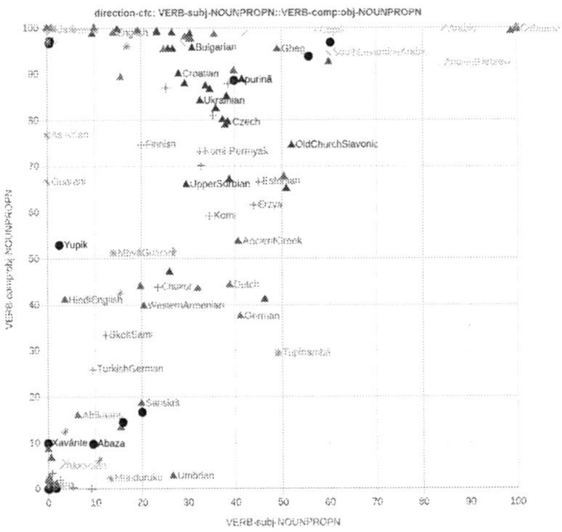

Figure 3: Two-dimensional scatter plots with verbal subjects and objects.

A head-initiality of 0 for a given language and construction shows a strictly head-final construction, a head-initiality of 100 indicates a strictly head-initial construction. Measuring head-initiality across the UD languages for the combination of core dependency relations (to be defined in the next section) gives the unidimensional scatter plot of Figure 2, where, unsurprisingly, Japanese is the most head-final language, and Arabic the most head-initial language of our language sample set.[7]

A second two-dimensional scatter plot (Fig. 3) opposes the head-initiality of nominal subjects in the x-axis (VERB-subj- NOUN|PROPN) and nominal direct objects in the y-axis (VERB-comp:obj- NOUN|PROPN). We allow both the UD POS noun and proper noun as arguments. We observe a typical triangular shape of the resulting distribution indicating that nearly all languages have the tendency to have direct objects more to the right than subjects. Put differently, hardly any language has a higher head-initiality on subjects than on direct objects. See Gerdes et al. (2021) for a discussion of how this observation generalizes to the well-known absence of OVS languages.

[7]Colors and shapes of the language points follow the original typometrics paper with colored *triangles* for the different subgroups of Indo-European languages, *plus* signs for agglutinating languages, orange *x* signs for Afroasiatic and Semitic languages, and *circles* and *stars* for other groups. Data, scatterplots, and detailed captions are on https://typometrics.elizia.net/. Note that only some languages are labeled. This has no semantics and is done automatically to increase readability.

4 Flexibility of languages

For a language L, *flexibility* measures the distance of a construction C from a rigid construction. In this paper, we only consider constructions involving a governor G and a dependent D by a particular relation. The construction has a wider or narrower range depending on whether the relation between G and D or the categories of G and D are more or less constrained.

flexibility(L,C)
= 2 × min(head_initiality(L,C),
100–head_initiality(L,C))
= twice the smallest distance of head_initiality(L,C) to 0 or to 100

The value of flexibility(L,C) ranges from 0 to 100 and measures the distance of C from a strictly head-initial or head-final construction. A very similar measure, *word order entropy*, has been proposed by Levshina (2019), inspired by Futrell et al. (2015).[8] She also considers the entropy for couples of dependencies, such as the relative position of subjects and objects.

For a given language L, we can compute the weighted average of flexibility(L,C) for a relevant set S of constructions C, which will be discussed below.

head_initiality(L) =
weighted average of head_initiality(L, C)on constructions C

flexibility(L) =
weighted average of flexibility(L, C) on constructions C.

A measure very similar to flexibility(L) has been introduced by Futrell et al. (2015), using conditional entropy. In information theory, the conditional entropy H(Y|X) quantifies the amount of information needed to describe the outcome of the random variable Y given that the value of the random variable X is known. The more H(Y|X) is close to 1, the more Y is independent from X, H(Y|X) being equal to 0. In Futrell et al. (2015), X is used to select a set S of constructions, while Y describes the word order on S. In other words, entropy, like

[8]Precisely, $\text{entropy}(L,C) = p.\log_2(p) - (1-p)\log_2(1-p)$, with p = head_initiality(L,C). This value also ranges from 0 to 100%, with value 0 for p=0 or 100% and 100% for p=50%. The only difference with our calculation is that entropy smoothes values for p around the 50% mark.

flexibility, measures the extent to which word order choices depend on syntactic constructions.[9]

Let us discuss our choices of S for head-initiality and flexibility. The computation of head_initiality(L) and flexibility(L) is sensitive to the range D of data considered. Unlike head-initiality(L), the computation of flexibility(L) is sensitive to the granularity of the partition of D into a set S of constructions: the finer the partitioning S, the higher the yield of flexibility(L). In our case, we have adopted a rather fine granularity, as we consider any *gov-rel-dep* triplet as a different construction, where *gov* is the POS of the governor, *dep* is the POS of the dependent, and *rel* is the relationship between them. We could have used an even finer granularity, by taking into account certain features, for example by distinguishing relative pronouns (PronType=Rel) from personal pronouns (PronType=Prs) or by isolating demonstratives (PronType=Dem).[10] Moreover, when we have a direct complement of the verb, we will distinguish nominal complement (dep=NOUN) and pronominal complement (dep=PRON), but not when it is a prepositional complement (dep=ADP). Sometimes the granularity can be excessive, as when UD/SUD distinguishes proper nouns (PROPN) and common nouns (NOUN).[11] It must also be remarked that Levshina(2018) restricts her computation for verbal constructions to verbs that are roots, arguing that word order can be quite different between main and subordinate clauses in some languages (German and Wolof for instance). Our preference is to keep all occurrences, but it is certainly interesting to do a partition between main clauses and subordinate clauses.[12]

Unlike flexibility(L), the computation of head_initiality(L) is obviously very dependent on the choice made for the head of each construction. It is this question that motivated us not to work with UD, but to choose the SUD variant where adpositions, subordinating conjunctions, and auxiliaries are chosen as heads.[13] For auxiliaries, the question is delicate, because while for Indo-European languages, they are clearly heads, this is less obvious in languages where they are particles. On the other hand, the wh-words of Indo-European languages are treated as pronouns in both UD and SUD, even though they also have a head role, which explains in part their peculiar placement.

For head-initiality(L), we decide to consider the relations of type *comp, mod, udep, subj, dislocated*, that we call the *core* relations. We have included the *dislocated* relation, because the boundary between governed and dislocated elements is not always well defined.[14] We have eliminated the *det* relation because the direction of the determiner-noun relation is controversial (see the discussion around the DP-hypothesis since Hudson 1984 and Abney 1987), as well as *clf* (for classifiers), which is used inconsistently. For flexibility(L), we could keep *det* and *clf*, because the choice of the governor of a given relation does not play any role: Flexibility only measures the proportion of dependencies going in the same direction and remains the same when all dependencies are inverted. However the *det* and *clf* have only a small influence on the final result (cf. Table D) and, to be precise, we decided to use the *core* relations for the computation of flexibility(L) as well. Other SUD/UD relations are of little interest for our study as their direction is fixed in the UD annotation guidelines. This includes *conj, fixed, goeswith*, etc. It should also be noted that we have not considered the relations between co-dependents at all. Yet, some

[9]The entropy view of flexibility is very elegant, but, as mentioned by Levshina (2019), Futrell et al. (2015) gives "one aggregate score" for each language, rather than considering individual constructions before aggregating them.

[10]Levshina (2019) also considers constructions restricted to one dependent word form. This is only possible if the corpus contains enough occurrences of the word, which commonly implies for many languages to parse raw corpora that are bigger than the manually annotated corpora of UD.

[11]On the other hand, UD does not usually distinguish prepositional dependents of the verb, which are all rel=*obl*, whether they are arguments or modifiers. This distinction is made only in a few treebanks, notably the native SUD treebanks (with the *comp* and *mod* labels). SUD uses the *udep* relation, for underspecified *obl* dependencies when the distinction in argument and modifier is not encoded.

[12]About the relations between constructions in main and subordinate clauses, see Schachter (1973).

[13]For instance, Futrell et al. (2015) based on computation on UD indicates that French and Italian are mostly head-final, while, based on SUD, they are head-initial at 76% and 77% respectively!

[14] For instance, in a pro-drop language such as Chinese, it is difficult to decide if preverbal objects are dislocated or not. See Note 3.

languages with a very strict head-final order, such as Japanese or Korean, can have much greater freedom in the placement of co-dependents, which is not taken into account in the present study.

Lastly, we chose to give each construction a weight equivalent to its frequency in the corpora, unlike Bakker (1998), who gives the same weight to each of the 10 constructions he considers (as well as Levshina (2019), who considers quantitative values for each construction but does an average with equal weight).

Figure 4 shows the head-initiality of SUD 2.11 languages in the x-axis and the flexibility in the y-axis. For treebanks with at least 1000 core relations, we observe that Ancient Greek, Tupinambá, Emerillon(Teko), Turkish-German (code switching corpus) and Old East Slavic are the most flexible languages (with flexibilities 59.3, 56.7, 55.2, 52.9, and 51.7 respectively), while Japanese, Hindi, Xibe, Kazakh and Telugu (flexibilities of around 0.5, 1.6, 2.1, 2.4, and 2.4 respectively) are the least flexible languages.

Languages with head-initiality equal to 0 or 100 have flexibility 0 and the closer they are to 50 the more likely they are to be flexible. But there are languages L with head_initiality(L) close to 50 and flexibility(L) close to 0, such as Bambara: these are *mixed order languages*. Languages with high flexibility(L), such as Ancient Greek, are *free order languages.*[15]

5 Comparison with Bakker's flexibility

Bakker (1998) proposes a computation of flexibility based on the same principles but does not take into account the greater or lesser flexibility of each construction for each language. In Bakker's computation, a language is either flexible or completely rigid.

flexibility[Bakker](C,L) =
0 if the construction C is completely rigid in L,
1 if it is flexible

flexibility[Bakker](L)=

(equal-weighted) average over 10 constructions C of flexibility[Bakker](C,L)

[15]Our measures are also dependent on the corpus chosen for the calculus and its genre. The flexibility measure of Ancient Greek is certainly increased by the fact that the corpus contains poetry and theater.

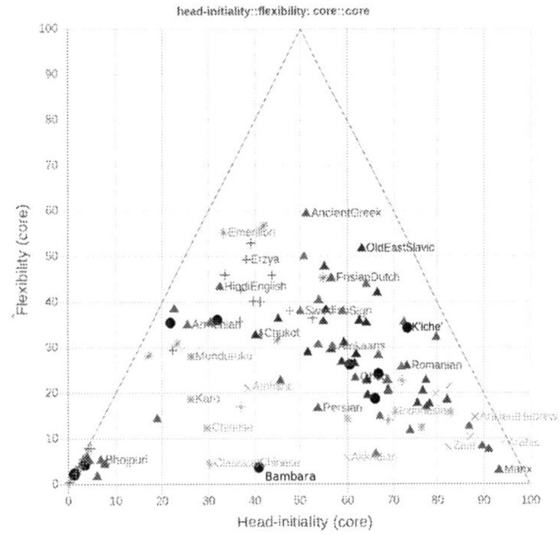

Figure 4: Head-initiality vs Flexibility (core)

Bakker gives the flexibility values for a sample of 86 European languages 47 of which are Indo-European. We propose to compare Bakker's values with a typometric index of the same type. Some of Bakker's constructions can be directly translated into SUD corpus queries, others can be approximated. For example, his "Adj/N" translates directly into the typometric measure NOUN-mod-ADJ. The Verb-Recipient relation (V/R) can only be approximated by VERB-comp:obl- ADP| NOUN (cf. Table A2 in Annex). The complete list of Bakker's constructions and their translation into typometric measures are provided in the construction flexibility Table A3 of the Annex.[16]

As Bakker's flexibility measure is categorical per construction, we have to arbitrarily set a threshold at 5%, considering

[16]Bakker (1998: 393ff) introduces another measure which he calls *consistency* and which is very dependent on the set of considered constructions, which are still the 10 same constructions (see Section 5):

```
consistency[Bakker](L) =
| #{ C / C is head-initial for L }
- #{ C / C is head-final for L } |.
```

It seems to us that the consistency of a language L is well captured by our head_initiality(L), which is not dependent on the partitioning P into constructions undertaken by the linguist. Moreover, Bakker (1998: 401-2) notes that flexibility[Bakker] and consistency[Bakker] are correlated, but this is obvious as soon as there are languages whose head-initiality is close to 0 or 100. Likewise, our flexibility and head-initiality are related, since `flexibility(L) ≤ 2 × min ( head_initiality(L), 100 - head_initiality(L) )`, which we have visualized as a triangle in Figure 4.

that languages with less than 5% variation for a given construction C are inflexible for C.

We can compare those 3 measures across the languages that we also find in UD: 1. Bakker's flexibility, 2. our recomputation of the flexibility à la Bakker, as a non-weighted average over Bakker's 10 constructions, with the 5% threshold as indicated above, and 3. our typometric flexibility.[17]

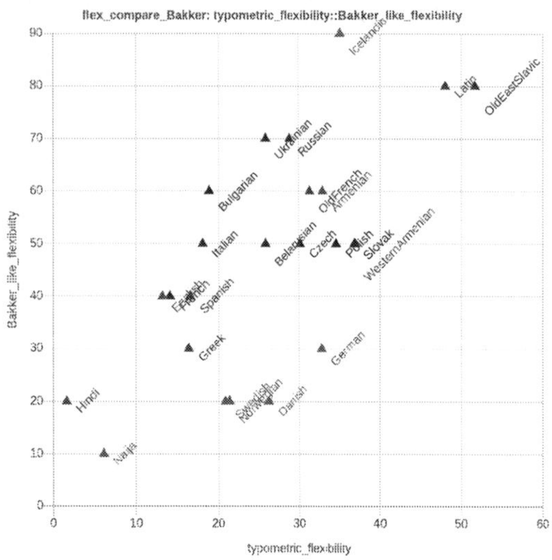

Figure 5: Typometric vs Bakker-like flexibility

The scatterplot of Figure 5 shows the strong correlation between the Bakker-like measure of flexibility and the typometric flexibility. The Bakker-like flexibility is also significantly correlated with Bakker's flexibility (Fig. C2), while there is only a weak correlation between the typometric flexibility and Bakker's flexibility (Fig. C1). See the complete results in Tables B in the Annex.

6 Flexibility of constructions

Having compared the overall flexibility of the languages, we can now see how the languages in a given sample S are distributed for each construction C and compare the constructions. Specifically, we are interested in how the head-initiality of the languages in our sample (the 138 languages in UD 2.11) is distributed for the different constructions C. Our hypothesis is that this distribution is reasonably well described by the following two values:

average_head_initiality$_S$(C) = average of head_initiality(L,C) over the Ls in S.

average_flexibility$_S$(C) = average of flexibility(L,C) over the Ls in S.

The less flexible C is on average, the more languages are attracted to 0 and 100. The average-head-initiality indicates whether 0 or 100 attracts more to one than the other. We propose two other values that will help us to better understand this attraction towards 0 and 100.

head_initial_weightS(C) =
average_head_initiality$_S$(C) /
average_flexibility$_S$(C)

head_final_weightS(C) =
(100 – average_head_initiality$_S$(C)) /
average_flexibilityS©

For a uniform distribution, flexibility = 50, head-initiality = 50, head-initial-weight = 1, and head-final-weight = 1. When head-final-weight > 1, the distribution is drawn towards 0 and when head-final-weight < 1, it is pushed away. The reverse holds for head-initial-weight. Our postulate is that the distribution of head-initiality is similar to a uniform distribution that has been distorted by stretching it from both sides.[18] Our head-initial and head-final weights give us an estimate of the strength of the force at each end.

We observe that for all the most frequent C constructions, both head_initial_weight$_S$(C) > 1 and head_final_weight$_S$(C) > 1 (see Table A3 in the Annex where all but one of the weights for the 10 Bakker constructions are greater than 1), which means that languages are attracted on both ends.

To give an idea of the different distributions we encounter, the three scatter plots below show three head-initiality distributions on the treebanks: 1. Num/N (NOUN-any-NUM),[19] 2.

[17]Some of Bakker's constructions, such as Dem/N or Pro/N, involve features that are not present in all UD treebanks (PronType=Dem and Poss=Yes in these two cases). Our computation is restrained to languages with all the required features.

[18]Levshina (2019), like us, uses the mean head initiality and the standard deviation to characterize the distribution of a head initiality for a given construction. The standard deviation is relevant for characterizing Gaussian distributions, but not for "stretched" distributions as here, particularly when elements tend to move away from the center and when these movements are asymmetric, with one end more attractive than the other.

[19]To be precise, SUD uses a special feature ExtPos, indicating the external POS of a word. Numerals, all categorized NUM in UD, are *nummod* or *det*

aux-v (AUX-comp:aux-VERB), and 3. Adj/N (NOUN-mod-ADJ). The first (Num/N) distribution tends towards 0 and is pushed away from 100 (weights 3.6 and 0.7), while the two other distributions are attracted both by 0 and 100, with a bigger attraction to 0 for Adj/N (weights 4.2 and 2.4) and to 100 for Aux/V (weights 1.7 and 2.8).

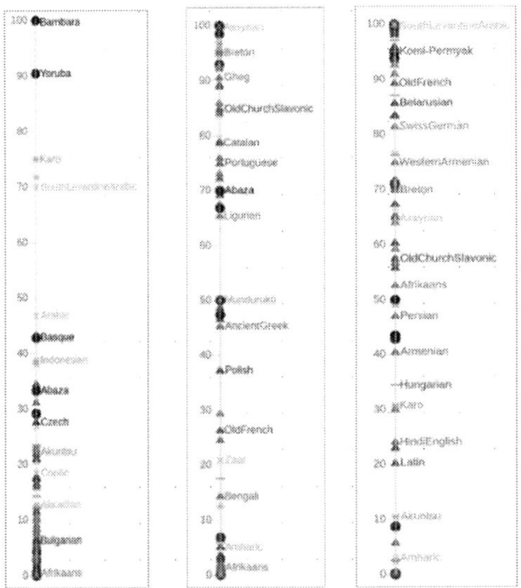

Num/N Adj/N Aux/V

Figure 6: Head-initiality language distribution for three constructions Num/N, Adj/N, Aux/V.

Again, we can compare our flexibility results with two measures: the flexibility measure proposed by Bakker (1998) and a Bakker-like measure that we calculate from our sample.

flexibility[Bakker](C)=
% of languages in Bakker's sample that are flexible for C.

flexibility[Bakker_like]$_S$(C) =
% of Ls in S with flexibility(L,C)>5.

Bakker restricts his study to a sample S of 86 European languages, 24 of them having enough data in UD to be compared.[20]

We find that V/O is the most flexible construction, followed by V/R and Adj/N. Two constructions do not behave at all as in Bakker's sample: Aux/V appears as the most flexible construction after V/O, while Rel/N appears as extremely inflexible.

Bakker also compares the flexibility of languages with head-initial and head-final basic order. Again we can introduce typometric Bakker-like measures. We consider that a language has head-initial basic order if more than 50% of core dependencies are head-initial.

head_initial_flexibility[Bakker_like]$_S$(C) = % of Ls in S with head_initiality(L,C)>50 that have flexibility(L,C)>5.

head_final_flexibility[Bakker_like]$_S$(C) = % of Ls in S with head_initiality(L,C)<50 that have flexibility(L,C)>5.

Bakker (1998: 392) "observed that head-modifier orders are, on the whole, more flexible than modifier-head orders." We have completely different results with our measures (see Table A3 in the Annex): Only for adpositions, languages with head-initial core order are more flexible than languages with head-final core order.

7 Predictivity

With these notions in place, it is now possible to measure which construction predicts best the overall core flexibility of a given language. For this, we measure the Spearman correlation between the distribution of flexibility(L,C) for various couples of construction C (Figure 8). We are particularly interested in the correlation with the *core* construction. Among the 10 Bakker constructions, the best predictors of the *core* flexibility is the *V/O* construction, unlike V/R. Note also some notable correlations: *Aux/V* and *V/O* that have a correlation of 0.59 as well as *subj* and *comp* that have a correlation of 0.53.

Bakker (1998: 392) however states that "the best predictors of overall flexibility are the flexibility of the recipient, genitive, numeral and relative clause. On the other hand, no prediction whatsoever can be drawn from the behavior of adpositions and articles." This is not backed up by our data with our weighted flexibility measure: The typometric genitive flexibility has a correlation of only 0.18 with

when they are used as a quantifier (*my 7 cats*). In other uses, they work as a proper noun (*line 7, page 7, year 2023*) and receive the feature ExtPos=PROPN. It is this feature, rather than the POS, that is used in all our computations. It remains that the use of *nummod* is not consistent across all treebanks.

[20]When looking at a particular construction C, we only consider a language L if the treebanks of L have at least 50 occurrences of C. For Bakker-like measures to be calculated for L, the threshold of 20 must be reached for each of the 10 constructions considered.

the core flexibility, numerals have a correlation of 0.01, and relatives of 0.07.

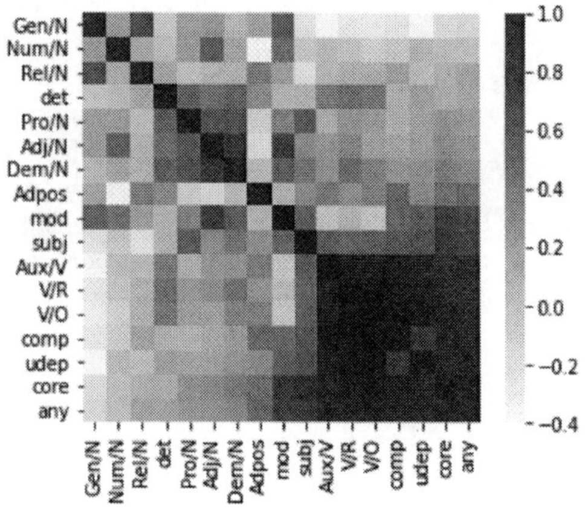

Figure 7: Heatmap of Spearman correlation between the distributions of flexibility(L,C) for various couples of construction C. See Table D of the Annex for detailed values.

Nonetheless, our data agrees with a common typologist view, most notably Dryer (1992), that sees V/O as a good predictor for word order constraints on other constructions.

Note also that the constructions with the biggest flexibility are the best predictors. This was expected because constructions with low flexibility tend to gather all languages around 0 and 100.

8 Conclusion

We have introduced a first measure, head-initiality, which measures the variable head-dependent word order on a language's treebank or on specific constructions. Based on this, we develop an operational notion of flexibility that renders the intuition that the average head-initiality can be far from 0 or 100 while the languages are strict per given construction.

We then show that our empirical notion of flexibility can be compared to previous definitions of flexibility of word order, notably to Bakker's work. Our notion of flexibility has the advantage that it can directly be computed from treebanks, that it does not require ad-hoc thresholds to categorize languages or constructions, and that it can be applied with any granularity of constructions.

Finally, we show which construction predicts overall word order flexibility of a language. For this, we rely on Spearman's rank correlation coefficient, which allows us to calculate a correlation between two distributions. We show that over UD's language sample, the highest correlation is obtained for nominal objects (V/O construction).

Since the Spearman correlation is a symmetric measure, we would like to continue our study by proposing an asymmetric measure that allows us to decide if one distribution can predict another. Our hypothesis, to be confirmed, is that constructions with the most uniform distribution, thus being flexible and well-balanced, provide better predictions of the behavior of other constructions. The V/O construction, which many authors take as a basic construction (see in particular the study of Dryer 1992) is thus an excellent candidate.

Acknowledgements

We would like to thank the three anonymous reviewers of the Gurt-Syntaxfest 2023 for their careful and patient examination as well as for the many valuable comments they made.

This research was supported by the French National Research Project (ANR) Autogramm.

References

Abney, Steven P. (1987). *The English noun phrase in its sentential aspect.* Doctoral dissertation, Cambridge: MIT.

Bakker, Dik (1998). Flexibility and consistency in word order patterns in the languages of Europe. In Siewierska A. (ed.) *Constituent order in the languages of Europe*, Berlin: Mouton de Gruyter, 383-419.

Chen, Xinying, and Kim Gerdes. (2017). Classifying Languages by Dependency Structure: Typologies of Delexicalized Universal Dependency Treebanks, *Proceedings of the 4th Conference on Dependency Linguistics (Depling).*

Dryer, Matthew S. (1992). The Greenbergian word order correlations, *Language* 68, 81-138.

Futrell, R., K. Mahowald, and E. Gibson (2015). Quantifying word order freedom in dependency corpora. In *Proceedings of the third international conference on dependency linguistics (Depling)*, 91-100.

Futrell, R., R. P. Levy, and E. Gibson (2020). Dependency locality as an explanatory principle for word order. *Language* 96(2), 371-412.

Gerdes, Kim, and Sylvain Kahane. (2016). Dependency Annotation Choices: Assessing Theoretical and Practical Issues of Universal Dependencies. *Proceedings of the 10th Linguistic Annotation Workshop (LAW X).*

Gerdes, Kim, Bruno Guillaume, Sylvain Kahane, and Guy Perrier. (2018). SUD or Surface-Syntactic Universal Dependencies: An annotation scheme near-isomorphic to UD. *Proceedings of the Universal Dependencies Workshop (UDW).*

Gerdes, Kim, Sylvain Kahane, and Xinying Chen. (2021). "Typometrics: From implicational to quantitative universals in word order typology. *Glossa: a journal of general linguistics* 6:1.

Greenberg, Joseph H. (1963). Some universals of grammar with particular reference to the order of meaningful elements. In J. H. Greenberg (ed.), *Universals of grammar,* Cambridge: MIT, 73–113.

Greenberg, Joseph H. (1966). *Language Universals.* The Hague: Mouton.

Guzmán Naranjo, Matías, and Laura Becker (2018). Quantitative word order typology with UD. In *Proceedings of the 17th International Workshop on Treebanks and Linguistic Theories (TLT),* 91-104.

Hawkins, John A. (1983). *Word Order Universals.* New York: Academic Press.

Hudson, Richard (1984). *Word Grammar.* Oxford: Basil Blackwell.

Levshina, Natalia (2019). Token-based typology and word order entropy: A study based on Universal Dependencies. *Linguistic Typology, 23*(3), 533-572.

Levshina, Natalia (2022). Corpus-based typology: Applications, challenges and some solutions. *Linguistic Typology, 26*(1), 129-160.

Liu, Haitao (2008). Dependency distance as a metric of language comprehension difficulty. *Journal of Cognitive Science, 9*(2), 159-191.

Nichols, Joanna (1992). *Linguistic Diversity in Space and Time.* Chicago: University of Chicago Press.

Schachter, Paul (1973). Focus and relativization. *Language* 49(1), 19-46.

Schmidt, P. W. (1926). *Die Sprachfamilien und Sprachenkreise der Erde: Atlas von 14 Karten.* Heidelberg: Winter.

Steinthal, Heymann. *Die Classification der Sprachen dargestellt als die Entwicklung der Sprachidee.* Dümmler, 1850.

Suitner, C., Maass, A., Navarrete, E., Formanowicz, M., Bratanova, B., Cervone, C., ... & Carrier, A. (2021). Spatial agency bias and word order flexibility: A comparison of 14 European languages. *Applied Psycholinguistics* 42(3), 657-671.

Tesnière, Lucien (1959). *Eléments de syntaxe structurale.* Paris: Klincksieck. [Transl. by Osborne, T., Kahane, S. (2015) *Elements of structural syntax.* Benjamins].

Wong, T. S., K. Gerdes, H. Leung and J. Lee. (2017). Quantitative Comparative Syntax on the Cantonese-Mandarin Parallel Dependency Treebank. *Proceedings of the conference on Dependency Linguistics (Depling),* 266–275.

ANNEX

Languages	Bakker-flexibility	Bakker_like_flexibility	typometric_flexibility
Armenian	40	60	33
Belarusian	-	50	26
Bulgarian	60	60	19
Czech	-	50	30
Danish	30	20	26
English	40	40	13
French	10	40	14
German	40	30	33
Greek	60	40	16
Hindi	-	20	2
Icelandic	40	**90**	35
Italian	**30**	50	18
Latin	**90**	80	**48**
Naija	_	10	6
Norwegian	40	20	21
OldEastSlavic	-	**80**	**52**
OldFrench	-	60	31
Polish	60	50	35
Russian	70	70	29
Slovak	50	50	37
Spanish	30	40	17
Swedish	40	20	21
Ukrainian	-	70	26
WesternArmenian	-	50	37

Table A1. Various flexibility measures for languages where a treebank-based verification of Bakker's measures is available as described in footnote 20.

Bakker's 10 relations	Corresponding construction
V/O	VERB-comp:obj-NOUN/PROPN
Adj/N	NOUN-mod-ADJ
Pro/N	NOUN-any-[Poss=Yes]
V/R	VERB-comp:obl-ADP/NOUN
Gen/N	NOUN-mod[gen]-ADP/NOUN
Rel/N	NOUN-mod@relcl-VERB
Adpos	ADP-comp-NOUN
Num/N	NOUN-any-NUM
Dem/N	NOUN-any[PronType=Dem]
Aux/V	AUX-comp:aux-VERB

Table A2: the 10 Bakker's relation and their corresponding constructions

Measures	V/O	Adj/N	Pro/N	V/R	Gen/N	Rel/N	Adpos	Num/N	Dem/N	Aux/V
freqSample	3.3	3.6	0.7	0.6	1.5	0.4	5	0.9	0.7	2.5
concerned_languages	113	96	51	59	68	42	103	85	64	87
typometric_flexibility%	26.2	16.2	15.9	31	20.2	2.5	5.5	22	10.3	25.7
Bakker-like_flexibility%	62.5	62.5	37.5	66.7	62.5	8.3	8.3	66.7	50	54.2
Bakker-like-flexibility(S)%	48.2	35.4	29.4	62.7	45.6	7.1	12.6	51.8	29.7	46
Bakker-like-head_initial(S)%	46.3	18.8	14.6	56.2	37	0	23.3	51.8	26.3	43.5
Bakker-like-head_final(S)%	49.3	68.8	90	65.1	51.2	7.9	8.2	50	57.1	46.9
head_initiality%	61	32	19	68	57	89	71	13	15	68
head_initial_weight	2.3	2	1.2	2.2	2.8	35.8	12.9	0.6	1.4	2.6
head_final_weight	1.5	4.2	5.1	1	2.1	4.3	5.3	4	8.3	1.3

Table A3. Measures for the 10 constructions considered by Bakker (1998). Among them *Bakker-like flexibility* is normalized over the 24 languages in Table A1, Others are normalized with the amount of languages in the row 'concerned languages'

Spearman	Bakker-flexibility	Bakker_like flexibility	typometric flexibility
Bakker-flexibility	1	0.458	0.479
Bakker_like flexibility	0.458	1	0.649
typometric flexibility	0.479	0.649	1

Pearson	Bakker-flexibility	Bakker_like flexibility	typometric flexibility
Bakker-flexibility	1	0.478	0.583
Bakker_like flexibility	0.478	1	0.692
typometric flexibility	0.583	0.692	1

Table B. Spearman correlation (left) and Pearson correlation (right) between Bakker's flexibility, Bakker-like flexibility and typometrics flexibility

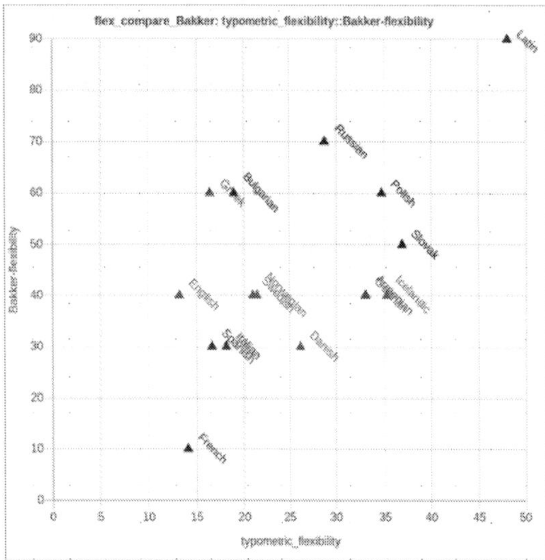

Figure C1: Typometric VS Bakker-flexibility

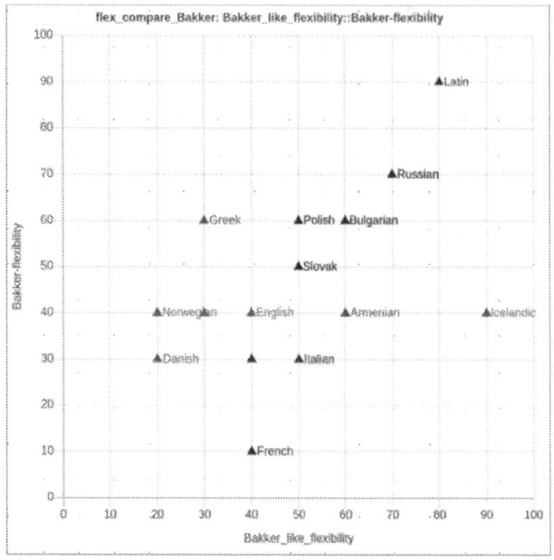

Figure C2: Bakker-like VS Bakker-flexibility

	Gen/N	Num/N	Rel/N	det	Pro/N	Adj/N	Dem/N	Adpos	mod	subj	Aux/V	V/R	V/O	comp	udep	core	any
Gen/N	1	0.197	0.654	-0.051	0.185	0.209	0.044	0.156	0.53	-0.268	-0.379	-0.281	-0.308	-0.254	-0.386	-0.184	-0.14
Num/N	0.197	1	0.086	-0.02	0.169	0.526	0.104	-0.4	0.423	-0.068	0.003	-0.023	-0.121	-0.087	0.04	0.008	0.01
Rel/N	0.654	0.086	1	0.09	-0.062	0.004	0.037	0.362	0.121	-0.292	0.003	0.069	0.062	0.145	-0.006	0.074	0.167
det	-0.051	-0.02	0.09	1	0.469	0.397	0.469	0.251	0.009	0.032	0.359	0.418	0.375	0.056	0.146	0.079	0.144
Pro/N	0.185	0.169	-0.062	0.469	1	0.532	0.583	-0.177	0.296	0.503	0.056	0.195	0.142	0.057	0.103	0.224	0.218
Adj/N	0.209	0.526	0.004	0.397	0.532	1	0.716	-0.267	0.68	0.229	0.171	0.257	0.107	0.087	0.124	0.273	0.256
Dem/N	0.044	0.104	0.037	0.469	0.583	0.716	1	-0.064	0.482	0.365	0.193	0.399	0.307	0.165	0.219	0.352	0.296
Adpos	0.156	-0.4	0.362	0.251	-0.177	-0.267	-0.064	1	-0.025	0.217	0.338	0.205	0.304	0.415	0.233	0.394	0.444
mod	0.53	0.423	0.121	0.009	0.296	0.68	0.482	-0.025	1	0.442	-0.119	-0.03	-0.123	0.407	0.462	0.684	0.664
subj	-0.268	-0.068	-0.292	0.032	0.503	0.229	0.365	0.217	0.442	1	0.478	0.421	0.453	0.492	0.545	0.722	0.688
Aux/V	-0.379	0.003	0.003	0.359	0.056	0.171	0.193	0.338	-0.119	0.478	1	0.839	0.844	0.907	0.842	0.809	0.838
V/R	-0.281	-0.023	0.069	0.418	0.195	0.257	0.399	0.205	-0.03	0.421	0.839	1	0.954	0.895	0.921	0.833	0.826
V/O	-0.308	-0.121	0.062	0.375	0.142	0.107	0.307	0.304	-0.123	0.453	0.844	0.954	1	0.941	0.93	0.858	0.86
comp	-0.254	-0.087	0.145	0.056	0.057	0.087	0.165	0.415	0.407	0.492	0.907	0.895	0.941	1	0.689	0.843	0.843
udep	-0.386	0.04	-0.006	0.146	0.103	0.124	0.219	0.233	0.462	0.545	0.842	0.921	0.93	0.689	1	0.85	0.864
core	-0.184	0.008	0.074	0.079	0.224	0.273	0.352	0.394	0.684	0.722	0.809	0.833	0.858	0.843	0.85	1	0.989
any	-0.14	0.01	0.167	0.144	0.218	0.256	0.296	0.444	0.664	0.688	0.838	0.826	0.86	0.843	0.864	0.989	1

Table D. Spearman correlation between the distributions of flexibility(L,C) for various constructions

Measure words are measurably different from sortal classifiers

Yamei Wang and **Géraldine Walther**
George Mason University
{ywang78, gwalthe}@gmu.edu

Abstract

Nominal classifiers categorize nouns based on salient semantic properties. Past studies have long debated whether sortal classifiers (related to intrinsic semantic noun features) and mensural classifiers (related to quantity) should be considered as the same grammatical category. Suggested diagnostic tests rely on functional and distributional criteria, typically evaluated in terms of isolated example sentences obtained through elicitation. This paper offers a systematic re-evaluation of this long-standing question: using 981,076 nominal phrases from a 489 MB dependency-parsed word corpus, corresponding extracted contextual word embeddings from a Chinese BERT model, and information-theoretic measures of mutual information, we show that mensural classifiers can be distributionally and functionally distinguished from sortal classifiers justifying the existence of distinct syntactic categories for mensural and sortal classifiers. Our study also entails broader implications for the typological study of classifier systems.

1 Introduction

Classifier systems constitute a major feature of East and South-East Asian languages (Li, 2013). Classifiers categorize referent nouns based on salient semantic features such as humanness, animacy, shape, or others (Aikhenvald and Mihas, 2019). In Mandarin, classifiers are obligatory when a noun is preceded by a number, a demonstrative, or a quantifier (Li and Thompson, 1989). For example, the classifier (in bold font) cannot be omitted in the following examples from Li (2013): 两 *liǎng* *(**个** *gè*) 学生 *xuéshēng* 'two students', 这 *zhè* *(**种** *zhǒng*) 动物 *dòngwù* 'this kind of animal', 每 *měi* *(**本** *běn*) 书 *shū* 'every book'. In other contexts, however, classifiers can be optional. In addition to *sortal classifiers*, which categorize nouns in terms of intrinsic semantic features, classifier systems also include *mensural classifiers* (or *measure words*), that are related to noun quantity. Table 1 lists a few common classifiers in Mandarin Chinese.

While sortal classifiers, like **张** *zhāng*, are typically associated with nouns displaying specific intrinsic semantic features, e.g., flat properties such as for the noun 地图 *dìtú* 'map', mensural classifiers like **组** *zǔ* 'group', **斤** *jīn* 'half kilogram', or **美元** *měiyuán* 'US Dollar' are usually characterized as being less restricted by the semantics of the nouns they combine with. In this paper, mensural classifiers like **组** *zǔ* 'group' will be referred as quantity, those like **斤** *jīn* 'half kilogram' and **美元** *měiyuán* 'US Dollar' will be referred as measurement and currency units respectively. In addition, Dryer et al. (2005) and Li (2013) indicate that sortal classifiers tend to be combined with countable nouns (e.g., 三 *sān* **本** *běn* 书 *shū* 'three books', 三 *sān* **只** *zhī* 碗 *wǎn* 'three bowls') while mensural classifiers refer to quantities of mass nouns (or "nouns with low countability") such as 三 *sān* **箱** *xiāng* 水 *shuǐ* 'three boxes of water' and 三 *sān* **斤** *jīn* 米 *mǐ* 'three half-kilograms of rice'. However those distinctions are not systematic: countable nouns can also be modified by mensural classifiers and mass nouns by sortal classifiers. For instance, the countable noun, 书 *shū* 'book' can be found in a nominal phrase such as 三 *sān* **箱** *xiāng* 书 *shū* 'three boxes of books', and the mass noun, 米 *mǐ* 'rice' can be modified by a sortal classifier in 三 *sān* **粒** *lì* 米 *mǐ* 'three grains of rice'.

Given their apparent similarities and differences, typological and general linguistic studies have long debated whether sortal and mensural classifiers should be considered as the same syntactic category (e.g., Lyons, 1977; Li and Thompson, 1989) or two different categories (e.g., Nguyen, 2004; Singhapreecha, 2001; Her and Hsieh, 2010). In these studies, suggested diagnostic tests rely on functional and distributional criteria, typically evaluated in terms of isolated example sentences

Proceedings of the Seventh International Conference on Dependency Linguistics (Depling, GURT/SyntaxFest 2023), pages 81 - 90
March 9-12, 2023 ©2023 Association for Computational Linguistics

Determiner	Classifier	Noun	Translation
一 *yī* 'one'	张 *zhāng* 'sortal classifier'	地图 *dìtú* 'map'	one map
这 *zhè* 'this'	组 *zǔ* 'group'	照片 *zhàopiàn* 'photo'	this group of photos
十二 *shíèr* 'twelve'	斤 *jīn* 'half kilogram'	米 *mǐ* 'rice'	six kilograms of rice
一亿 *yíyì* '100 million'	美元 *měiyuán* 'US Dollar'	公司 *gōngsī* 'company'	a 100 million US Dollar company

Table 1: Nominal phrases extracted from the Leipzig corpus of Mandarin Chinese (Goldhahn et al., 2012) using the CoreNLP Parser(Chen and Manning, 2014). The examples show noun phrases including the **sortal classifier** 张 *zhāng* and three measure words for **quantities** 组 *zǔ* 'group', **measurements** 斤 *jīn* 'half kilogram', and **currencies** *měiyuán* 'US Dollar'.

obtained through elicitation. We address this question in a more systematic and empirical way using data from large Mandarin corpora. We compare the distribution of sortal and mensural classifiers in terms of their contextual word representations and their function in terms of contribution to noun predictability. The idea that classifiers can be used to enhance the predictability of upcoming nouns is based on a study by Dye et al. (2017, 2018). The authors show that gendered determiners in German, which also partition the language's nouns into classes (masculine, feminine, and neuter), serve the communicative function of efficiently reducing the entropy of upcoming nouns in context. Similarly, our study adopts a communicative perspective on noun class partitioning and evaluates sortal vs. mensural classifiers in terms of their respective contribution to noun entropy reduction. If sortal and mensural classifiers prove to be distributed differently or to show differences in their degree of reducing the entropy of upcoming nouns, we will be able to successfully conclude that they can be considered separate syntactic categories. Otherwise, they would be better analyzed as two types within the same category.

Our study is based on 981,076 manually validated noun phrases extracted from a 489MB corpus of Mandarin Chinese that is part of the Leipzig Corpora Collection (Goldhahn et al., 2012), an open access collection of pre-cleaned data. We preparsed the data using the CoreNLP Chinese dependency parser (Chen and Manning, 2014). Our results show that mensural classifiers can be distributionally and functionally distinguished from sortal classifiers. Additionally two traditional subtypes of mensural classifiers (i.e., measurement and currency units) emerge as distinct from the other mensural classifier subtype (which we will refer to as *quantity*).

2 Measuring categorial differences

The goal of our study is to quantitatively evaluate whether distributional and functional properties of words traditionally labeled *sortal* vs. *mensural classifiers* suggest that they constitute a single or two separate syntactic categories in Mandarin Chinese. Based on 981,076 manually validated noun phrases extracted from a 489MB corpus, we analyze the syntactic distributions of sortal and mensural classifiers, as well as the differences in their communicative function for natural language use. We used contextual word embeddings as a measure of classifier distributions and mutual information (MI) (Cover and Thomas, 2012) as a measure of their contribution to facilitating noun predictability.

2.1 Data

We downloaded three of the 1M sentence corpora of Mandarin Chinese from the Leipzig Corpora Collection (Goldhahn et al., 2012)[1] and normalized the data by converting all Chinese characters into simplified Chinese using the Open Chinese Convert software.[2] We then applied the CoreNLP Chinese dependency parser (Chen and Manning, 2014) to our dataset. We used the dependency information to extract all complete nominal phrases containing nouns, classifiers, and other dependents such as determiners and adjectives, as well as the frequencies of all nouns and classifiers. 91 out of 1,079,190 nominal phrases were removed from the

[1]The types of corpora are 2007-2009 news, 2011 newscrawl, and 2015 China web: https://wortschatz.uni-leipzig.de/en/download/Chinese.

[2]https://github.com/BYVoid/OpenCC

data due to their unusual length (more than 35 characters)[3]. A sample of the remaining extracted nominal phrases is shown in Table 2.

Manual validation of the data revealed that despite the Mandarin Chinese CoreNLP parser's overall good performance[4] reported in Chen and Manning (2014), a significant proportion of words had been erroneously labeled as classifiers. We manually validated all 1,577 word types identified as classifiers by the parser. After excluding tokens containing symbols ('县、区、乡、'), non Chinese ('ま') or invalid characters ('\ue997'), numbers ('二九'), dialectal expressions ('拨儿'), and other similar cases, we were able to retain 315 classifier types. Excluded cases are listed in table 3. We labeled them as either sortal or mensural classifiers following the classification suggested in Chao (1965)'s reference grammar. Not all 315 classifier types are listed in Chao (1965). For those not listed in the grammar, we inferred the labels applying compatible classification criteria. As a result, 55 classifiers were labeled as sortal classifiers and 260 as mensural classifiers. We further categorized mensural classifiers into one of three subcategories: quantities (148), measurements (86), and currency (86) (see table 1 for examples of sortals, quantities, measurements, and currencies). The complete list of the classifiers with their corresponding labels is indicated in table 4.

Almost all discarded classifiers were hapaxes, such that at the end of the validation process, we were still left with 981,076 noun phrases out of the original 1,079,190. We analyzed the remaining classifiers in terms of their distributional properties (represented by contextual word embeddings) and functional properties (measured as mutual information (MI) (Cover and Thomas, 2012)).

Distributional information was obtained using the pre-trained Chinese BERT model from Hugging Face.[5] We extracted contextual word embeddings for all retained classifiers. Embeddings were based on the last-hidden state, where most of the contextual information is encoded.

Contextual word embeddings were adopted in order to be able to distinguish between tokens used as classifiers vs. identical tokens representing other parts of speech (e.g., 桶 *tǒng* 'bucket' represents a quantity in the phrase 一 *yī* 桶 *tǒng* 水 *shuǐ* 'one bucket of water' but is a noun the phrase 黄色 *huángsè* 的 *de* 桶 *tǒng* 'the yellow bucket'). Since the model returns one embedding per Chinese character, we were forced to discard classifiers represented by multi-character units[6]. This however only marginally changed our overall proportions for the two categories that lie at the core of this study: sortal classifiers vs. generic measure words. Overall, this step affected our four categories in the following way: sortal classifier tokens: 0% removed; generic measure word tokens: 1.4% removed; measurement tokens: 18.8% removed; and currency tokens: 99.3% removed. Because of their very specific use and homogeneous meanings, measurements and currency units are not usually considered contentious in the debate as to whether sortal and mensural classifiers constitute a unique or two separate categories. The removal of multi-character units from the currency units and measurement categories only removed a very small proportion of our overall classifier set and did not interfere with our main concern regarding the classification of sortal classifiers and generic measure words. At the end of this data cleaning process, our dataset contained 500,987 word embeddings corresponding to 221 distinct classifiers.

All noun frequencies (type: 324,920 and token: 27,596,565), frequencies of classifiers (type: 315 and token: 981,076), and their corresponding nouns (noun type: 45,159 and token: 981,076) in the retained nominal phrases were used to calculate the overall entropy of nouns and the Mutual Information between classifiers and their head nouns.

2.2 Method

Syntactic categories are commonly defined by the distribution and the function of the elements they contain. Words belonging to the same category are expected to display identical or similar distributional properties and functions. Our goal in this paper was to apply quantifiable measures of distribution and function to classifier tokens in order to objectively compare the distributional and functional properties of the types commonly identified

[3]Extracted phrases of more than 35 characters were judged to be abnormal by the author who is a native speaker. Given its small proportion, the removal of 91 our of 1,079,190 does not have a significant impact on the overall distributions.

[4]The unlabeled attachment score (UAS) and labeled attachment score (LAS) reported for the test dataset by Chen and Manning (2014) are 83.9% and 82.4% respectively. UAS indicates the percentage of words that have been assigned the correct head, and LAS shows the percentage of words that have been assigned the correct head and label.

[5]https://huggingface.co/bert-base-chinese

[6]Classifiers corresponding to multiple vectors.

Determiner	Classifier	Noun	Phrase
三 *sān* 'three'	部 *bù* sortal	片约 *piānyuē* 'film appointment'	三部片约 'three shooting sessions'
这 *zhè* 'this'	支 *zhī* sortal	团体 *tuántǐ* 'group'	这支出道 12 年的团体 'this 12-year-old group'
本 *běn* 'this'	周 *zhōu* 'week'	新闻 *xīnwén* 'news'	本周台湾旅游新闻 'Taiwan travel news of this week'

Table 2: Sampled nominal phrases extracted from the Leipzig corpus of Mandarin Chinese (Goldhahn et al., 2012) using CoreNLP Chinese Parser (Chen and Manning, 2014). The nominal phrase 三部片约 sān bù piānyuē 'three film shooting sessions' only contains a determiner, a classifier, and a noun. In addition to the determiner, classifier, and noun, the other two phrases also contain other modifying elements.

Discarded types	Examples
symbols	'II', '·', '〖'
characters with symbols	'县、区、乡、', '日圆、入不敷出'
invalid characters	'\ue997', '\ue08d
foreign characters	'ま', '4 G'
numbers	'二九', '陆仟捌佰零'
combinations of numbers and symbols	'二·一六', '八〇八二六〇'
combinations of classifier + noun	'号楼', '吨钢'
combinations of noun + classifier	'人次','人份'
combinations of classifier + classifier	'吨级', '架次'
reduplicated classifiers	'盘盘', '首首'
verbal classifiers	'下','遍','次'
dialectal phrases	'拨儿','斗子'
phrases with typos	'豪米','届'
words not convertible into simplified Chinese	'埸'
meaningless phrases	'圈共','岔起', '服轨'
words that cannot be classifiers	'跺', '啸', '恒星','烧烤', '富二代', '菩萨摩诃'

Table 3: Listed criteria used to manually validate parsed classifiers by using the CoreNLP parser (Chen and Manning, 2014)

as either sortal or mensural classifiers in the literature.

2.2.1 Exploring distributions

In order to evaluate the (dis)similarity between the distributions of our four classifier types, we compared their contextual word embeddings extracted from the pre-trained Chinese BERT model for all 221 single-character classifier types of our dataset. The embeddings produced by the model correspond to vectors with 768 dimensions for each token. We used the Uniform Manifold Approximation and Projection algorithm (UMAP) developed by McInnes et al. (2018) to perform high dimensionality reduction in order to better evaluate the (dis)similarity between the distributions of our four classifier types. UMAP maintains separability of categories: in a UMAP visualization, if two categories are separable in the projected space they will also be separable in the original space (Tunstall et al., 2022). We projected the 768-dimensional embeddings onto a 2-dimensional plane highlighting the differences in distributions for the four different classifier types.

The distributions of sortal and mensural classifiers are predicted to be alike if they occur with similar words around them, as suggested by several authors in existing literature (Lyons, 1977; Cheng and Sybesma, 1999; Paik and Bond, 2002; Bender and Siegel, 2004; Gebhardt, 2011, among others). Given the way the UMAP algorithm has been designed, if classifier distributions align, their UMAP projection should mostly overlap. Such an overlap would constitute an argument towards positing one single classifier category for all overlapping types. If classifier distributions do

Sortal:	**口, 扇, 盏, 出, 尊, 棵, 条, 枝, 所, 张, 粒, 头, 顶, 把, 面, 封, 管, 道, 件, 匹, 门, 枚, 堵, 座, 只, 架, 首, 朵, 家, 篇, 辆, 卷, 个, 行, 颗, 杆, 处, 桩, 幅, 顿, 部, 幕, 位, 艘, 根, 本**, 株, 宗, 栋, 则, 支, 幢, 台, 项, 袭
Mensural: quantity	**级, 片, 盘, 股, 壶, 脸, 排, 系列, 册, 手, 号, 层, 团, 段, 周, 版, 包, 瓶, 帮, 箱, 堂, 锅, 节, 岁, 剂, 组, 块, 种, 轮, 类, 杯, 天, 盆, 筐, 盒, 堆, 桶, 世, 边, 套, 名, 副, 担, 队, 对, 笔, 页, 派, 味, 划, 群, 截, 袋, 族, 栏, 脚, 区, 番, 点, 列, 章, 匣, 票, 分, 路, 班, 些, 站, 批, 月, 丝, 桌, 阶, 碗, 年, 重, 肚子, 双, 身, 代, 盅, 串, 样, 滴, 缸, 笼, 辈, 罐, 眼**, 撮, 匙, 届, 垛, 竹篓, 尾, 筒, 篓, 坨, 集, 帧, 墩, 柄, 户, 扎, 刻, 餐, 具, 起, 发, 针, 品, 日, 小捆, 瓮, 屉, 酒杯, 杓, 句, 场, 炉, 竿, 樽, 沓, 簇, 期, 茶匙, 箩筐, 记, 席, 缸子, 间, 缕, 池, 阕, 囊, 员, 帖, 伙, 拨, 曲, 束, 圈, 辑, 叠, 波, 摊, 份, 楼, 款
Mensural: measurement	**秒, 英里, 米, 克, 西西, 公尺, 亩, 公里, 毛, 丈, 英寸, 英尺, 公斤, 公分, 小时, 斗, 码, 海里, 加仑, 寸, 吨, 尺, 磅, 斤**, 平方米, 公吨, 呎, 平方英呎, 微米, 立方英尺, 兆瓦特, 毫克, 公克, 兆赫, 瓦, 兆, 度, 厘米, 平方公尺, 安培, 千伏, 平方公里, 元, 英吋, 盎司, 公升, 打, 立方米, 平方英尺, 盎斯, 平方尺, 海浬, 公厘, 克拉, 平方呎, 毫米, 毫升, 英哩, 千兆, 大卡, 千瓦时, 美分, 千伏特, 伏特, 英亩, 瓦特, 坪, 公顷, 摄氏度, 伏, 平方厘米, 海哩, 千克, 微秒, 浬, 兆瓦, 立方厘米, 平米, 瓩, 吋, 平方海里, 公倾, 千瓦, 华里, 角, 兆瓦时
Mensural: currency	**先令, 法郎, 卢比**, 克朗, 英磅, 马币, 比索, 新币, 缅元,, 瑞典克朗, 银元, 加元, 铢, 丹麦克朗, 韩币, 台币, 澳元, 澳币, 港币, 日圆, 镑, 新元, 泰铢, 美金, 欧元, 美元, 港元, 日元, 英镑, 韩元, 澳大利亚元

Table 4: List of all 315 manually validated and classified classifiers mainly based on Chao (1965)' reference grammar. Classifiers explicitly mentioned in the grammar are indicated in bold face.

not align, the UMAP projections should present as largely distinct. This would favor an analysis of more than one existing syntactic classifier category.

2.2.2 Evaluating functional contributions

Given that classifiers precede nouns within noun phrases, we also wanted to test whether classifiers, like German gendered articles (Dye et al., 2017), contribute to reducing uncertainty about upcoming nouns, and whether this reduction is equally operated by all types classifiers previously identified. For that purpose, we applied the information-theoretic measure of mutual information (MI) (Cover and Thomas, 2012) to all classifiers and their corresponding head nouns.

Mutual information (MI) indicates how much information (in bits) is shared between a classifier and its corresponding head noun. The higher the value of mutual information for a specific classifier-noun pair, the more systematically those nouns can be found together. In terms of processing, this systematicity contributes to significantly reducing the listener's (or reader's) uncertainty about the upcoming noun. Low mutual information would on the contrary indicate that classifiers are not particularly helpful for predicting (a class of) upcoming nouns.

If C and N represent the sets of all classifiers and nouns respectively, and c and n their corresponding elements, then MI between each type of classifier and its corresponding nouns is defined as follows:

$$
\begin{aligned}
I(N;C) &= H(N) - H(N|C) \\
&= \sum_{n \in N, c \in C} p(n,c) log \frac{p(n,c)}{p(n)p(c)}
\end{aligned}
\tag{1}
$$

We computed the mutual information between classifiers and nouns for each type of classifier. We then used a one-way ANOVA to evaluate the level of significance of the differences in MI across all four categories (sortal classifiers, quantities, measurements, and currencies).

3 Results

3.1 Distribution

The UMAP projections for the distributions of sortal classifiers and all three subtypes of mensural classifiers are plotted in Figure 1. Darker zones correspond to a higher proportion of projections in that area of the plane. Lighter zones correspond to fewer projections or an absence of projections in that area.

The plots show distinct patterns of distribution for all four different types of classifiers: while there may be some partial overlap in lighter regions, dark (high token frequency) regions are clearly separated out for all four subcategories. They all occupy different regions in the plane.

Currencies are especially well separated from the rest three subcategories. However, it is worth noting that the word embeddings for currencies are only a small subset of our full dataset since the majority of word embeddings for currencies are represented by more than one character corresponding to more than one vector in the BERT model. These multi-character tokens had been removed in the data pre-processing phase.

Both sortal classifiers and generic measure words (quantities) show a broader range of possible distributions. Yet the former are mainly clustered in the right region of the plane, while the latter are concentrated in the left half of the plane. The distribution of measurements is mostly situated in the middle.

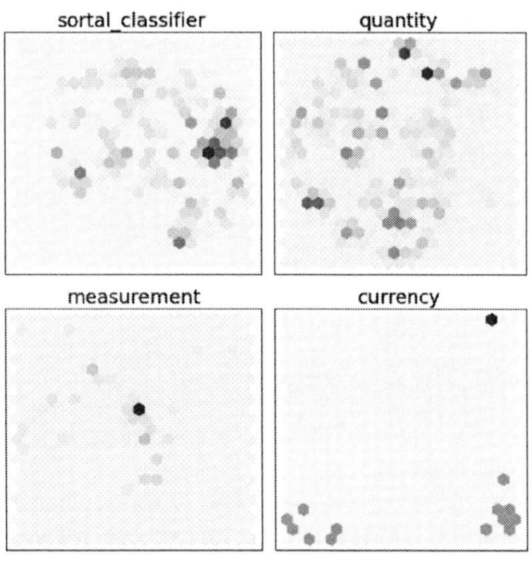

Figure 1: Visualization of the projections of 500,988 contextual word embeddings for all classifiers using UMAP (McInnes et al., 2018)

3.2 Function

For all classifier types, classifiers drastically reduce the entropy of upcoming nouns.

A one-way ANOVA test revealed that the difference in mean mutual information associated with each classifier type is significant across all four

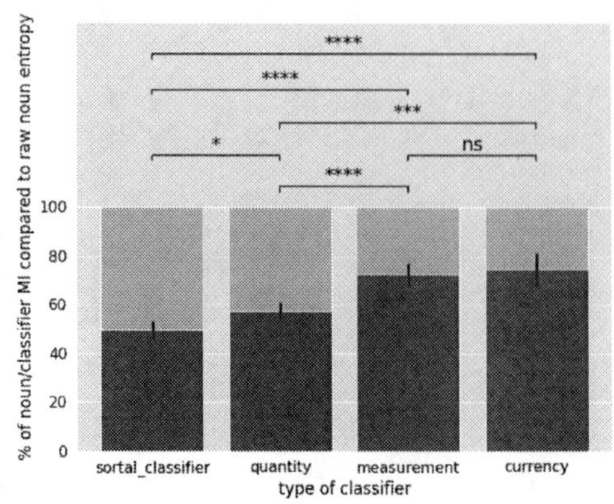

Figure 2: Percentages of Mutual information between nouns and classifiers over the entropy of noun. Error bars indicate bootstrapped (n sample = 10,000) *95% C.I.* of I(N; C). The number of asterisks denotes the magnitude of significance compared to a significance level of $p = 0.05$.

types.[7] We also used Tukey's HSD Test to perform multiple comparisons across the different types of classifiers.

We found that the mean mutual information between nouns and units of measurements is not significantly different from that between nouns and currency units.[8] Functionally, those two subtypes appear to play very similar roles: The overall entropy of nouns from our corpora lies around 12.29 bits. From Figure 2, it is apparent that both units of measurement (8.90 bits) and currencies (9.17 bits) greatly help with predicting upcoming nouns: knowing a measurement or currency accounts for around 75% of the original noun entropy. These two subcategories are significantly different from the other two.

MI involving units of measurements was significantly different from that involving sortal classifiers or generic quantities.[9] Not unsurprisingly, MI involving currency units also significantly differed from MI involving sortal classifiers or generic quantities.[10]

Even though the significance levels were not as high as for all other significant category pairs, differences in MI involving generic quantities vs.

[7] $F(3) = 25.46$, $P < 0.0001$.

[8] $P = 0.94$, *95% C.I.* = [-1.55, 1.02].

[9] $p = 0$, *95% C.I.* = [-3.80, -1.81]; $p = 0$, *95% C.I.* = [-2.63, -1.07].

[10] $p = 0$, *95% C.I.* = [-4.45, -1.70]; $p = 0.0001$, *95% C.I.* = [-3.35, -0.90].

those involving sortal classifiers still reached significance levels.[11] Our findings indicate that at the functional level, measure words can be distinguished from sortal classifiers. The presence of a measure word denoting generic quantities makes the upcoming noun more predictable than a sortal classifier in the same context. Classifiers denoting quantities (7.05 bits) account for 57% of the raw noun entropy, while sortal classifiers (6.09 bits) only account for 49%.

As a result, functional properties again suggest that mensural classifiers and sortal classifiers are better analyzed as two separate categories. Additionally, the results also suggest that the mensural classifier class is not homogeneous and that it may be better analyzed as at least two separate (sub-)categories: classifiers indicating generic quantities on the one hand and currency units and units of measurement one the other.

4 Discussion and relation to previous work

There is a longstanding debate as to whether mensural and sortal classifiers should be considered as the same grammatical category in Mandarin Chinese (or in classifier languages in general). Despite a general consensus that categorization should be performed on the basis of observable distributions and functions, researchers' conclusions diverge.

For some, sortal and mensural classifiers should be considered as one category since they can occur in similar contexts (e.g., Lyons, 1977; Cheng and Sybesma, 1999; Paik and Bond, 2002; Bender and Siegel, 2004; Gebhardt, 2011).[12] Others argue that sortal and mensural classifiers should be considered as distinct since they cannot be modified in the same way (Her and Hsieh, 2010; Singhapreecha, 2001; Nguyen, 2004). Her and Hsieh (2010) specifically argue that the difference between sortal and mensural classifiers is mainly semantic but has consequences on distributional properties: mensural classifiers are semantically substantive and block numeral quantification and adjective modification of the noun, whereas sortal classifiers are semantically null and not as restrictive.[13]

Similar differences are also claimed to exist in other classifier languages, such as Thai (Singhapreecha, 2001) or Vietnamese (Nguyen, 2004). In Vietnamese, for instance, mensural classifiers are described as sometimes occurring with modifiers inserted between the classifier and the head noun, whereas nothing can be inserted between a sortal classifier and its head noun. In general, previous literature arguing for separate categories for sortal and mensural classifiers tends to highlight that mensural classifiers can occur with more modifiers than their sortal counterparts. This is another way of saying that mensural classifiers are considered to allow a wider range of distributions than sortal classifiers.

Our results appear to corroborate that claim. Overall, in our results sortal and mensural classifiers do not appear to significantly overlap in their distributions, suggesting the existence of two distinct categories from a distributional perspective. But the UMAP plot in Figure 1 also shows more different distributions for mensural classifiers than for sortals, especially if generic quantities, currencies, and units of measure are analyzed as one group.

As an overarching category, mensural classifiers – including quantities, units of measurements, and currencies – appear to have a very diverse range of distributions. Given the very specific distributions for currencies and measurements, our data and the results of our analysis of classifier distributions appears to suggest that those might be better distributionally analyzed as three separate categories. Even if we only compare generic quantities to sortal classifiers, the range of projections associated with the mensural classifiers clearly exceeds that of the sortals, in line with conclusions drawn by proponents of separate syntactic categories.

From a functional perspective, some researchers have attempted to argue that mensural classifiers should be considered as belonging to the same syntactic category as their sortal counterparts because of the parallel roles they play within noun phrases (see Lyons, 1977; Cheng and Sybesma, 1999; Paik and Bond, 2002; Bender and Siegel, 2004; Gebhardt, 2011, among others).[14] The results of our

[11] $p = 0.03$, *95% C.I.* = [-1.86, -0.04].

[12] n Table 1, the sortal classifier 张 *zhāng* appears in a similar position as the mensural classifiers 组 *zǔ*, 斤 *jīn*, and 美元 *měiyuán* (between either a number or a determiner and a noun).

[13] Her and Hsieh suggest three diagnostic distributional tests to differentiate sortal and mensural classifiers: numeral/adjectival stacking modification, *de*-insertion, and *ge*-substitution.

[14] In Table 1 for example, both sortal classifier (张 *zhāng*) and mensural classifiers (组 *zǔ*, 斤 *jīn*, and 美元 *měiyuán*) can

study are closer in line with work suggesting that sortal and mensural classifiers are in fact functionally different.

Our study focuses on differences in the communicative function across classifier types. While we assume, based on evidence found for German gendered articles (Dye et al., 2017, 2018), that all classifiers will to some degree help anticipate the upcoming noun in the noun phrase they occur in, we wanted to test whether there would be a significant difference in the amount of MI effectively shared between the classifiers and their head noun. Such a significant difference would then suggest the existence of multiple syntactic categories associated with classifiers.

Related work by Liu et al. (2019) used MI to investigate how systematically classifiers can be predicted from the semantics of a given noun. The answer to that question would be relevant to questions related to classifier learning, but is distinct from our study. By focusing on the relation between noun entropy and its reduction in the presence of a classifier, we are specifically targeting the predictive value of classifiers in noun phrase processing.[15]

Our results show that there are significant differences in how much different types of classifiers help predict upcoming head nouns, with currency and measure units being the most predictive, classifiers denoting generic quantities ranking second, and sortal classifiers being the least helpful. Interestingly, while our results do suggest the existence of three different classifier categories from a functional perspective, the observed functional contributions are the opposite of what previous literature would have suggested.

Proponents of distinct classifier categories typically argue that while sortal classifiers are associated with nouns based on their referents' inherent properties (such as shape, humanness, animacy, etc.), mensural classifiers denote quantities not directly related to the nouns' meanings (see for example Jarkey and Komatsu, 2019; Unterbeck, 1994), suggesting that sortal classifiers would be more specifically linked to the nouns they combine with.[16] What we see in the results of our MI calculations is that all mensural classifier types share a greater amount of information with their head nouns than sortal classifiers do.

5 Conclusion

The distinction between sortal and mensural classifiers has been a long-standing debate in the fields of Chinese, (South-)East Asian linguistics, general linguistics and linguistic typology. Previous literature attempted to solve this problem using isolated example sentences and categorical grammaticality judgements. In this paper, we instead systematically re-evaluate the distributional and functional properties of classifiers using quantitative methodologies.

Using 981,076 noun phrases from a 489MB dependency-parsed corpus of Mandarin Chinese, we show that mensural and sortal classifiers are indeed measurably different both in their distributions and their functional contribution to noun phrase processing. We further find that mensural classifiers do not constitute a homogeneous class. Based on both their very specific distributions and they very significantly different functional contributions, units of measurement and currency can be classified as one if not two classes that are distinct from both sortal classifiers and generic measure words.

Our results also include two broader typological implications: since (i) sortal and mensural classifiers can be reliably identified as distinct categories in at least one language, (ii) the most promising line of analysis for further typological investigations into classifier systems will investigate whether languages with classifier systems cluster into two discrete types: those with separate categories for sortal and mensural classifiers, and those without a clear sortal/mensural split.

6 Appendix

Limitations and future work

In our results, currencies appeared as distributionally very different from both other mensural classifier types. However, when we extracted the contextual word embeddings of the classifiers for the distributional analysis, we discarded word embeddings for multi-token classifiers since they would

be used to quantify nouns.

[15]Lau and Grüter (2015) also investigate classifiers from a processing perspective, but using an experimental approached based on eye-tracking experiments involving L2 speakers of Mandarin.

[16]E.g., in table 1 the sortal classifier 张 *zhāng* combines with the referent/noun 地图 *dìtú* 'map' highlighting its flat properties, while the mensural classifier 斤 *jīn* quantifies the referent/noun 米 *mǐ* 'rice' by applying a specific measuring unit.

be represented by multiple rather than a single vector. This significantly reduced the number of representations for currencies. In the future, we might be able to use average vectors over multi-tokens or leftmost vectors to represent those discarded currencies, but further work will be needed to show their specific distributions. Regardless of this limitation, our study still revealed significant differences between the two largest subsets of classifiers: sortal classifiers and generic measures of quantity.

Our data does not cover all possible types of written and spoken genres. Yet, since a limited sample of genres already reveals distributional and functional differences between the two types of classifiers, those differences justify assigning sortal and mensural classifiers to separate syntactic categories in Mandarin Chinese. Future work could compare results across a broader variety of genres, notably to investigate classifier use in spoken Mandarin Chinese, where speakers may be more likely to either drop classifiers or make more extensive use of the most common generic classifier 个 *gè* at the expense of all other classifiers.

This project focuses on classifiers in Mandarin Chinese. In the future, we may be able to apply this methodology to other classifier languages to assess whether split classifier systems are the norm for languages with classifier systems or whether languages cluster into two discrete types: those with separate categories for sortal and mensural classifiers, and those without a clear sortal/mensural split.

Our code will be made available for replication and extension by the community.

Acknowledgements

This project was supported by resources provided by the Office of Research Computing at George Mason University (URL: https://orc.gmu.edu) and funded in part by grants from the National Science Foundation (Awards Number 1625039 and 2018631, and 2109578).

References

Alexandra Y Aikhenvald and Elena I Mihas. 2019. *Genders and classifiers: a cross-linguistic typology*. Oxford University Press.

Emily M Bender and Melanie Siegel. 2004. Implementing the syntax of japanese numeral classifiers. In *International Conference on Natural Language Processing*, pages 626–635. Springer.

Yuen Ren Chao. 1965. *A grammar of spoken Chinese*. ERIC.

Danqi Chen and Christopher D Manning. 2014. A fast and accurate dependency parser using neural networks. In *Proceedings of the 2014 conference on empirical methods in natural language processing (EMNLP)*, pages 740–750.

Lisa Lai-Shen Cheng and Rint Sybesma. 1999. Bare and not-so-bare nouns and the structure of np. *Linguistic inquiry*, 30(4):509–542.

Thomas M Cover and Joy A Thomas. 2012. Elements of information theory. 2012. *Google Scholar Google Scholar Digital Library Digital Library*.

Matthew Dryer, David Gil, and Martin Haspelmath. 2005. *The world atlas of language structures*. Oxford University Press.

Melody Dye, Petar Milin, Richard Futrell, and Michael Ramscar. 2017. A functional theory of gender paradigms. In *Perspectives on morphological organization*, pages 212–239. Brill.

Melody Dye, Petar Milin, Richard Futrell, and Michael Ramscar. 2018. Alternative solutions to a language design problem: The role of adjectives and gender marking in efficient communication. *Topics in cognitive science*, 10(1):209–224.

Lewis Gebhardt. 2011. Classifiers are functional. *Linguistic Inquiry*, 42(1):125–130.

Dirk Goldhahn, Thomas Eckart, and Uwe Quasthoff. 2012. Building large monolingual dictionaries at the leipzig corpora collection: From 100 to 200 languages. In *Proceedings of the Eighth International Conference on Language Resources and Evaluation (LREC'12)*, pages 759–765.

One-Soon Her and Chen-Tien Hsieh. 2010. On the semantic distinction between classifiers and measure words in chinese. *Language and linguistics*, 11(3):527–551.

Nerida Jarkey and Hiroko Komatsu. 2019. Numeral classifiers in japanese. *Genders and classifiers: a cross-linguistic typology*, pages 249–81.

Elaine Lau and Theres Grüter. 2015. Real-time processing of classifier information by l2 speakers of chinese. In *Proceedings of the 39th annual Boston University conference on language development*, pages 311–323.

Charles N Li and Sandra A Thompson. 1989. *Mandarin Chinese: A functional reference grammar*, volume 3. Univ of California Press.

XuPing Li. 2013. Numeral classifiers in chinese. In *Numeral Classifiers in Chinese*. De Gruyter Mouton.

Shijia Liu, Hongyuan Mei, Adina Williams, and Ryan Cotterell. 2019. On the idiosyncrasies of the mandarin chinese classifier system. *arXiv preprint arXiv:1902.10193*.

John Lyons. 1977. *Semantics: Volume 2*, volume 2. Cambridge university press.

Leland McInnes, John Healy, and James Melville. 2018. Umap: Uniform manifold approximation and projection for dimension reduction. *arXiv preprint arXiv:1802.03426*.

Tuong Hung Nguyen. 2004. *The structure of the Vietnamese noun phrase*. Boston University.

Kyounghee Paik and Francis Bond. 2002. Spatial representation and shape classifiers in japanese and korean. *The Construction of Meaning*, pages 163–180.

Pornsiri Singhapreecha. 2001. Thai classifiers and the structure of complex thai nominals. In *Proceedings of the 15th Pacific Asia Conference on Language, Information and Computation*, pages 259–270.

Lewis Tunstall, Leandro von Werra, and Thomas Wolf. 2022. *Natural language processing with transformers*. " O'Reilly Media, Inc.".

Barbara Unterbeck. 1994. Korean classifiers. *Theoretical issues in Korean linguistics*, pages 367–385.

A Pipeline for Extracting Abstract Dependency Templates for Data-to-Text Natural Language Generation

Simon Mille,[1] **Josep Ricci,**[2] **Alexander Shvets**[2] and **Anya Belz**[1]
[1]ADAPT Research Centre, Dublin City University
[2]Pompeu Fabra University Barcelona
{simon.mille, anya.belz}@adaptcentre.ie
josep.ricci01@estudiant.upf.edu, alexander.shvets@upf.edu

Abstract

We present work in progress that aims to address the coverage issue faced by rule-based text generators. We propose a pipeline for extracting abstract dependency template (predicate-argument structures) from Wikipedia text to be used as input for generating text from structured data with the FORGe system. The pipeline comprises three main components: (i) candidate sentence retrieval, (ii) clause extraction, ranking and selection, and (iii) conversion to predicate-argument form. We present an approach and preliminary evaluation for the ranking and selection module.

1 Introduction

Rule-based Natural Language Generation (NLG) systems have become increasingly unpopular since the NLP field switched first to statistical systems, then to neural: rule-based systems tend to have low coverage (limited robustness to new inputs), reduced suprasentential fluency, and on the whole need to be built manually, all of which in combination means they are no longer competitive in shared task competitions and other NLP research contexts. However, their output can generally be guaranteed to have high accuracy and grammaticality, which continues to make them the system of choice in many commercial contexts.[1] Moreover, they can be efficient in terms of data and energy requirements, and suitable for low-resource languages. That is, on their own or in combination with, e.g., language-model-based modules, rule-based NLG potentially has an important role to play in the current NLP landscape if shortcomings such as the coverage issue addressed here can be overcome.

[1]E.g. Arria NLG's NLG Engine.

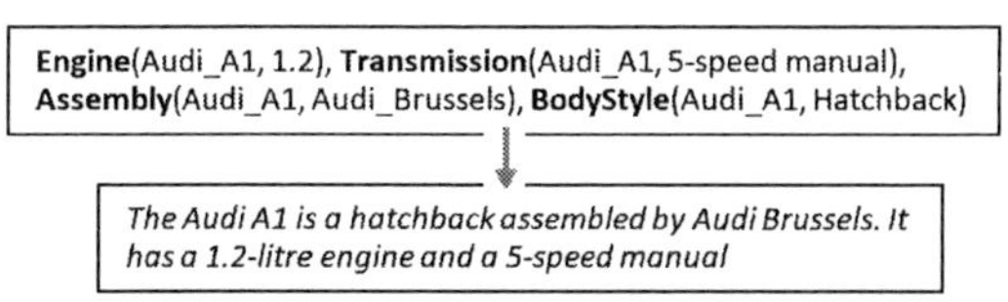

Figure 1: A DBpedia triple set from WebNLG+ and a corresponding generated text. Triple = Property(DB-Subj, DB-Obj), where the DB-Subj is an entity, and the DB-Obj another entity, a numeric, a date, etc.

WebNLG+. The present work was prompted by the WebNLG+ shared task (Castro Ferreira et al., 2020), in which part of the test set inputs contained features not seen in the training or development data. The WebNLG+ dataset is a benchmark for data-to-text NLG consisting of aligned DBpedia triple sets and texts. DBpedia triples are the building blocks of the inputs, and consist of three related elements called a *Property*, a *Subject* and an *Object* in Semantic Web terminology. A Subject (denoted by *DB-Subj* in this paper) is usually an entity that has a Property and a value for this Property, which is the Object (*DB-Obj*). E.g. in Figure 1, the entity *Audi_A1* is associated with 4 properties: *Engine*, *Transmission*, *Assembly* and *BodyStyle*. The semantics of each property is defined by DBpedia editors,[2] but in most cases, *the Property of the DB-Subj is DB-Obj* makes it clear (e.g., *the Transmission of the Audi_A1 is 5-speed manual*).

The coverage issue. Unlike their neural counterparts, rule-based generators submitted to the WebNLG+ challenge such as RDFJSREALB (Lapalme, 2020), DANGNT-SGU (Tran and Nguyen, 2020) or FORGe (Mille et al., 2019b) are not able to cope with new (previously *unseen*) properties. FORGe, which we are aiming to extend, operates on dependency structures at several levels of representation (syntax, semantics), and needs partially lexicalised predicate-argument (*PredArg*) structures in the PropBank style (Kingsbury and Palmer, 2002) to use as input for generation (see Figure 2b). In other words, if a mapping between

[2]See http://mappings.dbpedia.org/index.php/How_to_edit_the_DBpedia_Ontology.

Proceedings of the Seventh International Conference on Dependency Linguistics (Depling, GURT/SyntaxFest 2023), pages 91 - 101
March 9-12, 2023 ©2023 Association for Computational Linguistics

property and PredArg structure as shown in Figure 2a-b does not exist, the generator cannot introduce the appropriate words and, unless a backup mechanism is in place, it will fail to generate a text.

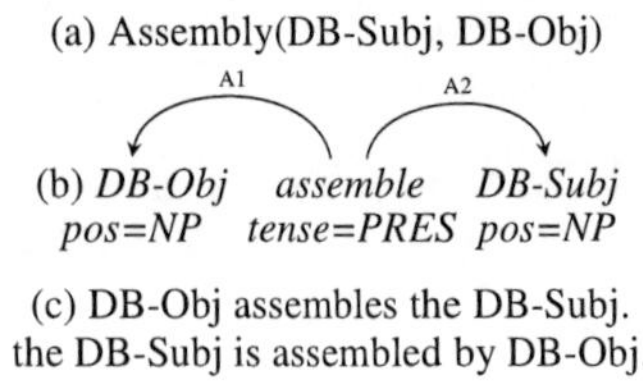

Figure 2: (a) The Property *Assembly*, (b) a corresponding PredArg template (graph with no linear order information), and (c) two possible verbalisations of the property *via* the template. A1/2 = first/second argument.

Thus, the overall problem that we are tackling is the following: given (i) the rule-based FORGe generator that covers all properties in the WebNLG+ training data, (ii) a file which contains the mappings between these properties and their respective PredArg template, (iii) an input triple set that contains one or more properties not currently covered by the generator, automatically extend the mapping file in ii with new unseen property/template pairs that will enable FORGe to generate a text that verbalises all input properties.

Proposed solution. Our aim is the automatic extraction of property/template pairs via a pipeline for retrieving and ranking candidate clauses from Wikipedia that correspond to a given DBpedia *instantiated property* (i.e. a triple), and converting them to predicate-argument representations. We are at an early stage of this research: the pipeline and components have been defined and connected, and we have identified two main challenges in our approach: one is candidate clause extraction, i.e. how to find a sentence or a clause that exactly matches the input triple, the other is the identification of such candidates, i.e. if provided with a list of candidates clauses that contains a match, is it possible to identify it. In this paper, we focus on the second challenge, since if we are not able to identify target candidates, the approach cannot work. In the remainder of the paper, we present the different components and resources used in our pipeline, and provide an encouraging preliminary quantitative and qualitative evaluation of a transformer-based candidate ranking and selection component.[3]

[3]The code and data are available at https://github.com/mille-s/PredArg-Template_Extraction.

2 Related Work

A number of papers have tackled the extraction of templates from text to be used as input for NLG. Duma and Klein (2013) mine and prune sentence templates from Wikipedia articles, but (i) extract templates given an entity (instead of a property as in our case), and (ii) manage to obtain a template for about 20% of the target entities. Ell and Harth (2014) achieve impressive coverage with their (multi-property) sentence templates, but also suffer accuracy problems, with the text faithfully representing the input in only about half the cases. Our general approach is conceptually similar to Perera and Nand (2015)'s, who use an open Information Extraction (IE) tool to identify candidate sentence spans that verbalise a given property, and then acquire lexicalisation information via VerbNet, resorting to default strategies when a predicate is not covered by VerbNet. Hoang et al. (2022) suggest several general approaches to align triple components and textual elements, namely string, substring, hypernym and synonym matching; for property matching, they also use a pre-trained vector model to calculate the distance between words. Other recent work on this topic uses keyword matching (Kaffee et al., 2022) or cosine similarity (Abhishek et al., 2022) for aligning triples and text in under-resourced languages. In order to assess the strength of the alignment, Abhishek et al. (2022) apply a Natural Language Inference (NLI) model to detect (lack of) entailment between the triples and the candidate sentences.

One difference between our approach and most of the related work on template mining for NLG is that we want to extract predicate-argument templates (Figure 2b), and not full-sentence templates. However, the approaches have a lot in common, since we extract the predicate-argument structures from sentences. The main issue with most of the approaches above is the lack of accuracy. Recently, Transformers have been shown to improve accuracy for Question-Answering (Karpukhin et al., 2020), including for the specific task of aligning text and structured data (Oguz et al., 2022) and also for fact checking, for instance for comparing tables and text (Zhang et al., 2020). In our approach, we therefore explore another way of aligning linguistic predicates and properties via Transformer-based meaning similarity scoring.

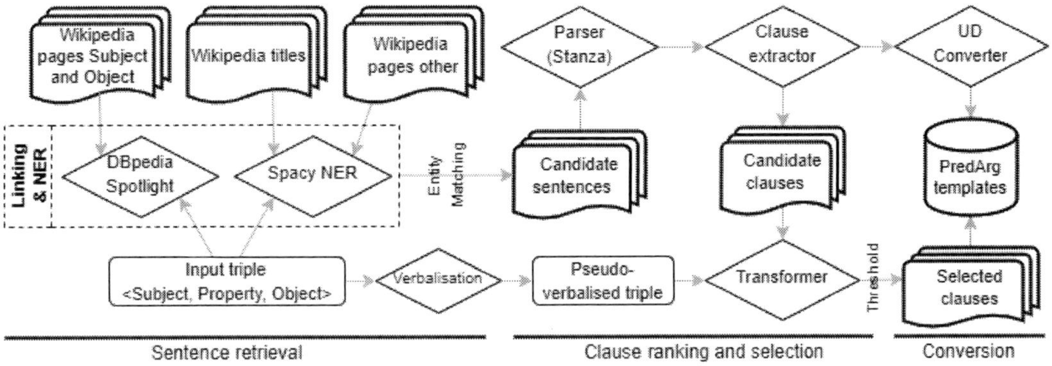

Figure 3: Overview of the pipeline for PredArg template extraction (see Appendix A for module output illustrations)

3 Template Extraction Pipeline

In this section, we describe the components that allows us to extract one or more PredArg template(s) given one input DBpedia triple.[4] Figure 3 shows a complete view of the pipeline (see Appendix A for module outputs). The three main components of the pipeline (indicated across the bottom in Figure 3) are: (i) Candidate sentence retrieval, (ii) Candidate clause ranking and selection, (iii) conversion to predicate-argument template.

3.1 Candidate sentence retrieval

The first step is to find candidate sentences for a given input triple; since DBpedia triples are often verbalised in Wikipedia texts, we use the Wikipedia contents as a candidate source. Via the HuggingFace dataset,[5] we have access to the title and the cleaned (plain) text of each article. We first find the Wikipedia articles of both the DB-Subj and the DB-Obj (if any), and then run the entity linking tool DBpedia Spotlight (Mendes et al., 2011) on the input triple's DB-Subj and DB-Obj and on the article text to find sentences that mention both the DB-Subj and the DB-Obj.

In order to find more candidate sentences and possibly get better candidates, we also perform a relaxed search. We get a named entity type for the DB-Subj using Spacy NER,[6] and parse Wikipedia article titles until we find an article about an entity of the same type as the DB-Subj. We then proceed to run Spacy NER on the DB-Obj and the found article so as to find sentences that contain two entities of the type of the DB-Subj and DB-Obj, and replace these entities with the ones from the original input for the ranking phase.

3.2 Candidate clause ranking and selection

In this section, we detail how we extract minimal clauses and calculate their semantic similarity with the input triple using a Sentence Transformer bi-encoder model[7] (Reimers and Gurevych, 2019), so that candidates scored above a given threshold are kept while others are discarded (see Section 4). Existing sentence similarity approaches return a score for a pair of sentences; in our case, we need a similarity score between a triple and a clause, so we fine-tuned the model to this task using a dataset created for this purpose.

Fine-tuning. We created a fine-tuning dataset with pseudo-verbalisations of input triples aligned with sentences from the WebNLG+ training set as follows. For each triple *T*, we compiled 4 sets of sentences that correspond to 4 levels of similarity with *T*: 1 (sentences that verbalise exactly *T*), 0.66 (sentences that verbalise a triple that has 2 elements in common with *T*, either DB-Subj and Property, DB-Subj and DB-Obj, or Property and DB-Obj), 0.33 (1 element in common with *T*), and 0 (no element in common with *T*), see Table 1.

We obtained 7,645 triple/sentence pairs in total for the set of similarity 1, 24K pairs for 0.66, 399K for 0.33 and 23M for 0. To balance the dataset, we randomly picked 7,645 pairs from the sets 0.66, 0.33 and 0. Finally, we converted each triple to a typed pseudo-verbalised form (Pasricha

[4]Since FORGe performs triple aggregation during the generation, we don't need to extract PredArg templates that correspond to multiple triples.

[5]https://huggingface.co/datasets/wikipedia

[6]https://spacy.io/api/entityrecognizer

[7]https://huggingface.co/sentence-transformers/nli-distilroberta-base-v2

Triple: Location(Agra Airport, India)	
1.00	**'Agra Airport is in India.'**, **'Agra airport is located in India.'**
0.66	**'Agra Airport is located in** Uttar Pradesh.', 'The Taj Mahal **is in India.'**, etc.
0.33	'AGR is the ATA Location Identifier for **Agra Airport.'**, 'AC Hotel Bella Sky Copenhagen **is in** Copenhagen.', 'Mother Theresa is from **India'**, etc.
0.00	'Agnes Kant is a national of the Netherlands.', 'FC Köln played the 2014-15 season in the Bundesliga.', 'Ampara Hospital has 476 beds.', etc.

Table 1: Sentences with different similarity levels; in **bold**, the elements in common with the triple.

et al., 2020): *Location(Agra Airport, India)* $\rightarrow$ *<AIRPORT> Agra Airport <PROP> location <PLACE> India.*[8] In our use case, when an unknown property is detected in the input, we will not have at hand a verbalisation of the triple that contains it since the objective of our pipeline is to discover such verbalisations. Therefore, the pseudo-verbalisation here is an adequate strategy: the pseudo-verbalised input triple will be compared to the candidate clauses.

Clause extraction. The sentences retrieved (see Section 3.1) are usually long, in the Wikipedia style; we thus reduce each sentence to the minimal subtree that contains a finite verb and two elements of the same types as the the DB-Subj and the DB-Obj respectively. Each candidate sentence is parsed with the Stanza Universal Dependency parser (Qi et al., 2020); the output syntactic structures are then processed to extract the minimal subtree via our own graph-transduction grammars. The original sentence span that corresponds to this clause subtree is selected (see Appendix A for illustration).

3.3 Conversion to PredArg templates

The predicate-argument structures of the selected clauses from the previous step are created. For this, we use the grammar-based UD Converter released for the Surface Realisation Shared Tasks (Mille et al., 2019a), which given a UD parse returns a predicate-argument structure. The specific DB-Subj and DB-Obj are replaced by generic [DB-Subj] and [DB-Obj] placeholders.

4 Experiments and preliminary results

In this paper, we provide a first evaluation of the ranking component; we believe that there are many ways of finding more candidate sentences (see Section 5), but predicting which candidate is suitable (or not) is particularly crucial in our pipeline.

[8] See Appendix B for details on the data and fine-tuning.

Evaluation setup. For the evaluation, we compare two models, the off-the-shelf Transformer (Reimers and Gurevych, 2019) and our fine-tuned version of it, on two datasets, (a) the WebNLG+ development subset of single-property inputs (401 triples), and (b) the subset of the WebNLG+ test set comprising all and only items with properties not seen in the WebNLG+ training data (113 triples). The objective is to obtain performance upper and lower bounds for the fine-tuned model by examining how accurate it is at selecting the right candidate (a) for properties seen during fine-tuning, and (b) for unseen properties, which is the most realistic scenario for PredArg template extraction. For each input triple, there are 1 to 3 exactly matching sentences (the corresponding reference sentences in the WebNLG+ dataset), which are the *target sentences* that we want the model to prefer (rank highest) for the input triple. For use as the non-matching candidates, which should be dispreferred (ranked lower) by the model, we select all other sentences that verbalise one-triple inputs, and all sentences that verbalise two-triple inputs; the total Dev and Test candidate pools contain 1,834 and 2,887 sentences respectively. This way, we ensure that we have candidates with a significant meaning overlap with the target sentences (one-triple inputs can share elements with one another, see Section 3.2, and two-triple inputs can include elements or even full triples of the one-triple inputs).

Results. On the development data (top half of Table 2), the fine-tuned model ranks all the target sentences at the top in 98.5% of the cases, and one of the target sentences at the top in 99.5% of the cases. The average similarity score of the correctly top-ranked sentences is 0.963, and the first non-target sentence is on average scored 0.346 points below. The off-the-shelf model is effective at placing one, but not all, target sentences at the top, and the difference in scores between the target and non-target sentences is half of what it is for the fine-tuned model (0.170 and 0.346 respectively).

To assess to what extend the models capture the semantics of the properties, we repeated the experiment above but modifying the input triples in two ways: replacing the property name by another randomly selected property (Avg. top P_{Mod}), and inverting the DB-Subj and DB-Obj (Avg. top P_{InvSO}). The off-the-shelf model has a harder time discriminating between correct and wrong properties than the fine-tuned model (similarity scores of

0.785 and 0.684, respectively, for the off-the-shelf model, 0.963 and 0.754 for the fine-tuned model). However, neither of the models is able to discriminate cases where the DB-Subj and DB-Obj are switched, yielding even higher scores on average than with the original triple (Avg. top P_{InvSO}).

We then looked for the threshold at which a model gets the best F1 score when selecting a candidate sentence. We tested all thresholds (in steps of 0.01 from 0 to 1) for each model on the Dev set and obtained values of 0.73 and 0.87 for the off-the-shelf and fine-tuned models respectively, which yield a F1 of 0.798 and 0.955 respectively. On the unseen test set, these thresholds yield a significantly lower F1 score, the fine-tuned model reaching an F1 of only 0.694 and the off-the-shelf model 0.429. Note that a better F1 can be achieved on these unseen triples by selecting different thresholds (both higher, at 0.93 and 0.78 respectively).[9]

Error analysis. We examined all the false positives and false negatives for the best threshold on the Dev set (0.87), and found the following errors.[10] *False positives (53 errors)*: (i) a sentence that corresponds to 2 triples was selected, because one or more elements of the second triple are very similar with the input triple's DB-Subj, DB-Obj or Property (75% of errors); (ii) the selected sentence verbalises a triple that is almost identical to the input triple (25%). *False negatives (35 errors)*: (i) mismatch between a DB-Subj, Property or DB-Obj and their corresponding verbalisation due to an accent, a comma in a number, quotation marks, parentheses, casing (57%); (ii) a triple element is verbalised with a word judged semantically distant (29%); (iii) a reference sentence is wrong (14%). Only false negatives (i) and (iii) in the stem from errors or lack of normalisation in the data; the other errors are due to the model.

Discussion. We were surprised by the decrease in the score between the Dev and the Test sets, especially for the off-the-shelf Transformer, for which we would expect no difference between seen and unseen properties. We hypothesise that the Test set is more challenging: (i) the reference sentences seem less similar (0.910 on Test VS 0.932 on Dev when running the off-the-shelf Transformer on the gold sentences for triples of size 1); (ii) some problematic cases are more frequent (e.g. the DB-Subj or DB-Obj has content in parentheses in 34% of the Test triples, VS 12% in the Dev set); (iii) there are more candidate sentences for the Test set (see Evaluation setup). There are likely other factors.

All properties of Dev. Set (401 triples)		
	Off-the-shelf	*Fine-tuned*
Accuracy$_{All}$ (%)	91.02	98.50
Accuracy$_{One}$ (%)	98.25	99.50
Avg. top P_{OK}	0.785	0.963
Margin	0.170	0.346
Avg. top P_{Mod}	0.684	0.754
Avg. top P_{InvSO}	0.803	0.971
F1 (thresh.)	0.798 (0.73)	0.955 (0.87)
Unseen porperties of Test Set (113 triples)		
	Off-the-shelf	*Fine-tuned*
Accuracy$_{All}$ (%)	56.64	73.45
Accuracy$_{One}$ (%)	87.61	96.46
Avg. top P_{OK}	0.787	0.929
Margin	0.110	0.212
Avg. top P_{Mod}	0.702	0.776
Avg. top P_{InvSO}	0.815	0.952
F1 Dev thresh.	0.429	0.694
F1 (best thresh.)	0.537 (0.78)	0.745 (0.93)

Table 2: Evaluation of the ranking module (WebNLG+). **Accuracy**$_{All/One}$ = % of cases with all/one good candidate(s) ranked at the top; **Avg. top P**$_{OK}$ = Average score (0 to 1) of correctly top-ranked n candidates for a given input triple; **Margin** = difference in % between top ranked candidates and first non-correct candidate; **Avg. top P**$_{Mod/InvSO}$ = Average score (0 to 1) of the top-ranked candidate for a given input triple in which the property name was randomly changed / the DB-Subj and DB-Obj were inverted; **F1**: best F1 score for candidate selection obtained via the indicated threshold.

5 Future work

We are currently developing the approach reported here further, including investigating how to increase the F1 for candidate selection on unseen data, for instance by using cross-encoders for the final ranking of the top candidates or NLI to filter out bad candidates (Abhishek et al., 2022). To find more and better candidates, we will apply co-reference resolution on the Wikipedia pages, test Open IE approaches to identify text spans (Perera and Nand, 2015), and explore the use of Simple Wikipedia (Duma and Klein, 2013) and WEXEA (Strobl et al., 2020). We will further develop our prototype clause extractor, and will apply our approach to other languages to test its portability.

[9]Fig. 6 and 7 in Appendix C show the F1/Threshold plots.

[10]See Tables 3 to 8 in Appendix D for examples.

Acknowledgements

This research was funded via (i) ADAPT/DCU by the MSCA-PF-EF 2021 grant awarded for the action 101062572, and (ii) UPF by the EC-funded research and innovation programme Horizon Europe under the grant agreement number 101070278 and by the Erasmus+ programme.

References

Tushar Abhishek, Shivprasad Sagare, Bhavyajeet Singh, Anubhav Sharma, Manish Gupta, and Vasudeva Varma. 2022. Xalign: Cross-lingual fact-to-text alignment and generation for low-resource languages. *arXiv preprint arXiv:2202.00291*.

Thiago Castro Ferreira, Claire Gardent, Nikolai Ilinykh, Chris van der Lee, Simon Mille, Diego Moussallem, and Anastasia Shimorina. 2020. The 2020 bilingual, bi-directional WebNLG+ shared task: Overview and evaluation results (WebNLG+ 2020). In *Proceedings of the 3rd International Workshop on Natural Language Generation from the Semantic Web (WebNLG+)*, pages 55–76, Dublin, Ireland (Virtual). Association for Computational Linguistics.

Daniel Duma and Ewan Klein. 2013. Generating natural language from linked data: Unsupervised template extraction. In *Proceedings of the 10th International Conference on Computational Semantics (IWCS 2013)–Long Papers*, pages 83–94.

Basil Ell and Andreas Harth. 2014. A language-independent method for the extraction of RDF verbalization templates. In *Proceedings of the 8th International Natural Language Generation Conference (INLG)*, pages 26–34, Philadelphia, Pennsylvania, U.S.A. Association for Computational Linguistics.

Thang Ta Hoang, Alexander Gelbukh, and Grigori Sidorov. 2022. Mapping process for the task: Wikidata statements to text as wikipedia sentences. *arXiv e-prints*, pages arXiv–2210.

Lucie-Aimée Kaffee, Pavlos Vougiouklis, and Elena Simperl. 2022. Using natural language generation to bootstrap missing wikipedia articles: A human-centric perspective. *Semantic Web*, 13(2):163–194.

Vladimir Karpukhin, Barlas Oguz, Sewon Min, Patrick Lewis, Ledell Wu, Sergey Edunov, Danqi Chen, and Wen-tau Yih. 2020. Dense passage retrieval for open-domain question answering. In *Proceedings of the 2020 Conference on Empirical Methods in Natural Language Processing (EMNLP)*, pages 6769–6781, Online. Association for Computational Linguistics.

Paul Kingsbury and Martha Palmer. 2002. From TreeBank to PropBank. In *Proceedings of the Third International Conference on Language Resources and Evaluation (LREC'02)*, Las Palmas, Canary Islands - Spain. European Language Resources Association (ELRA).

Guy Lapalme. 2020. RDFjsRealB: a symbolic approach for generating text from RDF triples. In *Proceedings of the 3rd International Workshop on Natural Language Generation from the Semantic Web (WebNLG+)*, pages 144–153, Dublin, Ireland (Virtual). Association for Computational Linguistics.

Pablo N Mendes, Max Jakob, Andrés García-Silva, and Christian Bizer. 2011. Dbpedia spotlight: shedding light on the web of documents. In *Proceedings of the 7th international conference on semantic systems*, pages 1–8.

Simon Mille, Anja Belz, Bernd Bohnet, Yvette Graham, and Leo Wanner. 2019a. The second multilingual surface realisation shared task (SR'19): Overview and evaluation results. In *Proceedings of the 2nd Workshop on Multilingual Surface Realisation (MSR 2019)*, pages 1–17, Hong Kong, China. Association for Computational Linguistics.

Simon Mille, Stamatia Dasiopoulou, and Leo Wanner. 2019b. A portable grammar-based nlg system for verbalization of structured data. In *Proceedings of the 34th ACM/SIGAPP Symposium on Applied Computing*, pages 1054–1056. ACM.

Barlas Oguz, Xilun Chen, Vladimir Karpukhin, Stan Peshterliev, Dmytro Okhonko, Michael Schlichtkrull, Sonal Gupta, Yashar Mehdad, and Scott Yih. 2022. UniK-QA: Unified representations of structured and unstructured knowledge for open-domain question answering. In *Findings of the Association for Computational Linguistics: NAACL 2022*, pages 1535–1546, Seattle, United States. Association for Computational Linguistics.

Nivranshu Pasricha, Mihael Arcan, and Paul Buitelaar. 2020. NUIG-DSI at the WebNLG+ challenge: Leveraging transfer learning for RDF-to-text generation. In *Proceedings of the 3rd International Workshop on Natural Language Generation from the Semantic Web (WebNLG+)*, pages 137–143, Dublin, Ireland (Virtual). Association for Computational Linguistics.

Rivindu Perera and Parma Nand. 2015. A multi-strategy approach for lexicalizing linked open data. In *International Conference on Intelligent Text Processing and Computational Linguistics*, pages 348–363. Springer.

Peng Qi, Yuhao Zhang, Yuhui Zhang, Jason Bolton, and Christopher D. Manning. 2020. Stanza: A python natural language processing toolkit for many human languages. In *Proceedings of the 58th Annual Meeting of the Association for Computational Linguistics: System Demonstrations*, pages 101–108, Online. Association for Computational Linguistics.

Nils Reimers and Iryna Gurevych. 2019. Sentence-BERT: Sentence embeddings using Siamese BERT-networks. In *Proceedings of the 2019 Conference on Empirical Methods in Natural Language Processing and the 9th International Joint Conference on Natural Language Processing (EMNLP-IJCNLP)*, pages

3982–3992, Hong Kong, China. Association for Computational Linguistics.

Michael Strobl, Amine Trabelsi, and Osmar Zaiane. 2020. WEXEA: Wikipedia EXhaustive entity annotation. In *Proceedings of the 12th Language Resources and Evaluation Conference*, pages 1951–1958, Marseille, France. European Language Resources Association.

Trung Tran and Dang Tuan Nguyen. 2020. WebNLG 2020 challenge: Semantic template mining for generating references from RDF. In *Proceedings of the 3rd International Workshop on Natural Language Generation from the Semantic Web (WebNLG+)*, pages 177–185, Dublin, Ireland (Virtual). Association for Computational Linguistics.

Hongzhi Zhang, Yingyao Wang, Sirui Wang, Xuezhi Cao, Fuzheng Zhang, and Zhongyuan Wang. 2020. Table fact verification with structure-aware transformer. In *Proceedings of the 2020 Conference on Empirical Methods in Natural Language Processing (EMNLP)*, pages 1624–1629, Online. Association for Computational Linguistics.

A Sample outputs of all components

In this section , we illustrate each step of the whole pipeline.

Input triple
Alan_Bean || birthDate || "1932-03-15"

Entity linking (DBpedia Spotlight)

- DB-Subj: Alan Bean
  - kb$_{id}$: 11139903761698166211
  - dbpedia link: http://dbpedia.org/resource/Alan_Bean
- DB-Obj: "1932-03-15"
  - kb$_{id}$: 0 (No dbpedia entity found)

Entity type assignment (Spacy)

- DB-Subj: Alan Bean
  - Entity label: 380 (PERSON)
- DB-Obj: "1932-03-15"
  - Entity label: 391 (DATE)

Typed pseudo-verbalisation
We first check if the DB-Subj or DB-Obj are a number –using regular expressions- or a time period –using the python module dateutil.parser. If not, we do the DBpedia query:

- DB-Subj (Alan_Bean): None
- DB-Obj (1932-03-15): TIMEPERIOD

Since the DB-Obj has a type, we then query DBpedia for the DB-Subj only, and choose the first returned type (in bold below):

{{'uri': **'http://dbpedia.org/ontology/Person'**},
{'uri': 'http://dbpedia.org/ontology/Animal'},
{'uri': 'http://dbpedia.org/ontology/Astronaut'},
{'uri': 'http://dbpedia.org/ontology/Eukaryote'},
{'uri': 'http://dbpedia.org/ontology/Species'}}

We can then proceed to produce the pseudo-verbalised triple as follows:

<PERSON> Alan Bean <PROP> birth date <TIMEPERIOD> "1932-03-15"

Sentence extraction (Entity matching) and parsing (Stanza)
To get Wikipedia pages, we retrieve (i) the page of the DB-Subj, (ii) the page of the DB-Obj if any, and (iii) 1,000 random article about an entity that has the same type as the DB-Subj (matching the Spacy tag of the title with that of the DB-Subj). We then look for candidates on the pages, based on the type predicted by DBpedia Spotlight (pages of DB-Subj and DB-Obj) or by Spacy (other pages). We detokenise the DB-Subj and the DB-Obj for them to be parsed as one single named entity.

```
1	The	DT	Definite=Def|PronType=Art	2	det
2	seat	NN	Number=Sing	11	nsubj
3	of	IN	_	5	case
4	Wheeler	NNP	Number=Sing	5	compound
5	County	NNP	Number=Sing	2	nmod
6	,	,	_	2	punct
7	in	IN	_	8	case
8	Texas	NNP	Number=Sing	5	nmod
9	,	,	_	11	punct
10	is	VBZ	Mood=Ind|...	11	cop
11	Wheeler	NNP	Number=Sing	0	root
12	,	,	_	11	punct
13	where	WRB	PronType=Rel	16	mark
14	Alan_Bean	NNP	subject=true	16	nsubj:pass
15	was	VBD	Mood=Ind|...	16	aux:pass
16	born	VBN	Tense=Past|...	11	acl:relcl
17	on	IN	_	18	case
18	1932-03-15	CD	NumForm=Digit|...	16	obl
19	.	.	_	11	punct
```

Figure 4: Sample UD structure (selected columns)

Clause Extraction (graph transduction grammars)
The output of the clause extractor is the minimal subtree that contains both the DB-Subj and the DB-Obj, with additional trimming (e.g. a relative pronoun before the DB-Subj is removed): 'Alan_Bean was born on "1932-03-15"'

Clause ranking (Transformer)
The similarity of the extracted clause with the input triple is then calculated: 'Alan_Bean was

born on "1932-03-15"' -> 0.8853045701980591'. If the clause is above the defined threshold, it is selected for the template. See more examples of ranking and selection in Appendix D.

Conversion to PredArg (UD Converter)
Figure 5 shows the delexicalised predicate-argument template extracted from the selected clause.

1	bear	VERB	Tense=Past|...	0	ROOT	
2	[Subject]	PROPN	subject=true|...		1	A2
3	[Object]	NUM	NumForm=Digit|...		1	Time

Figure 5: Sample PredArg template (selected columns)

B Details on the fine-tuning step

Our method for triple pseudo-verbalization is based on the one in (Pasricha et al., 2020); we adapted a couple of aspects not detailed in the paper: (i) we implemented our own simple functions for checking if a DB-Obj is of type number or date, and (ii) we took the first ontology type (starting with *dbo:*) in the *rdf:type* section of the DBpedia page for the other types.

The finetuning dataset is built from the one-triple items in the test set of the WebNLG+ dataset.[11] For finetuning the model, we sample 7,645 items for each of the 4 similarity categories as explained in the paper. The sample is divided 70/15/15 for training, development and test sets, respectively. The train batch size is 16, and the train loss is Cosine Similarity Loss. It uses the Embedding Similarity Evaluator (which uses the development set) with evaluation steps = 1000, and some warm-up steps (10% of the training data), with num_epochs = 4.

C Plots F1-score clause ranking and selection

Figures 6 and 7 show a plot of the F1-score in function of the selection threshold for candidate sentences.

D Sample classification errors

Tables 3 to 8 show examples of mis-selection of candidate sentences for an input triple. In cyan, correctly selected target sentences; in orange, erroneously selected (false positive) or discarded (false negative) sentences.

[11] https://drive.google.com/file/d/1BM-W0GTa931jdNp1De_vHcfa8GGdPhTL/view?usp=sharing

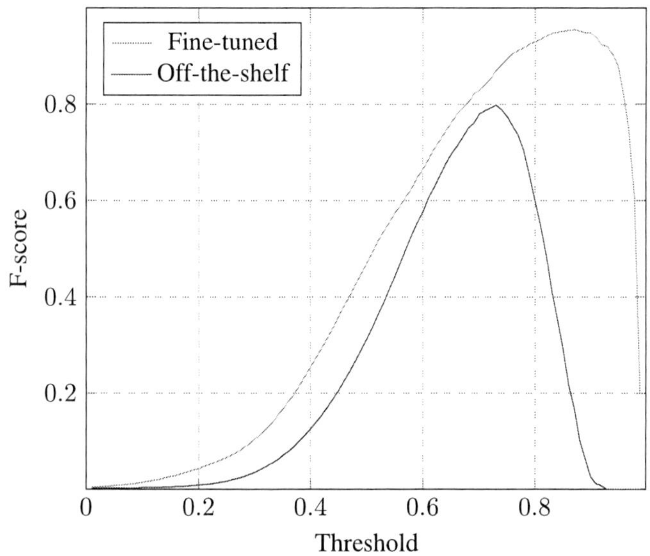

Figure 6: Threshold definition for clause selection (Development set)

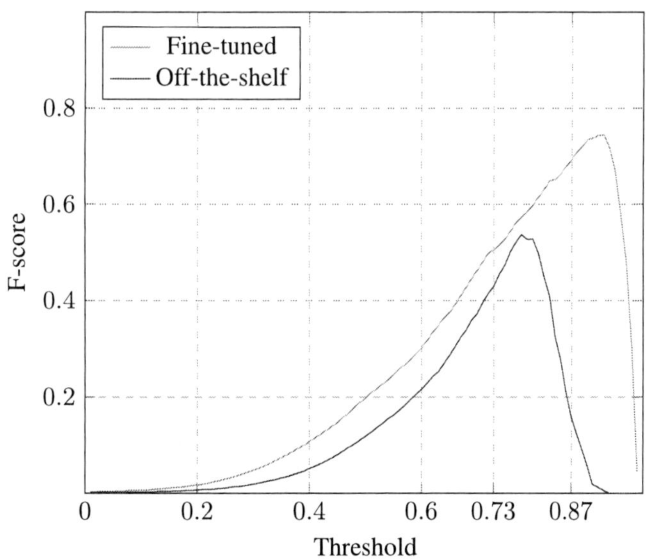

Figure 7: F1 score for clause selection (Test set)

Input
<AIRPORT> Athens International Airport <PROP> location <PLACE> Spata
Target sentences
Athens International Airport is located in Spata.
Athens International Airport is in Spata.

Top-ranked sentences	**Score**
Athens International Airport is located in Spata.	0.958
Athens International Airport is in Spata.	0.955
Athens International Airport, which is located in Spata, serves the city of Athens.	0.949
Athens International Airport is in Spata and serves the city of Athens.	0.943
Athens International Airport in Spata serves the city of Athens.	0.934
Agra Airport is in Agra.	0.523

Table 3: False positive Dev Type (i) (Non-target sentence > 0.87)

Input
<PLACE> Ann Arbor, Michigan <PROP> leader title <PERSONFUNCTION> Mayor
Target sentences
Mayor, is the title of the leader in Ann Arbor, Michigan.
The leader title of Ann Arbor, Michigan, is Mayor.
Ann Arbor, Michigan is led by the Mayor.

Top-ranked sentences	**Score**
The leader title of Ann Arbor, Michigan, is Mayor.	0.994
Ann Arbor, Michigan is led by the Mayor.	0.990
Mayor, is the title of the leader in Ann Arbor, Michigan.	0.988
The City Administrator leads Ann Arbor in Michigan.	0.908
A City Administrator leads Ann Arbor, Michigan.	0.897
Albany, Georgia is led by a Mayor.	0.657

Table 4: False positive Dev Type (ii) (Non-target sentence > 0.87)

Input
<AIRPORT> Alpena County Regional Airport <PROP> runway length <NUMERIC> 1533.0
Target sentences
The runway length of Alpena County Regional Airport is 1,533.
The runway length of Alpena County Regional airport is 1533.0.

Top-ranked sentences	**Score**
The runway length of Alpena County Regional airport is 1533.0.	0.995
The runway length of Alpena County Regional Airport is 1,533.	0.567
The Adolfo Suárez Madrid–Barajas Airport is in San Sebastián de los Reyes and has a runway length of 3500.0 metres.	0.474
Located in Alcobendas, Adolfo Suarez Madrid-Barajas Airport has a runway with the length of 3500.0 metres.	0.470
The Adolfo Suárez Madrid–Barajas Airport located at San Sebastian de los Reyes has a runway length of 3500.	0.466
Ann Arbor, Michigan has a population of 1580.7 per square kilometre and a total area of 74.33 square kilometres.	0.464

Table 5: False negative Dev Type (i) Number (Target sentence < 0.87)

Input
<FOOD> Bakso <PROP> ingredient <FOOD> Noodle
Target sentences
Bakso contains noodles.
Noodle is an ingredient in Bakso.
The dish Bakso contains noodles.

Top-ranked sentences	Score
Noodle is an ingredient in Bakso.	0.989
The dish Bakso contains noodles.	0.857
Bakso contains noodles.	0.820
Vermicelli is an ingredient in Bakso.	0.640
Vermicelli is an ingredient of the dish Bakso.	0.636
Vermicelli is included in bakso.	0.553

Table 6: False negative Dev Type (i) Casing (Target sentence < 0.87)

Input
<PERSON> N. R. Pogson <PROP> nationality <MUSICALARTIST> England
Target sentences
N. R. Pogson was English.
N.R. Pogson was an English national.
N. R. Pogson is British.

Top-ranked sentences	Score
N.R. Pogson was an English national.	0.913
N. R. Pogson is British.	0.909
N. R. Pogson was English.	0.574
People from the United Kingdom are called British people.	0.482
British people is a demonym for people in the United Kingdom.	0.458
The native people of the United Kingdom are known as the British people.	0.441

Table 7: False negative Dev Type (ii) (Target sentence < 0.87)

Input
<PLACE> Swords, Dublin <PROP> is part of <SETTLEMENT> Dublin (European Parliament constituency)
Target sentences
Swords is a part of the Dublin European Parliamentary constituency.
Swords belongs to the Dublin constituency of the European Parliament.
Swords, Dublin is part of the Dublin European Parliament constituency.

Top-ranked sentences	Score
Swords, Dublin is part of the Dublin European Parliament constituency.	0.893
Swords is a part of the Dublin European Parliamentary constituency.	0.835
Swords belongs to the Dublin constituency of the European Parliament.	0.774
Trane is located in Swords, Dublin, Ireland.	0.638
Trane is located in Swords, Dublin, which is in Ireland.	0.625
The location of Trane is in Swords, Dublin, Ireland.	0.620

Table 8: False negative Dev Type (iii) (Target sentence < 0.87)

Author Index